I0815114

THE MOROCCAN COOKBOOK

Ghillie Başan

THE MOROCCAN COOKBOOK

Exploring the food of an ancient cuisine

LORENZ BOOKS

Contents

Above **My children being taken to and from the Kasbah du Toubkal on a mule.**

Opposite top row, left to right **Saharan tea ceremony using rainwater brewed over charcoal; A picnic under the shade of a juniper tree in the Atlas Mountains; Riding a moped through a covered street.**

Opposite middle row, left to right **The colours and patterns of Moroccan handmade pottery identify its region; A farmer selling his sun-ripened sweet melons in Rissani market; 5pm 'casse croute' when the women of the family drink tea and enjoy the bread and pastries they have proudly baked.**

Opposite bottom row, left to right **Looking down to the village of Imlil with the Atlas Mountains beyond; Bundles of cinnamon sticks at a spice stall; Bringing in the camels at dusk to camp, during explorer Alice Morrison's expedition across Morocco and the Sahara.**

Introduction

While I walked up to the Kasbah du Toubkal, a magnificent mountain retreat in the Atlas Mountains, my young children were transported on the back of a gentle mule. Chatting and giggling, they were blissfully unaware of the draining heat, but I was thankful when we arrived at the walls of the ancient refuge. In the shelter and shade of the pretty courtyard garden, a vision of colour from lush green herbs and scented pink roses, we were greeted warmly with a cool sprinkling of rose water to refresh our hands, faces and necks and the most succulent dates I have ever tasted dipped in a bowl of milk – traditional Berber hospitality. Welcome to Morocco!

Hospitality is of utmost importance in Morocco. Offering, sharing and receiving are intertwined, and, even in the humblest of homes, a guest will be offered dates to dip in milk, or a simple glass of milk flavoured with rosewater, sometimes with scented petals floating on top. Freshly baked or griddled bread, sweetmeats or fruit may also be offered, and wherever you go in the country a glass of hot, sweet mint tea is the essence of hospitality, friendship, family gatherings and trade. This is just the beginning. What has yet to come is a feast for the senses. Spicy and scented, fruity and sweet, offering creative combinations of cumin and ginger, honey and cinnamon, saffron and rose, chillies and turmeric, nuts, olives and preserved lemons, all served in painted earthenware bowls and tagines. It is no wonder that the cuisine has been described as the 'perfumed soul' of the culture.

A table laden with a Moroccan feast can tell the fascinating story of the country and its people, and the influences from the cultures that have left their mark. At the root of the culinary culture are the indigenous Amazigh, the Berber communities, with their traditions of tagines and couscous; the nomadic Bedouins from the desert who brought dates, milk and grains; the Moors expelled from Spain who relied heavily on olives and olive oil and brought with them the Andalucian flavours of paprika and herbs; the Sephardic Jews with their preserving techniques; the Arabs who introduced their sophisticated cuisine from the Middle East along with Islamic culinary restrictions; the slaves from central Africa with their tribal secrets; the Ottoman influence of kebabs and pastry making; and the finesse of the French. Sensually intertwining ancient and medieval within the modern, the cuisine is regarded as the most exquisite and refined of the Maghreb, the North African region comprising Morocco, Tunisia, Algeria, Libya and Mauritiana.

POTASSE
PHILDAR
10 DH/Pcs

History and culture

Morocco, the land of the setting sun, is the western part of the Arab world and provides a geographical door to the rest of Africa, influencing trade, culture and food. Its culinary traditions have been shaped by a history of invaders and settlers from the ancient Romans and Arabs to the Ottomans, Spaniards and the French. This vibrant history and culinary culture are splendidly vivid as you travel through the country.

Above **With its long coastline and proximity to the tip of Spain, Morocco's geographical location acts as a culinary door to the rest of Africa.**

Opposite **In Marrakesh, the Place Djemaa el Fna fills with the hussle and bustle of stalls and people as the sun goes down.**

The land of the setting sun

In Arabic, The Kingdom of Morocco is referred to as Al Maghreb – full name Al Mamlakah al Maghribiyah, meaning 'the Western Kingdom' in reference to it being the western part of the Arab world and, therefore, the place where the sun sets. With an extensive coastline for fishing, fertile coastal plains, lush valleys fed by the streams that flow from the melting snows of the high Rif and Atlas Mountains, deserts with date-palm oases, and a climate and topography similar to California, it is not only a place where the suns sets but one that is blessed with abundant harvests of olives, figs, oranges, lemons, melons, aubergines, peppers, tomatoes, courgettes, pulses and grains, and good grazing for sheep and goats.

The geographical location of Morocco also provides a culinary door to the rest of Africa in addition to the lively mix of Spanish, French, Arab and Ottoman influences that have shaped its history. The Mediterranean coast extends for about 500km to the Algerian border, and Tangier, the second-largest port in the country, is the easiest entry point as ferries operate regularly from the south of Spain. In the first half of the twentieth century Tangier was stylish and liberal with its own laws and administration, and encouraged a very lively bar and gay scene so it attracted many wealthy exiles, refugees, novelists and artists until Independence in 1956 when the face of the city changed and most of the expat community moved to Spain or France. Beyond Tangier and Tetouan, the next big city along the Mediterranean coast, the terrain is wilder and more isolated as this is where the Rif Mountains begin, acting as a natural boundary between Europe and Africa and cutting off Morocco from Algeria and the rest of the Maghreb. For this very reason, the region has been fairly closed to outside influences throughout history, and remains fairly tribal. The infertile soil and stony terrain has meant it has often been short of food supplies and, although some cereal crops are grown, most of the farmland has been taken over by cannabis cultivation, even though the plant grows wild all over the slopes.

Heading south from the Mediterranean you reach two of Morocco's imperial cities, Meknes and Fes. Although Meknes is an important market centre and just south of it lies one of Morocco's wine-growing regions which, under French rule, was very productive, as Morocco and Algeria provided a third of the table wine drunk in France, the real gem from a cultural point of view is Fes. It is the most complete medieval city of the Arab world and from a culinary perspective it is regarded as the jewel in the crown. Fes has dominated Moroccan trade, culture and religious life since the end of the tenth century, and its cuisine is a unique reflection of the diversity of its inhabitants, which have included Berbers, Jews, Arabs,

0 45 0
14

Andalusians, the French and other Europeans. The city itself may be a shadow of its former glory nowadays but the people of Fes, the Fassis, are regarded as intellectual and sophisticated, many are heads of government, and they have their own cuisine and way of life. Often elaborate in style, Fassi food combines the subtle secrets of the imperial kitchens with all the cultural influences that have come and gone in the city. One of the Fassi specialities is the crispy, feather-light pigeon pie, *b'stilla*, which is aromatic and sweet, and reputed to be the best in Morocco.

The capital of Morocco, Rabat, is situated on the Atlantic coast above Casablanca, the country's largest port, said to be busier than Marseilles, on which the French modelled it. In fact the influence of the French is very dominant on this coastline, and, with the wide streets and westernized style of the Ville Nouvelle surrounding and overshadowing the medina (the old, walled city), both Rabat and Casablanca look like Marseilles, and French is spoken as often as Moroccan Arabic. When it comes to food, there is a cosmopolitan mix of restaurants and cafés with menus in French and a fusion of Moroccan-French dishes, but you can find cheap, traditional fare in the medinas and mellahs, the Jewish quarters.

Further down the coast and more relaxed and a little less French is Essaouira, a charming, walled fishing town. It is famous for its white-washed and blue-shuttered houses, its boat builders and sardine fishermen and, of course, its sandy beaches. Fresh fish is definitely on the menu, and the street food at the port is an Essaouira institution, as the catch is practically flung from the boats onto the grills.

The cinnamon-coloured city of Marrakesh is the door to the desert and the gateway to both Berber and African culinary traditions, with the lively Place Djemaa el Fna at its heart. Here, where gold and African slaves from Sudan, Senegal and the ancient kingdom of Timbuktu were once traded, the snake charmers, costumed water-sellers and story-tellers work their trade in a cloud of smoke emanating from the stoves furiously grilling kebabs and kefta. Not so long ago you could exchange a camel for a brace of slaves in this square; now you can tuck into a paper cone containing freshly roasted chickpeas, sprinkled with cumin and salt, and observe the street theatre for next to nothing.

With the old medina rebuilt and not overshadowed by the new city, Marrakesh feels more like a series of villages, or quarters formed by the migrants coming in from the countryside. Both Marrakesh and Fes have an established Jewish quarter, known as the Mellah, meaning 'salt' due to its use in their long-established techniques of preserving food and without which the Moroccans would not have their ubiquitous preserved lemons. The people of Marrakesh, the Marrakchis, are well known for being warm and laid-back, more open to different ways of life, and women seem to enjoy more freedom here, often riding mopeds through

Top **The rocky terrain of the Rif Mountains cuts off Morocco from the rest of the Maghreb.**

Bottom **The view from Sale of the harbour at Rabat, the capital of Morocco, situated on the Atlantic coast.**

the narrow streeets. But, compared to the cosmopolitan style of food and culture in Casablanca, and the Spanish influence in Tangier and Tetouan, the architecture of Marrakesh – the low buildings with bright doors and flat roofs – and its cuisine strongly reflect the city's distinctive Berber roots.

You can see the beginning of the Atlas Mountain range from Marrakesh, and it is well worth heading to them, passing through the fertile, river-fed Ourika Valley known for its saffron crocuses, fruit and nut trees, straggly Berber villages and countryside markets. It is a far cry from urban life and, like the Rif Mountains and southern oases, it is quite striking to see how little outside influences have changed the way of life. Here both the nomadic and settled Berber tribes have held on to their ancient cultural and culinary identities, including their own dialects. For anyone travelling in Morocco it is refreshing to see how friendly and open the Atlas Berbers are, and the women are less restricted than those in the north of the country or on the rural plains as they are able to wander around unveiled, wear bright clothes, and work in the fields and in the market in Asni. The Atlas Berbers are also used to welcoming visitors as this is good trekking country, so villages like Asni and Imlil have developed around this trade. Many trekkers want to climb Djebel Toubkhal, the highest peak in North Africa, and many local men are happy to guide them or operate trek and tour companies and arrange for them to stay in the homes of Berber families, or you can follow the trail up to the Kasbah du Toubkhal, originally the private home of a feudal caid and now a tastefully decorated refuge decked out with colourful Berber rugs and cushions. There are glorious views of the pointed, snow-capped peaks, and over the tree canopy of the Toubkhal National Park on to the patchwork of terraced fields and stacked houses made from mud and stone and then the streams and river below. It is quite chilly and windy up there, even on a hot summer's day, but you soon warm up with the traditional Berber greeting of dates dipped in milk and steaming, rich and redolent tagines.

Once you cross the southern Atlas you are in the Sahara where the sky is big, the air hushed and time seems to stand still. At first the desert sand seems far away as the landscape begins with rocks and dry scrub, and the kasbahs, the fortified tribal villages, are made of mud. There are river valleys, date palm oases – the dates of the Zagora oasis are some of the finest in Morocco – and dwindling crops of henna, barley, and citrus fruits. The majority of Morocco's saffron is grown in the Taliouine region, and scented roses are cultivated in the lush 'Valley of Roses' in the province of Quarzazate for rose water. But what you are also seeing when you cross the Atlas Mountains and head south are the beautiful, ancient caravan routes that were once travelled by slaves and traders in gold and spice to the markets of Fes and Marrakesh from old Sudan, Niger and Timbuktu.

Top **One of the cinnamon-coloured Berber villages en route to the snow-capped Atlas Mountains.**

Bottom **A camp of the nomadic Bedouin in Morocco's Sahara Desert.**

An ancient heritage

The first inhabitants of the Maghreb are thought to have dwelled in the Sahara as hunter-gatherers. Recorded history begins around 1100BCE with the ancient Phoenicians, who set up trading colonies along the coastlines, from where they traded saffron, which was used as a dye in ancient Egypt. As most of their colonies were built on defensable headlands, it is thought that they probably had little contact with the indigenous population who inhabited the inland fertile plains and harsh mountainous terrain, where they lived off honey, beans, lentils and wheat. The Carthaginians were the next to take over the African trading routes and developed some of the ports into considerable cities, exporting grain and grapes, as well as minting their own coinage. After Carthage was sacked in the Punic Wars, the Romans incorporated parts of the region into their vast Empire as the province of Mauritania. Driven by the agricultural success of the Carthaginians, the Romans increased the wheat and fruit production and encouraged the cultivation of olive trees and the production of olive oil. However, the Romans didn't penetrate the Rif and Atlas mountains, as their main interest was in exploiting the fertile vineyards and wheat fields in the north and gaining access to the rich agriculture of Tunisia, Algeria and Spain as well. Later, when the Roman legions withdrew, the Vandals took power in southern Spain and controlled some of the North African ports, until their defeat to the Byzantine Empire.

Early archeological records show that the Amazigh, the Berber, are descendants of an ancient race that has inhabited much of North Africa between Egypt and the western coast of Morocco since Neolithic times. Originally farmers, living alongside the semi-nomadic Taureg, also of Berber descent and called the 'blue people' because of their indigo clothing and the stain it leaves on their skin, and the desert Bedouin, the Berbers would have made an impact on the food of the region long before the invasion of the Arabs.

Eastern and western influences

The greatest influence on the history of the region was the new force rising in the East – the Arabs and Islam. After the death of the Prophet Mohammed in 632CE, the Arab invasion came in waves between the seventh and fourteenth centuries. The first wave described the region as 'paradise', as their eyes swept over the productive landscape of extensive orchards and fields of grain. With each wave came big changes to the culinary landscape: eastern spices such as cumin, ginger and cinnamon

Opposite **The fortified town of Ait ben Haddou near Ouarzazate on the edge of the Sahara Desert in Morocco.**

from their far-reaching trade routes in the Indian Ocean, rice from India, saffron from Persia, the notion of sweet and sour with the fruit-inspired meat dishes of ancient Persia and the sophisticated cuisine of Baghdad, and the tradition of mezze – a spread of small dishes to whet the appetite, called *kemia* in modern-day Morocco. Most importantly of all, they converted the population of the Maghreb to Islam and the Arabic language.

In Algeria, the Berbers, including integrated Jews and Coptic Christians from Egypt, resisted the Arab invasion at first but, by the early part of 700CE, most of the inhabitants had embraced Islam and North Africa effectively came under Arab rule. With their Berber recruits, the Arabs began to look for new territories to conquer and convert and, like the Romans and Byzantines before them, their main thrust was towards Spain. So began the significant and lasting cultural and culinary influence of the Moors (the term for people of mixed Berber and Arab descent) on southern Spain, Portugal and Sicily. Around the time that Columbus was landing in the Americas, the Moors were forced from al-Andaluz (Andalucia) to return to Morocco, which led to the Spanish culinary and cultural influences they had acquired spreading from Tangier and Tetouan to the courts of Fes and south to Marrakesh. By the time the Ottoman Empire spread across North Africa, the cuisine of Morocco was established, so the sophisticated cooking from the palace kitchens of Istanbul did not alter but added to it with flat breads, savoury and sweet layered and coiled pastries, milk puddings, minced meat balls, grilled chunks of meat threaded onto skewers and the introduction of chillies from the New World.

The French, who colonised North Africa at the end of the nineteenth and beginning of the twentieth centuries, also had a lasting influence on the culinary culture. Nicknamed the Pieds Noirs, 'Black feet', by the Arabs who coined the expression from the sight of the highly polished boots of the soldiers, they brought silky soups and scented broths, sophisticated fish dishes, café culture, wine-making, and their own language to the region. Along with the French immigrants who spread themselves all over North Africa, a wave of Italians came to Tunisia and also of Spaniards to the northern part of Morocco. Many of the French immigrants settled in the new, sparkling white city, Casablanca, with its wide avenues and busy markets, and remained there immersed in an Arab culture but leading a very French way of life until 1956 when Morocco gained independence and many left the country. Culturally, they joined ranks with the Sephardim, descendants of the Jews who had been expelled from Spain and Portugal at the end of the fifteenth century, who had settled mainly in Fes, Marrakesh and Essaouira on the coast. As a result, the Pied Noir cooking created its own identity, combining French roots with Jewish dietary laws, and all the dishes were given French names, most of which survive today.

Top **Rows of the traditional blue wooden fishing boats in the port of the walled town Essaouira on the Atlantic coast.**

Bottom **The modern Post Office building on Avenue Mohammed V in Rabat is considered to be an architectural landmark.**

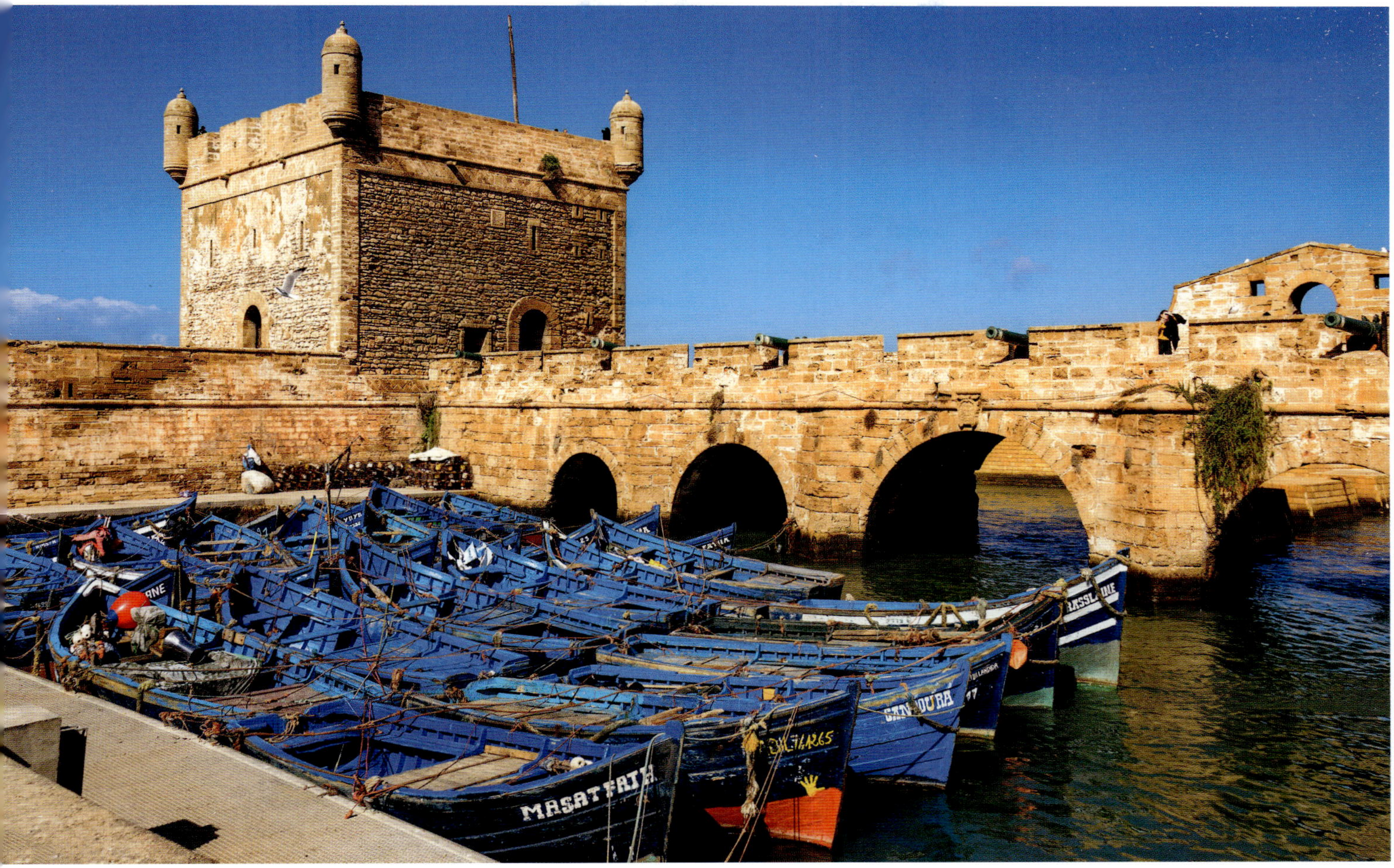

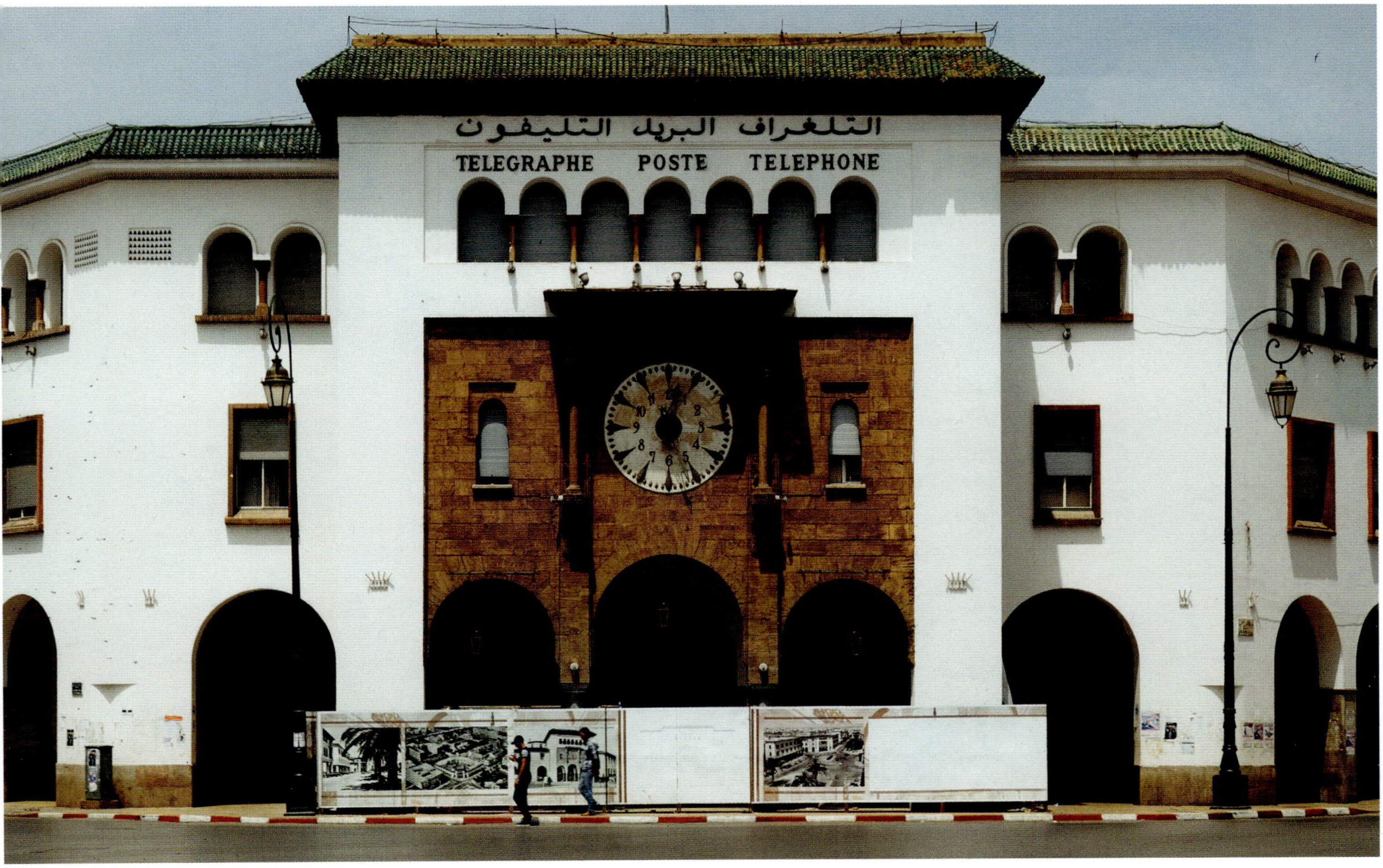

التلغراف البريد التليفون
TELEGRAPHE POSTE TELEPHONE

Berber traditions

The Berbers are proud of their ancestry and, although they had to convert to Islam and adopt new religious and culinary customs, they are keen to make the point that they are not of Arab descent. It would be fair to say that Moroccan cuisine is rooted in Berber traditions and their great dynasties, such as the Almoravides and Almohads, who ruled Muslim Spain between the eleventh and thirteenth centuries. During this period of Berber rule, with the imperial seats in Morocco and the territories expanding throughout Spain, Tunisia, Algeria and parts of Senegal, the region was thrust into a new realm of cultural and culinary sophistication. The old imperial cities of Marrakesh, Fes, Meknes and Rabat still reflect some of this glory and the legacy of the royal kitchens is evident in the refined tagines and pastries, some of which echo the cuisines of medieval Baghdad and Moorish Spain.

Berber communities speak their own languages and dialects but the majority also speak Arabic and, in some areas, French, and they fiercely uphold some of their own culinary customs. Perhaps the most important of these is the *moussem*, a religious gathering of Berber communities, some travelling great distances as a pilgrimage to honour a saint. A moussem can be a religious holiday, a trade fair or a seasonal harvest but most of all it is a festive celebration of cultural identity, often held in tented enclosures where traditional dishes such as couscous and tagines are cooked in vast quantities and shared. Another feature of Berber culinary life is the *diffa*, an extravagant banquet, which might be part of moussem, but might also be the feast to mark a special occasion such as a wedding, birth or circumcision. Depending on the wealth of a family, the traditional dishes will include a selection of *kemia*, appetizers and salads; *harira*, a thick, nourishing broth; *b'stilla*, the classic pastry stuffed with saffron-scented chicken; *mechoui*, which can involve a whole lamb or kid, or a large joint, slow-roasted on a spit over embers in a deep pit; a lamb or chicken tagine with olives and preserved lemon; a mound of couscous served on its own; and a selection of sweet pastries.

The traditional dishes of the mountain and desert Berbers are simple and rustic, almost as if the cuisines of the royal dynasties simply passed them by. An example of this simplicity is the Berber speciality, *tangia*, which consists of meat cooked in an earthenware amphora-shaped vessel. Like *mechoui*, this is one of the few dishes prepared by the men of a village or neighbourhood. The Marrakesh version, *Marrakchi tangia*, is reputed to be the most succulent. The lamb, which is flavoured with saffron and preserved lemon, is sealed in the amphora with parchment paper that is tied with string and cooked very slowly in the embers of a fire. The resulting texture of the meat is so tender it literally melts in the mouth like butter, with a delicate aromatic taste. It is a dish well worth trying.

Top **Berber villages and terraced fields on the slopes of the Atlas region.**

Bottom **A Berber family enjoying a traditional meal in their home.**

The impact of Islam

After the Arab invasion and the adoption of Islam by the majority of Moroccans, a number of religious rituals and restrictions entered the cultural and culinary landscape. These continue to be practiced by Muslims in accordance with the Islamic laws set out in the Qur'an, and include slaughtering an animal by cutting its throat; that blood must not be consumed; the prohibition of slaughter for any other God or consuming an animal killed for any reason other than food or that is already dead; and that no part of the pig is permitted.

There are a number of religious festivals associated with Islam, the most prominent ones being Ramadan, the holy month of fasting, and Aid el Kebir. Ramadan is the ninth month of the Muslim calendar, commemorating when the Qur'an was revealed to the Prophet, and requires fasting from dawn to sunset. It is therefore a time of reflection and purification but, once the sun sets, the culinary activity begins in the street markets and in the home. The aroma of special breads baked and griddled to break the fast, meat roasted in the *tannur* and cauldrons of *harira* lingers in the air along with the sweet scent of almond and honey pastries. Ramadan brings good business to street hawkers, and families gather together in their homes. At the end of the month when the moon is first sighted, a celebration of feasting begins with Aid el Fitr, which brings Ramadan to a close as people visit each other bearing gifts of sweets and pastries, and give dates, grain and money to the poor.

Two lunar months after Aid el Fitr is Aid el Kebir, 'the Big Holiday', to mark the near-sacrifice of Ismail (Isaac) by his father, Ibrahim (Abraham). When he is stopped by a voice from heaven, Ibrahim sacrifices a ram to Allah instead, so the Muslim tradition calls on the head of a family to slaughter a ram to mark the event. Also known as Aid el Adha, 'the Feast of the Sacrifice', the festivities can last for as long as a week as rams are led through the streets by a rope, carried around on shoulders, stuffed into the boot of a car, or draped over a moped to take home to slaughter in the ritual manner. In some households the fire is lit in the *tannur* to prepare *mechoui* with the whole beast or large joints, or the animal is divided into various cuts for different dishes– the head is prized for steaming and will be served to a guest or the most important member of the household; the rams testes and penis are generally grilled and regarded as an honour to eat; the offal is threaded onto skewers for *kouah*; the hind legs are roasted; and the cuts in between end up in *harira* and Mrouzia tagines, and some get minced for kefta. It is a family or community affair, one of merriment and sharing.

Another day to donate to the poor is Aid el Achoura, or Ashura, the tenth day of the new year, which for some is a day spent mourning and fasting, for others a day of celebration, but there is a carnival atmosphere with bonfires, shows and sweet sellers, and people eat *fakia*,

Top **The Hassan II Mosque in Casablanca is the largest functioning mosque in Africa and has the tallest minaret (210m/689ft) in the world with a laser on the summit projecting a beam towards Mecca.**

Bottom **Colourful, ornamental tiles in a Moroccan courtyard.**

Above **St Peter's Cathedral in Rabat.**

Opposite top **In the Rif Mountains, the old town of Chefchaouen, or Chaouen, is known for its striking blue-washed buildings.**

Opposite bottom **Heavenly pink rose production in El Kelaa M'gouna, the Valley of Roses, in the Oases of the Dades Valley.**

a mixture of dried fruit and nuts, and couscous with chicken or with preserved meat prepared with the leftovers from Aid el Adha.

The birthday of the Prophet Mohammed is marked by a religious holiday, Aid Al Mawlid Annabaoui, when businesses and schools close and the sacks of couscous vanish from the markets as families rush home to prepare the sweet couscous dish, *seffa*, as well as other sweets and cakes to distribute amongst the community. Some men spend the day at the mosque, while others celebrate by wearing colourful clothing and visiting each other. It is a day of respect for the Prophet and his values – forgiveness, love, helping those in need – and the old medinas become charged with energy, religious chants and drums and, of course, food.

Although the majority of Moroccans are Muslim by faith, they are aware of the diverse cultural identities within the country and they live in harmony with the Moroccan Jews who share many of the same culinary beliefs, such as the importance of hospitality and the sharing of bread, regarded as sacred in both religions, and distributing to the poor. And, although their practices and religious laws may differ, the Moroccan Muslims and Moroccan Jews share many cultural festivities and feasts, such as Aid el Adha. Rosh Hashanah, the Jewish New Year, is celebrated.

Regional festivals

Moroccans celebrate national holidays throughout the country. There are festivals to mark the birthday of the King and for his ascension to the throne; in November there is Independence Day. But there are also festivals that draw people from afar because they all involve music, dancing, street parades and food – and there are a lot of these in Morocco! Every month of the year there is something going on: moussems to pay tribute to saints; spiritual Sufi festivals; an annual Marrakesh arts festival held in July; and the Meknes Fantasia, an annual equestrian performance to celebrate traditional folklore.

Regional harvest festivals are important social gatherings for villagers. In the Mediterranean region on the edge of the Rif Mountains there is a festival in Berkane, a village surrounded by orchards, to honour the harvest of clementines in May; a festival to celebrate the bounty of the sea on the beaches of Al Hoceima in July; and an olive festival in December, held in the olive groves in Rafsai. Inland from Agadir on the Atlantic coast, there is a week-long honey festival in Imouzzer das Ida Outanane, a village renouned for its waterfalls, in August and, in the same month, there is an apple and pear festival in Imouzzer du Kandar, just south of Fes. Also in the foothills of the Middle Atlas, just south of Fes, there is a three-day cherry festival in June when Sefrou, an ancient walled town, comes alive with a colourful market, torchlight processions and the selection of Miss Cherry. And in Tafraoute, situated at the foot

of Djbel Lekest and surrounded by rocky, wind-eroded terrain, there is a charming festival in February to celebrate the almond trees in blossom – a spectacle of colour against the ochre walls of the town which brings together the villagers from the valley in a market atmosphere with food, dancers, musicians and storytellers.

Below **Young Berber girls of the Ait Haddidou tribe, in the Upper Atlas mountains.**

Bottom **Henna is used to decorate the hands and feet in times of celebration. It is also used to toughen the skin, and women will put it all over the palms of their hands and the soles of their feet to protect them when working in the fields.**

Rose Festival | This festival starts with the main road in the town of El Kelaa M'gouna being blanketed with freshly picked roses as the heady aroma of honey and treacle fills the air. Who would have thought that roses would grow in the Dades Valley – some of the harshest and most desolate terrain in the southern valleys where the steep, rust-red gorges are carved out of the river – but they do. They grow wild and are also cultivated in their thousands, and every Spring the 'Valley of Roses' bursts into pink, fragrant bloom. Legend has it that the roses came to Morocco with a Berber merchant from Damascus and the species that grows here is Rosa Damscena, the ancient Syrian rose famous for its intense perfume. The valley produces between 3000 to 4000 tons of roses very year and the petals must be picked in the early morning before the sun burns them. Roses are loaded into crates on backs of tractors, trucks and mules, petals are gathered in baskets and everyone heads to El Kelaa. The villagers drink rose tea, splash their hands and faces with rosewater and fix roses in buttonholes or in arrangements around their wrists and the festivities begin. Around 20,000 people come to this small town to enjoy the celebration of roses and rose produce, such as the distilled rosewater, rose perfume, soap and jam. The roses are the main attraction, displayed in canvas tents where growers and buyers haggle over terms, but there are stalls of apples, dates, almonds and walnuts, and kebabs grilling over charcoal. And at the end of the Festival, girls from the villages dress in their best kaftans and decorate themselves with roses to be selected as the Rose Queen. Naturally, the winner is showered in rose petals.

Imilchil Wedding Festival | The pretty village of Imilchil is already a popular stop for visitors exploring the high Atlas and southern oases routes but there is one event in September that puts it on the cultural and culinary map as well – the legendary Wedding Festival. Traditionally, it is a homecoming event for the herders who have spent the summer in faraway grazing grounds, so the ensuing cattle fair for livestock traders adds to the chaos of the bustling market and people who have gathered for match-making at the wedding festival that takes place at the same time. For the Amazigh, the Berber tribes, this tradition is a homage to love and has been centred around the belief that any marriage blessed by the saint Sidi Mohammaed El Maghani will be long and prosperous, so the festival takes place near his tomb in the form of a tent city with a market, music, dancing and feasting. The women who are looking for a partner in life dress in traditional attire and wear their finest silver jewellery, and the men who are available dress in white with turbans. For a largely Muslim nation with its Islamic restrictions on women this is a liberating festival as the young are allowed to meet and marry freely.

Date Festival | Also in the region of the iconic Draa Valley, but closer to the desert and the Algerian border, is the little town of Erfoud, where the Festival of Dates is held in October every year. As this is one of Morocco's richest regions for dates and therefore known as the 'Country of the Dates', the economy of Erfoud relies on the date harvest and the festival that goes with it, and the locals make sure that they put on a good show so that people come from afar. It is a lovely excuse to enjoy traditional Berber music and tribal performances, fashion parades, dancing and, of course, food. This arid region is perfect for cultivating dates so there are many varieties – the succulent Medjool is regarded as king –and the dishes showcasing them are just as varied, from stuffed dates to date tagines, date couscous (the speciality of the region), and *kalia*, meat that is buried in the hot sand to slow-cook and served with dates. It is a three-day affair and as with other rural festivals centred around harvests, such as the Cherry Festival and the Rose Festival, it ends with the selection of the Date Queen.

Camel Festival | In late May or early June, the Tan-Tan Moussem, also known as the Goulimine Camel Festival, is held in the deep south in the western Sahara in the desert town of Tan-Tan. It is an annual gathering of nomadic peoples of the Sahara – more than thirty tribes – some travelling from Mali, Mauritania and Niger. Originally a spontaneous meeting of peoples as part of the herding calendar to buy, sell and exchange camels and goods, it first took the form of a moussem in 1963 to celebrate the life of Mohamed Laghdaf, who resisted French and Spanish colonialism and is buried in Tan-Tan. Due to turmoil in the region it was banned for several decades but revived in 2004. Now the moussem is the biggest gathering of nomadic peoples in north Africa and is still an important event for tribes to meet, trade and exchange but also a celebration of craft, food and cultural identity. One of the highlights is the equestrian *tbourida*, where Berber tribesmen, dressed in billowing robes, ululate a war cry and shoot their rifles towards the sky. The focus of the moussem, however, is the trade of hundreds of dromedary (Arabian) camels. The long procession with nomads astride or leading the camels and singing traditional songs, and the women dressed in tribal costumes, their hands covered in intricate henna tattoos, is a sight worth seeing. Tents are set up to display food, herbal remedies, weaving and crafts, and, like all Berber moussems, there are musical performances, chanting, dancing and plenty to eat – griddled flat breads, dates to share, and sheep or goats slow-roasted in a pit.

Top **Young woman in traditional costume at the Erfoud date festival.**

Above **Oases are scattered throughout the deserts of Morocco. Where there is water, there is life.**

The souks

The country markets and the souks of the old Medinas are the lungs of Morocco. Magical and enticing, filled with arresting aromas, they are noisy bustling venues for haggling, planning, utensil buying, conducting business, entertainment and gossip – and snacking. The crowds, the chaos, the smells, the donkeys and camels, the tooting trucks and mopeds, the shade of rural tented stalls or the cool of old city, stone passageways and high-ceilinged, indoor storage areas stacked with crates and sacks, all add to the excitement of shopping. From the medieval souks of Fes and Marrakesh to the Berber markets in the foothills of the Atlas Mountains, there is a sense of life revolving around food and shopping as both men and women stop at stalls to rake through items of clothing, to inspect the skills of local craftsmen, and to fill their baskets with local produce and items fashioned from nature and the ground. A local stone is used for shampoo; a murky-looking sludge, prepared from plants, is sold as soap; tiny saucers made from red clay are offered as lipstick – if you wet your finger you can apply the natural colour to your lips; ground plants, insects and lizards are sought after as aphrodisiacs. You can buy a solid cone of white sugar and a block of yellow butter; long stalks of leafy herbs tied in large bundles; plump purple and green olives piled high in plastic tubs; and you can smell the scent of the dried lavender heads and pink rose buds while you nibble on toasted almonds or dried apricots. There are hanging carcasses and the complete decapitated head of a cow; live hens clucking furiously in their cages; the freshly stripped fleece of a lamb; the full-length skin of a python; tiny live tortoises; and whole, dried chameleons.

To experience the breadth of culinary diversity and the loud chaos of locals, travellers and visitors gathered in one place, it is worth visiting the Place Djemaa el Fna, meaning the 'Assembly of the Dead' after the heads of conspirators were displayed there by one of the sultans. Situated at the heart of Marrakesh, bridging the old medina quarter with the newer sections of the city, it is a large open area that acts as a hub for trade and cultural expression by combining street theatre with street food. It might seem relatively quiet in the morning as traders set up their stalls and people wander through the square or sip mint tea at a café on the edge of the square but, from mid-afternoon and well into the night the Place takes on the atmosphere of a carnival with the beating of drums and bells, the tuneless flute playing of the snake-charmers, performing monkeys, fire-eaters, storytellers, costumed water-sellers in fringed hats clanging brass cups, henna tattoo artists, acrobats and

Opposite **The old medina in Fes is little changed since medieval days, a wonderful maze of tiny lanes with overflowing stalls selling everything under the sun.**

Maroc
TELEBOUTIQUE

musicians. For centuries the Place was a giant food market as traders came from the mountains every day with their goods but now they share the space with the theatre, the snack stalls and busy cafés and rooftop restaurants around the edge. There are juice stalls with oranges arranged in geometrically shaped piles; there are busy nut stalls as the almonds, pistachios or chestnuts are roasted and scooped into paper cones; and there are huge cauldrons of spicy snail broth or *harira* brewing over stoves alongside makeshift grills on which the liver, heart and kidneys of sheep and goats are cooked on skewers. If those stalls don't lure you in, you can move on to the frying fish or steaming spiced tagines.

For stalls selling local produce, natural remedies, spices and everything you need for a tagine, the kitchen, your comfort and the furnishing of your home, you only need to wander out of the Place and venture into the extensive maze of a souk where you will find chunky jewellery and leather bags, belts and slippers, colourful kaftans, scarves and dance outfits, drums and water pipes, bowls and cooking spoons carved out of local woods, and beautiful glass lamps and tribal-designed carpets and cushions. Around the corners, almost hidden away, you'll come across small shops stacked from floor to ceiling with tubs of pink, green, purple and black olives; large tins of pressed olive oil and bottles of the nutty argan oil; and brightly coloured jars of preserved lemons and pickled cucumbers, turnips, carrots and pears. For your tagines and sweet pastries, there are shops displaying roasted and ground almonds, walnuts and pistachios, crates of plump dried apricots, prunes and figs, and boxes of fresh red or yellow dates alongside the dark brown dried dates, some soft and succulent, perfect for dipping into milk and melting in your mouth. Jars of honey are never far away from the dried fruit and nuts as they are often combined in sweet and savoury dishes and there is a delightful choice, ranging from the light and fragrant orange blossom or lavender to aromatic sage or the rich, treacle-like chestnut honey.

Long wooden carts laden with seasonal fruit and vegetables, such as aubergines, courgettes, carrots, oranges and watermelons, are often parked in cool, airy areas of the souk and the donkeys that pull the carts will be tethered nearby. Sacks of dried pulses and grains are also in this part of the souk where women gather to select the right grade of semolina for the all-important couscous. Mortars and pestles, some with intricate Berber designs, sit beside baskets of dried lavender and rose buds, bundles of dried herbs such as sage and lemon verbena, and sacks of spices, which are sold in seed and bark form as well as finely ground and often displayed in high cone-shaped mounds beside the pyramids of ground natural dyes for clothing and hair. Selecting the special spice blend, *ras el hanout*, can be tricky as every spice merchant tells you his, or hers, is the best. As you walk around the souk, perhaps the biggest surprise of all are the walls of sweet-smelling mint tied in big bundles and stacked so high you can't see the person selling them. These luscious green bundles are, of course, destined for the national mint tea.

Above **Welcome to the best sweet shop in the market. Walk up the main alleyway of the Marrakesh souk and you will find this stall on your right. You get to try before you buy.**

Opposite, clockwise from top left **A colourful spice shop in Marrakesh where you can also buy little clay pumices covered in crocheted wool to scrub your back in the hammam; Ornate, painted doorways are a feature of Morocco's towns and cities; A narrow street in the indoor souk of Marrakesh; Traditional, colourful lanterns in the souk.**

Moroccan eating

When travelling in Morocco, it is difficult to stop yourself eating. The cooking in the streets always smells so enticing and the cooking in a home is accompanied by rituals of hospitality, starting with the offering of a sweet date or sweetmeat to welcome you. When you are a guest in a Moroccan household your comfort is looked after with refreshments and plenty of food. Sometimes too much food, but it is rude to refuse!

Street food | Food sold and eaten on the streets of Morocco gives the towns and villages a terrific ambience. The souks, old medinas, tiny, narrow streets, busy boulevards, ports, bus and train stations are alive with food-centred activity. Street vendors sell their specialities from ramshackle stalls or from baskets and trays carried through the crowds. Aromatic breads and filled savoury pastries appear from nowhere. Donkeys and traders alike are bent over with their burdens, laden with sacks of grain, while vegetables arrive from the fields in horse- or donkey-drawn carts. Amongst the dust, slanting sunlight and long shadows, the scenes are almost medieval as veil-covered women gather in groups to haggle and men splattered in dirt with lit cigarettes dangling from their mouths scurry about unpacking loads, setting up stalls and preparing food. The smell of fire, smoke and cooking fills the air and lingers long into the night.

At dawn, light and golden fritters are deep-fried in vast cauldrons and sold in sheets of paper. Also in the mornings, people gather in cafés to gulp down bowls of steaming chickpea and lentil soup –*harira* – or plates of thick, hot pancakes – *baghira* – dripping with honey. The enticing smell of freshly baked bread and rolls emanates from almost every corner and every stall, where people stop to buy a few aromatic buns or a wedge of *acuajada*, a Spanish-style omelette. Dried fruit and nuts, spices and dried herbs are always on display ready to nibble or sprinkle over a snack. No matter what time of day or night, there is always something delicious to eat.

Mezze or kemia | The ancient tradition of mezze was probably introduced to Morocco by the Arabs in the seventh century. Derived from the Persian word *maza*, meaning taste or relish, this course was intended to delight the palate before the main meal. This style of eating remains one of the most enjoyable and creative in the Middle East and North Africa but, in Morocco, the word 'mezze' is not as commonly used as 'kemia' or, in some regions, 'mukabalatt'.

Some *kemia* dishes are simply *amuse-gueule*, palate ticklers, such as roasted nuts, a plate of pickles with a local cheese, a bowl of plump

Top left **Freshly baked flat breads being sold in the street in Fes.**

Top right **A quick street snack of corn bread dipped in a local spice mix.**

Bottom **The lively food stalls in the Place Djemaa el Fna at night.**

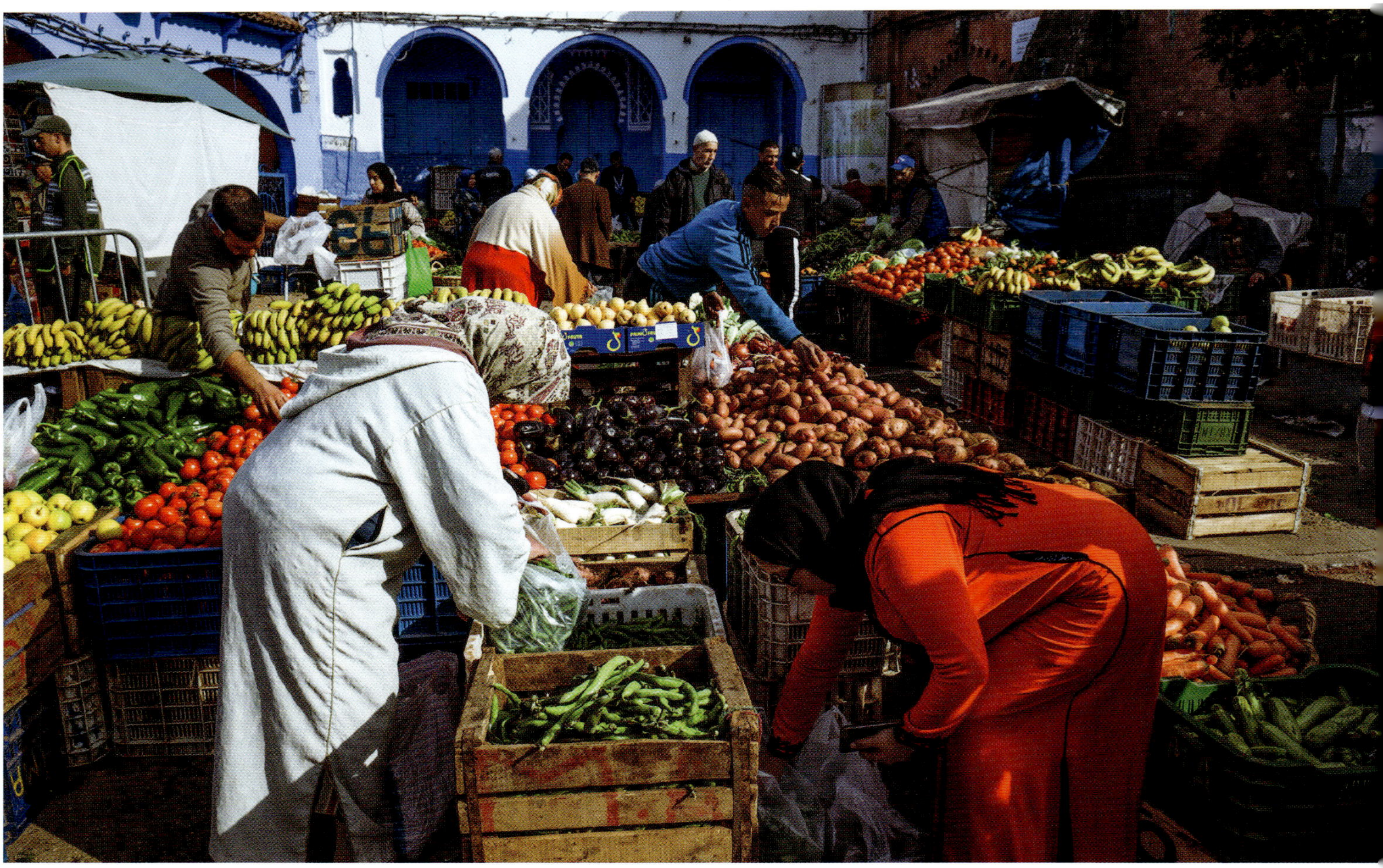

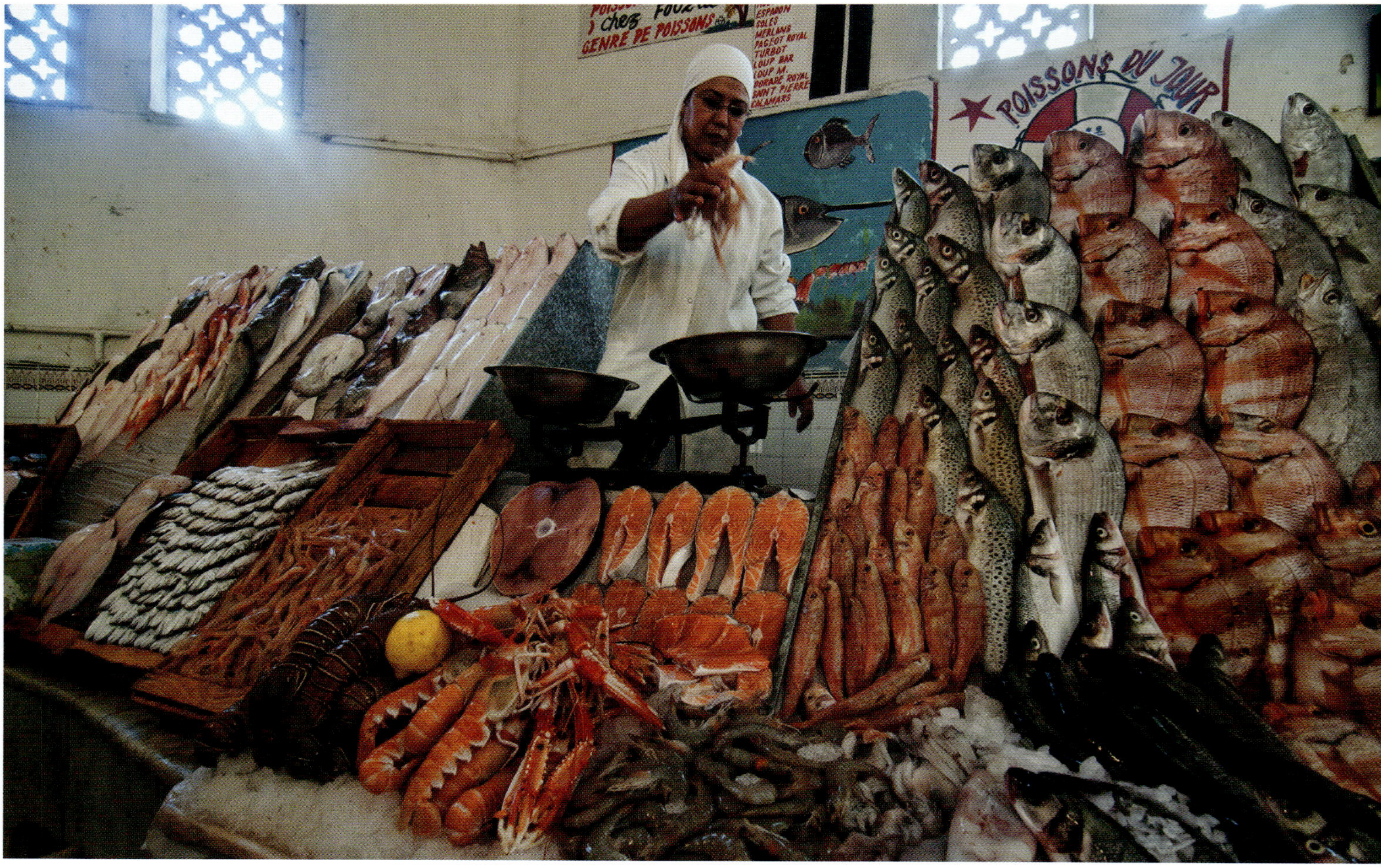
chez
GENRE DE POISSANS
ESPADON
SOLES
MERLANS
PAGEOT ROYAL
TURBOT
LOUP BAR
LOUP M.
DORADE ROYAL
SAINT PIERRE
CALAMARS
POISSONS DU JOUR

olives marinated in herbs or spices, or cubes of sweet watermelon. Others are more complex, involving fresh fruit and cooked vegetables in salads sharpened by the bite of salty preserved lemon; garlicky dips prepared with roasted aubergines or broad beans; savoury pastries stuffed with cheese, minced beef or lamb flavoured with ginger or cinnamon, or fish pounded with onions and herbs; small whole sardines soused in vinegar and spices; pan-fried offal spiked with garlic and fiery harissa; mini grilled fish or meatballs. And, as with the tradition of mezze, the enjoyment of *kemia* is relaxed. There is no rush as you tuck into the dishes, with chunks of bread to mop up the olive oil and savoury juices.

When preparing a Moroccan meal, try to select *kemia* dishes that are quite different from each other, with contrasting yet complementary tastes and textures, as this part of the meal is where the fun begins. These dishes might be followed by a fruity, spicy lamb tagine but equally they might be followed by a cut of plain chargrilled meat. The flavours of the *kemia* dishes may be the most important part of the meal.

Fresh and seasonal | Fresh vegetables are abundant in Morocco, and market traders sell a variety of produce from the local farms, as well as imported crops. Mediterranean staples, such as aubergines, courgettes, tomatoes and artichokes are put to good use alongside hearty root vegetables such as potatoes, carrots and yams. Vegetables can be roasted, pan-fried or baked, caramelizing their skins and sealing in the natural sweetness of their flesh. Beans add protein and texture to vegetable-rich tagines, and a medley of spices and seasonings turn simple ingredients into show-stopping dishes. Ripe fruit is usually eaten fresh, often as a dessert, or cooked in a tagine, but the vegetables and herbs are destined for a variety of delicious mezze dishes, side dishes or refreshing, crunchy salads.

Salads are never served on their own. Instead, several may be offered at the beginning of a meal as part of the mezze spread or they may accompany tagines to balance the flavours and texture. If the tagine is sweet and fruity, the salad will be crunchy and spiced with chilli; conversely a spicy tagine will be tamed with a sweet, refreshing salad. The vegetables, herbs and flavours are so versatile that there is plenty of scope for experimenting with combinations of your own. Both the salads and side dishes make irresistible courses or light meals served by themselves, with crusty, fresh bread to soak up all the deliciously oily, garlicky and spicy juices. Other vegetables that marry particularly well with Moroccan flavours include leeks, cauliflowers, borlotti beans, courgettes and squash. Try them combined with fruit, such as apples and pears, or with nuts and olives, a sprinkling of spicy and aromatic ras el hanout or cinnamon and, of course, a little chopped preserved lemon.

Fresh from the seas, swordfish, tuna, monkfish, sea bream, red mullet, shark, sardines and fresh anchovies are in constant supply, from the

Top **Women shopping for fruit and vegetable in the medina of Chafchaouen old town.**

Bottom **Fresh fish for sale in the Marche Central in Casablanca.**

Strait of Gibraltar and the Atlantic Ocean. Fish is commonly marinated in the aromatic spice paste, chermoula, where the distinctive spice mix works beautifully with the delicate flesh. Fish is grilled, pan-fried or baked – or cooked in tagines. Prawns, mussels and scallops are given special *k'dra* treatment in an extravagant dish fit for a feast.

Mewshi | Meshwi is meat and poultry (as well as fish and vegetables) that is roasted and grilled over an open fire, pan-fried or baked in the oven, cooking from the outside to leave the middle moist and tender.

The most popularly cooked animal in the Muslim world is the sheep. On the day of Aid el Kebir, the festival marking the sacrifice of Ismail, sheep are gathered by the roadsides and in the markets for sale as each household will slaughter one and use every bit of it in different dishes. The good cuts of meat are grilled and roasted; the lesser cuts are cooked slowly in tagines or soups; the head is baked in the local ovens; the trotters are cooked in a tagine with chickpeas; and the bones, joints and gristle are boiled with spices to make the meat conserve, *mrouzia*. Another traditional method for a whole sheep or goat is *mechoui*, cooking on a spit over a charcoal fire burning in a pit. The meat is spiced with garlic and cumin, and cooked very slowly, with frequent basting to ensure it is moist and tender; a dish reserved for ceremonial occasions.

Puddings and pastries | To dine Moroccan style, after wiping away the last grains of couscous from the fingers, select from the season's fruit. The choice of fresh fruits is vast, ranging from different types of dates, grapes and sweet melons, to strawberries, peaches, apricots, ruby-red pomegranates, yellow plums, plump cherries, bursting figs, white and purple mulberries, pineapples, mangoes, prickly pears and cactus fruit. Some fruits, such as quinces and plums, lend themselves to poaching in syrup with spices, an ancient method of preserving.

More homely desserts and sweet snacks are often based on creamy yogurt or milk. The yogurt is sprinkled with sugar or drenched in honey and can be served with fruit. The milk puddings are also quite plain, often lifted with a touch of saffron or flower water.

Sweet pastries and cakes are usually enjoyed as snacks from a street stall or pastry shop. Some are complicated and time-consuming to make, the special kneading techniques requiring years of practice. Today's busy cooks buy ready-prepared *ouarka*, the paper-thin dough used to make many of the sweet pastries. If there is a good pastry shop in the neighbourhood, it is even easier to pop out and buy ready-made. There are rich pastries for feast days; sticky, honey cakes and fried pastries bathed in scented syrup for Ramadan; simple cookies decorated with nuts to offer to guests; and cakes filled with almond paste for a touch of refinement. One of the most famous Moroccan pastries is *m'hanncha*, coiled like a snake and sprinkled with cinnamon and icing sugar.

Top **Meat and vegetables cooking over charcoal in a street stall.**

Bottom **Sweet pastries and cakes in a Moroccan market.**

البيئة حياتنا، نحافظ عليها
Association
Nass
Lhomma
Jamaa El Fna
جامع الفنا
Bank Al Maghr
بنك المغرب

Tagines and couscous

We have the Berbers to thank for tagines and couscous. It is their unique contribution to Moroccan culinary culture and a predominant feature wherever you go. In the seventh century, when Arab soldiers settled in the region, they brought spices such as cinnamon, ginger, caraway and cumin that were quickly included in the traditional tagines. They also introduced the idea of matching sweet with sour, using honey and fruit. It is this sweet and sour taste, combined with warm aromatic spices, that gives the Moroccan tagines their own distinct character.

Couscous is also considered to be Morocco's national dish. In different forms, it is a traditional staple of the whole of the North African region, right down to Senegal and across to Chad. Further east in Egypt and parts of the Middle East, it is known as *moghrabiyyeh*, meaning 'the dish of the North Africans'.

Top **A maker and seller of newly fired earthenware tagines in Marrakesh.**

Bottom **Decorated tagines in the market in Marrakesh.**

Tagines | Essentially, a tagine (*tajine*) is a long-simmered stew, usually meat-based, cooked slowly over charcoal, and deeply aromatic and full of flavour. It is also the name of the earthenware cooking vessel with a conical lid designed to allow the food to cook in its own steam. The *slaoui* is the round base of the tagine on which its conical or curved lid sits. The design of the lid can vary in different Berber villages. Many people eat directly from this tagine base but there are also decorative ones for serving, and the slaoui might get used for serving other dishes too.

The tagine *slaoui* can sit on top of a charcoal stove, the *kanoun*, or go in the oven. The kanoun that you see in the villages is made of sun-baked clay but some are made of iron or copper and, once the charcoal is lit in the base it is replenished from time to time to keep it going for hours so that the heat is gently dispersed all around the tagine *slaoui*, enabling the ingredients to cook slowly in the steam, which builds up inside the lid. This way the ingredients remain beautifully tender and moist in a broth that reduces to a sauce, sometimes sweet and buttery and best mopped up with bread. When you travel through rural areas, you often see tagines lined up regimentally by the side of a road, or at the edge of a country restaurant, steaming gently on top of their charcoal stoves, enticing you to stop and tuck into tender lamb with artichokes and peas, beef with aubergines and dates, or perhaps the chicken with green olives and preserved lemon which is deliciously tart and refreshing, flavoured with local herbs.

There are different types of tagine dishes, distinguished by the cooking fat, the spices, or the quantity of onions that form a velvety sauce on cooking. The *tfaia* tagines are usually prepared with smen and served with almonds and boiled eggs. *Qamama* tagines are cooked with lots of onions, honey and lemon until the onions caramelize and melt in your mouth; regarded as superior, great praise is heaped on the cook if the tagine is golden and caramelized. *M'quali* tagines are flavoured with saffron and ginger; *mchermel* tagines require the main ingredient to be marinated first and then cooked in the marinade; and *m'hammar* tagines means a 'red' tagine due to the quantity of paprika in the cooking sauce. Classic tagines include lamb with prunes and almonds, and chicken with olives and preserved lemon. Another type of tagine known as a *k'dra* is cooked in the aged butter, smen, the preferred cooking fat of the Berbers, which adds its distinctive flavour. In some regions the name *k'dra* also refers to the large tin-lined copper pot the ingredients are cooked in.

The method employed in tagine cooking varies from the countryside to the cities. In the north, in cities like Tangier and Casablanca, where the Spanish and French influences are evident, the meat is often browned in butter or oil and the spices and onions are sautéed before adding the liquid and slow cooking, whereas the traditional way of preparing a Fassi and Marrakchi tagine is to heat the water or broth with the raw ingredients, cook slowly, and add the butter or smen at the end. In rural areas, a tagine is often served as a communal dish with the meat or chicken eaten first and then the sauce mopped up with bread, so the hot *slaoui* is placed on a *qa'tajine*, a copper dish to protect the table. For special occasions or in wealthy households and restaurants, the contents of the cooking tagine might be transferred to a serving one, decorated with pretty blue, turquoise, green, yellow and red patterns, which enhances the overall pleasure when serving guests.

When you go to a tagine stall to buy the cooking or serving vessel, you might see several styles and sizes – some represent a Berber tribe, a particular village, or a region of Morocco. To be used for cooking, they must be glazed. Before use, the standard clay tagine is treated by soaking it in water for 24 hours; some people season it by placing bay leaves and dried sage in the base along with a roughly chopped onion, garlic, and a generous dollop of olive oil, then fill it with water and gently heat it to remove the earthenware taste from the base and prepare it for prolonged cooking over heat; others swear by heating milk in the base to scalding point and leaving it to cool.

Traditionally, the tagine is placed on top of an earthenware charcoal stove, the *kanoun*, so that the base is a distance from the heat and the coals can be kept smouldering for a long period of time. On conventional stoves and gas hobs you need a diffuser as the base of the tagine is too close to the heat and will develop cracks.

The secret of a good tagine is to simmer the meat until it is very tender, allowing the oil or butter to mingle with the liquid to produce a velvety sauce, which must be served piping hot. This combination of rich, sweet and spicy flavours in a thick sauce can be unbelievably delicious.

Below **A traditional dish of couscous served topped with vegetables.**

The liquor is best mopped up with chunks of bread. Traditionally, the tagine would just be one of many courses in a meal served with a salad or bread but couscous or rice alongside turns it into a meal in itself.

Top **Sifting and sorting the couscous grains to get the right size.**

Above **Rolling couscous in the hand to dip into sauce or broth.**

Couscous

Heaped couscous is recognized as the signature dish of Maghrebi cuisine, originally created by the Berbers using durum wheat introduced by the Carthaginians. Couscous is of fundamental value to Moroccan culture for dietary, religious and symbolic reasons, as the Moroccans believe it is a food that brings God's blessing upon those who consume it. It is therefore prepared in every household on Muslim holy days and on Fridays, the Islamic day of rest, when it is traditionally distributed to the poor as well. At festive and religious feasts, such as the traditional *diffas*, or the Berber *moussems*, a mound of couscous is served as the magnificent crown to end the meal. There is a Moroccan saying that 'each granule of couscous represents a good deed', so it is not surprising that thousands of granules are consumed in a day.

Although referred to as a 'grain', couscous is not technically one; instead it could be more accurately described as Moroccan 'pasta', as it is made with semolina flour and water and then hand-rolled, sieved and dried before it is steamed in a traditional *keskes* and *gdra* or a modern couscoussier (see also pages 70–71). Traditionally, there is quite a bit of effort in making couscous, in washing and soaking it, aerating it by hand in a *gsaa* – a large, round wooden or earthenware bowl – and then alternating the steaming and aerating with a little oil or butter. The familiar commercial varieties that are available today tend to be pre-cooked or instant, making preparation quicker and easier as once the grain has absorbed an equal volume of water, it simply needs steaming until heated through.

Traditionally, couscous is served as a course on its own. It can look spectacular, particularly when piled up in a cone-shaped mound for banquets and topped with stuffed pigeons, dates and almonds, or decorated with strips of colourful vegetables and topped with sweet onions and raisins tinged yellow with saffron, and it is often accompanied by little side dishes, such as spicy chickpeas, marinated raisins, and harissa paste. Eating couscous in a traditional manner is an experience in itself and requires a little practise. Like everything else, couscous is eaten with the fingers of the right hand. It is a communal dish so, once the mound has been set on the ground, or on the low table, diners literally ram their right hands, palm upwards, into the grains to extract a handful and then, using the thumb and first two fingers, deftly roll the grains to form small tight balls that might incorporate some small pieces of meat or vegetables, and flip them into their mouths. If there is a lot of sauce or broth with the couscous, a little bowl of perfumed water is provided to clean the fingers at the end of the meal. At home, you might prefer to use a fork.

The traditional kitchen

Food and family are the heartbeat of Moroccan culture. Much of the day-to-day life is centred round food, with visits to the markets, tea in the cafés, street snacks and religious festivals. To sample the best of Moroccan cuisine, however, it is essential to be invited into a home where the women of the household have lovingly prepared a myriad of tantalizing dishes. Eating on the cheap in Morocco will enable you to sample couscous, spicy tagines, savoury pastries, kebabs and kefta, but you will only skim the surface of the complexity and depth of flavours of the richly authentic dishes prepared in the homes. As the recipes are still handed down from generation to generation, with very little recorded on paper, no two dishes will ever be the same – it all depends on the love and skills of the cooks, usually the women of the household, relying on the eye as a scale of measurement and the tongue for the complexity of seasoning, each dish reflecting the mood of the cook.

Traditionally, the kitchen was a very feminine place – a place for gossip, for healing, for bonding – and cooking was regarded as a woman's gift from god. Men rarely entered this private culinary zone and guests were not invited in. Much of this rings true today in rural areas but in the old imperial cities, where the atmosphere is more cosmopolitan and women study and work in demanding professions, they of course want to eat out or hire a cook, and there is a growing number of male kitchen apprentices and well-known male chefs.

In Morocco's hidden past, wealthy Arab and Berber men from the imperial cities of Fes, Meknes and Marrakesh would purchase women of African origin, descended from slaves who were brought into the country from the Sudan and parts of central Africa, to cook for them and look after the children. Sometimes they were bought to be a third or fourth wife and, if she bore any children, they would usually be brought up in the household, but the female offspring would be expected to carry on the tradition of cooking.

Shrouded in mystique, dressed in robes and a turban, their long sleeves tied around the wrists with a silk cord and bangles jangling around her wrists and ankles, creating a mystical tinkle from the depths of the dark, spartan kitchen, these women were kept in a form of bondage and usually remained illiterate. Nowadays, the descendants of these women, or any young girls and women who work in households, have laws to protect them and some run kitchens in prestigious restaurants and hotels, or work for catering companies that hire them out to wealthy families to prepare a *diffa* for a large wedding or religious feast. The catering company itself may be headed by a man, as business is still a man's domain in many regions, and he will make all the arrangements

Top **For crispy-crusted tannour bread, a delicacy from the mountains, the dough is plastered against the walls of the clay oven which is then sealed and reopened when the bread is ready.**

Bottom **Women preparing a meal together in Merzouga.**

Above **A traditional teapot and glasses for the refreshing mint tea.**

with the family, while the women are busy in the kitchens for several days, purchasing all the food from the markets, slaughtering the sheep, preparing the *ouarka* for the savoury and sweet pastries, and chopping and grinding ingredients using traditional Maghrebi kitchen tools.

In a conventional Moroccan home, palatial or modest, old or modern, the family meal is served at a low table surrounded by benches or cushions. The presentation of the food and the eating of it are regarded as an art and a pleasure, so there is no hurry. In most homes, it is customary to eat using your hands so, at the start of a meal, a jug of perfumed water is passed around to refresh the face and fingers of the right hand. Generally, the thumb and first three fingers are used, just as the prophets are reputed to have done. There is a skill to scooping up the food with fingers, particularly in rolling couscous into a little ball and placing it into the mouth without even touching the lips. If you are not accustomed to eating with your hands, it is in fact very pleasurable as it enables you to appreciate the texture of the food as well as the flavour. The dishes are placed in the centre of the table, often in the earthenware dishes in which they were cooked, and everyone tucks in. As dish follows dish, it is vital to pace yourself and eat slowly so that you can enjoy each mouthful. Burping at the end of a meal is regarded as a sign of appreciation for all the good food and hospitality – it is customary to follow it with the words 'nhemdou Allah', 'we praise God' – and it is a cue for the food to be cleared and to recline comfortably on the cushions while the mint tea is served to refresh the palate and aid the digestion.

When cooking for guests, it is customary to make vast quantities of food so that they will be completely satisfied and unable to finish. Not finishing is in fact a polite thing to do as the leftover food will be enjoyed by members of the extended family. A meal of this nature can take several hours to prepare and the women of the house may be absent from the social gathering for the duration of the cooking. A traditional celebratory meal, a *diffa*, begins with a simple selection of appetizers and salads, *kemia*, which might include a bowl of olives, a cooked vegetable salad dressed with olive oil, a pounded vegetable or pulse dip, and savoury pastry served with flat bread. The first main dish to be served is the impressive *b'stilla*, filled with chicken or pigeon and dusted with icing sugar and cinnamon; the second dish is usually a *choua*, a steamed shoulder of lamb flavoured with cumin, or *mechoui*, a whole roast lamb or goat cooked over glowing coals in a pit in the ground. Next come a variety of tagines, each one different, served with flat bread to mop up the tasty sauce. The last tagine is always sweet, usually made of lamb, caramelized onions and honey. Just to make sure that no guest leaves with any space unfilled, the grand finale is a steaming mound of couscous, also eaten with the fingers. A simple plate of prepared fresh fruit marks the end of the meal before the hot mint tea served in decorative glasses.

The room where the food is cooked displays none of the splendour or exoticism of the actual dishes. Even in the grandest of riads, the kitchen is the most basic room in the house, semi-dark and cool in the stifling heat of summer but damp in the winter months. The cooking utensils are simple, consisting mainly of glazed earthenware tagines and copper pots, wooden spoons and a mortar and pestle, or grinding stone, for spices. A folded carpet is placed on the floor to serve as a seat.

The blessing of Allah may be called upon before the cooking commences and incense is often thrown into the fire to drive away the devil, *jnoun*. The dripping water in the courtyard fountain and the bashing of the pestle and mortar bring the darkness of the kitchen to life as the women chat and sing, while they fill the atmosphere with warmth and the aromatic aromas of fresh coriander, ginger, garlic and spices perfumed with a whiff of rose or mint. Modern city kitchens might lack this ambience but most Moroccan women take pride in their cooking and presentation of their food wherever they are.

Below **A modern couscoussier.**

Bottom **A potter at work in Fes.**

Cooking equipment and utensils

As well as the tagine, some cooking equipment and utensils will feature in every kitchen. Simple and effective, each item has a traditional purpose and rustic charm. Copper and brass pots, tin-lined copper pans for specific pastries, brown and ochre pottery, hand-carved wooden mortar and pestles, wooden spoons and trays, grass baskets, metal and silk sieves, iron or silver skewers, leather bottles, colourful serving dishes and pretty tea glasses with intricate designs, a still for distilling orange blossom and rose water, and a teapot. All of these utensils can be bought in the countryside markets and old city souks.

Kanoun | The portable, charcoal-fed *kanoun* is a small stove made of sun-baked clay on which the tagine sits, and in some wealthy households there may be a larger stove for baking and roasting too, otherwise the neighbourhood communal oven is used.

Gdra or K'dra | Usually made of copper or earthenware, the *gdra* is the lower part of the traditional pot for couscous in which the meat and vegetables are cooked. Sometimes, the copper pot is used on its own to cook for a big group and served in it so the dish might get called a *k'dra*, but this word is also used for tagines made with smen.

Keskes | Used solely for cooking couscous, this is the copper or tin pot that slots into the top of the *gdra*. It is perforated in the base to allow the steam from the ingredients below to gently cook the couscous grains. Together, the *gdra* and the *keskes* form the complete cooking utensil for making couscous, and is also known as the couscoussier (see also page 70).

Gsaa | The *gsaa* is a perhaps the most versatile utensil in the traditional kitchen. Large, wide and round, usually made of sun-baked clay which might or might not be glazed, it is used for kneading and resting bread and pastry doughs, for shaping kefta and biscuits, for aerating couscous, for picking over nuts and olives, and for soaking or washing small ingredients. Every kitchen has a *gsaa* and in some rural areas they are fashioned from the trunks of oak, walnut and olive trees and from date palms in the southern oases.

Tbeck | A large, shallow basket used to sort the grains of couscous according to size.

Mejmar | This is the copper or iron charcoal barbecue used for grilling. They come in different shapes and sizes, such as a round one for *tbsil dial ouarka*, the round dish used to make the thin flat breads, and the rectangular one with notched edges for slotting the *m'ghazel*, the iron skewers, into for kebabs, kefta and fish.

Ghorbel | The traditional village ghorbel is fashioned from perforated leather, stretched taut and wide to act as a sieve to separate the bran from crushed wheat when preparing semolina. The more modern utensil is made from metal.

Khabia | Used for both preserving and storing, the *khabia* is an earthenware jar, glazed on the inside, and varies in size. There will usually be several in a traditional kitchen to store flour, olives, preserved lemons or preserved meat and for preparing lben (see page 62).

Chkoua | A *chkoua* is a bottle made from tanned goatskin for carrying and keeping water. It is particularly useful for working in the fields, or for walking to market as it can be tied to clothing and it keeps the water cool. If a household has to fetch fresh water, it will be carried and kept in a chkoua. In rural areas, the *chkoua* is also used to prepare lben.

Ied ettas | As Moroccan meals are usually eaten with fingers, there is a utensil for cleaning them before and after a meal. Made of brass or silver plate, this ewer has a long slender spout, making it easy to pour the water, which might be scented with rose or orange blossom water. While everyone is eating it sits on a *tass*, a little pan on the table.

Siniya | Every kitchen has a *siniya*, a tray made of copper, brass, silver plate or wood, sometimes ornate and with legs a few inches high. This is the tray for the tea utensils – the pot, the glasses, the spoons and the sugar – so it is often polished and shiny. The *berrad* is the simple silver or metal teapot found in every household. It doesn't have to be fancy but the tea should always be served in ornate glasses.

Top **A traditional artisan fashioning copper pots and dishes in the old medina market in Fes.**

Bottom **A market stall displaying wooden cooking utensils and a range of baskets.**

Key ingredients

Olive oil, argan oil, scented waters, spices, herbs, preserved lemons, honey, olives and pickles are entrenched in the Moroccan kitchen. Aroma, flavour and texture are important features of everyday dishes but they differ according to the regions and seasons. All of the key ingredients for Moroccan food are found in the souks and markets of the cities and villages.

Spices

Moroccan cooks use every spice that ever found its way across the Sahara desert or over the Mediterranean, blending the influences of the different cultures that have their left their culinary mark: Berber, Arab, Moorish, Jewish, French, Ottoman and Spanish. Many of the spices now so intricately entwined in the cuisine first came to the region with the Arab traders along the caravan routes, carrying with them pungent spices from China, the East Indies, Persia, Egypt and Zanzibar. Cinnamon, ginger, cumin and coriander are perhaps the most traditional spices in Moroccan cooking, along with chillies, which were brought back from the New World by the Spaniards and distributed throughout the Middle East and North Africa by the Ottomans. The cooking of the imperial kitchens of the Berber dynasties relied on a delicate marriage of olive oil and spices and some of the best examples of this are to be found in Fassi cooking, the dishes from Fes, whereas rural Berber cooking tends to be more pungent and fiery with powerful tones of cumin, ginger and turmeric, flavoured with smen, honey and sugar, and in some cases icing sugar.

Ras el hanout | Of all the Moroccan spices and flavourings, the most eloquent and refined, the one that stands above all the rest, is ras el hanout, literally 'the head of the shop'. A legendary mix of at least thirty different spices, it is a synthesis of spices reflecting the centuries of trade and the geographical position of Morocco, as in that mix there are also seeds, bark and dried leaves from deepest Africa. The story behind it claims that a warrior, presumably one of the Arab invaders, created the mix with all the scents and flavours of the countries he had passed through. Rich in flavour and known to contain various aphrodisiacs, as well as several unknowns, each spice merchant has their own recipe and the price will vary according to the rarity of the spices included. And there is quite a list – cardamom seeds from Sri Lanka; nutmeg and mace from Java; galangal from the Far East; guinea pepper, an aphrodisiac from the Ivory coast; cinnamon from India and Sri Lanka; cloves from Zanzibar; ginger and curcuma from India; cyparacee, a strong-smelling stalk from Sudan; orris root from high in the Atlas Mountains; white ginger from Japan; ash berries from Europe; monk's pepper, an aphrodisiac from Morocco; belladonna berries; fennel flowers; lavender; black pepper; and rose buds. Although it is impossible to fully recreate ras el hanout, there is a recipe on page 74.

Aniseed (Nafaa) | The sweet, aromatic components of aniseed are often enjoyed in Moroccan breads. Otherwise the seeds are used in spice blends or – sparingly – in dishes with fennel seeds, or in place of them.

Opposite **Pyramids of ground spices in the Marrakesh spice souk.**

Opposite **Clockwise from top left: cumin and coriander seeds; fresh green peppers; cinnamon sticks; and dried red chillies.**

Black pepper (Ibzar) | Black pepper is employed as a spice, not just as a seasoning, to mitigate the sweetness of a dish. It was used to give a warm heat to a dish before chillies arrived in the region. However, it is still used in generous amounts in tagines and *meshwi*, and is probably used as often as white pepper in Morocco.

Hemp (kif) | Hemp seed is used to flavour some sweetmeats, particularly *majoun*, but you have to be careful buying from some street sellers in ports like Tangier as, although marijuana and hashish are illegal, it is present and does find its way into these little cakes.

Caraway (Kerouiya) | A warming spice and digestion aid like cumin, caraway is often added to vegetable and pulse dishes. Depending on the spice merchant, it can be a key flavour in harissa and in tabil, an aromatic spice mix from neighbouring Algeria and Tunisia but enjoyed in Morocco where it is used in some street meat dishes and the savoury pastry, *brik*.

Cardamom (Qaqulla) | Coffee and sweetmeats are sometimes flavoured with green cardamom and, because of its warm pungency, it is a great favourite in ras el hanout.

Chillies (Felfa harra) and Sweet paprika (Felfa hloua) | Although chillies entered Moroccan cuisine in the sixteenth century, they are used fresh or dried in harissa, and dried and ground in ras el hanout – the two key Moroccan spice flavourings. Fresh chillies are often used in salads and both sweet and hot paprika are added to spice blends, dusted over pastries and salads and stirred into tagines.

Cinnamon (Karfa) | Cinnamon is perhaps the most used spice of all in Moroccan cooking. It is used liberally in both sweet and savoury dishes – in broths, meat tagines, couscous, orange and carrot salads, combined with icing sugar and dusted over pigeon *b'stilla*, mixed with nuts for sweet pastry fillings, added to baking of all types and sprinkled over fruit – in fact, sprinkled over just about anything.

Coriander (Kezbour) | The word *kezbour* is used for both the seeds and the leafy herb (cilantro) and both are used a lot in Moroccan cuisine. Roasted and ground, they are added to almost every spice mix and marinade and, with caraway seeds, provide the key flavouring in tabil.

Cumin (Kamoun) | Cumin seeds are widely used throughout Morocco, usually dry-roasted first to warm the natural oil and release their aroma before being ground, using a mortar and pestle. Spice mixtures, such as the local merchant's spice for kefta, combine roasted cumin with roasted coriander seeds and sweet or hot paprika.

Tabil | A North African spice mix consisting mainly of coriander and caraway seeds balanced with a little chilli, its heat depending on the spice merchant who might have a heavy hand with the amount of chilli (see recipe on page 74).

Fennel (Besbass) | Fresh fennel is used in salads and some tagines but fennel seeds are popular as a flavouring in harissa and in meat broths, tagines and bread. Like cumin, the seeds aid digestion and are used to make a healthy tea or syrup to soothe coughs.

Fenugreek (Helba) | The warm fragrance of toasted fenugreek seeds, or ground fenugreek, is different to the usual bitter taste but it is that characteristic that Moroccans enjoy, particularly in tagines where the balance of bitter and sweet is key. Nursing mothers also turn to fenugreek as it is believed to induce lactation as well as lower blood sugar levels.

Ginger (Skinjbir) | Traditionally, fresh ginger isn't used as much as the dried and ground spice, which is employed in many spice mixes and baking. But, as fresh ginger contains health properties and aids the digestion, it is used in the tagines and broths of more modern Moroccan cooking.

Saffron (Saafrane) | Saffron plays an integral part in Moroccan cooking but, although it is cultivated in the south, it is expensive, so a cheap grade of ground saffron mixed with wild flowers, or ground turmeric, is sometimes used as 'poor man's saffron' for colouring purposes. In the villages of the south, the women have a lovely tradition of making golden saffron tea.

Turmeric (Khlerkoum) | The earthy taste and imparted orange-yellow colour is favoured more in Berber cooking than in dishes influenced by the French or Spanish. The slow-cooked meat and poultry tagines with turmeric are quite distinct and at least one will be included in a *diffa* (feast). The anti-inflammatory and antioxidant health benefits play a role too, as Berbers have an ancient relationship with herbal remedies.

Harissa | This fiery paste is popular throughout North Africa. It can be served as condiment, or as a dip for warm crusty bread, and it can be stirred into tagines and couscous to emit its distinct chilli taste. The recipe on page 77 is for the basic paste, to which other ingredients such as fennel seeds, fresh coriander and mint, dried orange rind or rose petals can be added. Jars of ready-prepared harissa and rose harissa are available in African and Middle Eastern stores, as well as some supermarkets and delicatessens.

Top **Worth its weight in gold, a herbalist carefully weighs dried saffron in the Atlas Mountains.**

Bottom **The beautiful purple crocus flowers are harvested in the south of Morocco for their precious saffron stamens.**

Herbs

There are lots of herbs indigenous to the different regions of Morocco, some used specifically for medicinal remedies, others for culinary purposes. Aside from sage (salmiya) and thyme (zaatar), both of which appear in herbal teas, salads and tagines, the most commonly used and recognizable are fresh coriander, mint and parsley.

Coriander (Kezbour) | Fresh coriander (cilantro) is probably the most-used herb in Moroccan cooking. It is a key component of fresh pastes and marinades like chermoula, it marries well with chilli by toning down the heat and refreshing the palate, and it is added liberally to soups, salads and tagines.

Mint (Naana) | Fresh mint, in particular sweet spearmint and peppermint varieties, has one hugely important destination – the ubiquitous Moroccan mint tea. Every market has large bunches of mint for this national drink and some of finds its way into refreshing salads and vegetable dishes too.

Parsley (Maadhouse) | Along with fresh coriander and mint, generous quantities of parsley are added to Moroccan salads and tagines. Parsley, in particular, cuts the spice and refreshes the breath, but it also marries beautifully with cumin and chilli and is often combined with coriander in the fresh spice paste, chermoula (page 77). The parsley used in Morocco is the flat leaf variety.

Scented waters

The culinary etiquette of eating with one's fingers requires the washing of them before a meal and the refreshing of them afterwards, and the scent of the two most commonly used distilled waters, orange blossom (zhar) and rose (ma'ouard), leaves the hands smelling sweet and fragrant. Both waters are also used in beauty products and perfume, and play a part in religious ceremonies. When it comes to their culinary uses, they are interchangeable so you can use the one you prefer. In the parts of Mediterranean and Atlantic coast where oranges grow, the preference is often for orange blossom water and, similarly rose water is preferred in the rose-growing regions, such as the M'Goun Valley in the south. Orange blossom water is sometimes splashed over salads and both are occasionally added to tagines, but the scent and flavour of the distilled sweet pink rose petals and the fragrant white orange blossom are highly desired in sweet dishes, such as stuffed dates, nut-stuffed pastries, cakes and milk puddings.

Top **The piles of fresh and dried herbs at the Moroccan stalls are sold by the bunch for savoury dishes and teas.**

Bottom **Both fruit and the flowers of the orange tree have their unique culinary uses in Morocco.**

Olives

I think Moroccans are the unsung olive kings of the globe, and Marrakesh is the place to go for its lively olive stalls. In amongst the jars of pickles and sheaves of mint, you will find yourself in olive heaven, spilling out of giant plastic tubs or heaped in mounds – skinny, cracked green ones; plump violet ones flavoured with garlic and turmeric; crinkled black ones cured in salt; fiery yellow ones spiked with coriander, cumin and chilli; and brown, purple, orange and pink ones, as well as various shades in between. Olives for nibbling, olives for cooking, olives for marinating; olives to be tucked into tagines, tossed into salads, and baked in bread; olives to be pressed for oil or bound in preserves; olives to be stuffed with almonds, garlic, or peppers. Moroccan cooks add olives to everything, and every village has its own special combination of flavourings, each city has its own particular variety of olive, and the olive sellers personalize their olives with their secret marinades.

From mid-September to October, the green olives are picked. Some are cracked and soaked in salted water; others are pitted and stuffed with almonds and pimento. The violet- and beige-coloured olives, which are picked in November, are often slashed with a sharp knife and soaked in brine, and the black olives remain on the tree to ripen until the late November and December. When the black olives are harvested, they are usually rolled in salt and stored in wicker baskets, which are weighted down with a heavy stone to force the fruit to weep and the salt to penetrate and crinkle the skin. After several months, the olives are rinsed and laid out to dry on rooftops and terraces before being stored in olive oil, or tossed in a piquant marinade.

Olive oil

Morocco exports a vast quantity of olives every year and supplies Spain and France with the bulk of theirs but, until recently, they were not big exporters of olive oil. In spite of the industrious planting of olive trees carried out by the Romans – all the way from the Mediterranean coast in the north to the edge of the Sahara in the south – and possibly the Phoenicians before them, Moroccans grew fewer trees and produced less oil than their North African and southern Mediterranean neighbours. Part of the reason for this is the archaic harvesting and pressing techniques of rural Morocco where donkeys or camels still powered the grinding stones and few young people remained in the villages to help the ageing generation.

Today, the story has changed. Morocco is now the sixth-largest producer of olive oil and the cold-pressed, deliciously fruity 'liquid gold' wins global awards. With good arid soil in the coastal areas and up the

Top **Marrakesh is the place to go for its olive stalls displaying a huge variety of size and colour.**

Bottom **Morocco is a major producer of olive oil as the trees grow well in the good arid soil of the coastal region and up the slopes of the mountain ranges.**

slopes of the mountain ranges of the Rif and Atlas, much of the Moroccan countryside is ideal for olive growing. The hills around Fes are tinged grey-green with the prolific spread of olive trees, which are celebrated in a local festival at harvest time. The bulk of modern-day production takes place in the Atlas Mountains, where the trees thrive in the variable climate and soil of the valleys and hillsides of the foothills. Olive oil may not be cheap, but it is favoured for tagines and salads, and to rub though couscous grains so that they become light and airy, almost floating.

Argan oil

Those photographs of goats in a tree are true! If you have travelled to Souss in the southwest region of Morocco, you will probably have seen the goats climbing the argan trees and clambering along the branches to reach the fruit. Ancient survivors in dry, arid soil and indigenous to Morocco, the argan trees are stout and gnarled and very thorny, making it difficult to harvest the fruit for the prized kernels but, if you have goats, they will willingly do this for you by eating the fleshy exterior of the fruit which resemble large, green olives and then spitting out, or excreting, the nut. In the traditional manner, the village women remove the nuts from the droppings, or from the fruit that has fallen to the ground, and leave them to dry in the sun before cracking each one open to extract the kernels which are rich in nutrients and protein. The kernels are then roasted and manually stone-ground to produce a thick paste, which separates from the nutty-tasting, lightly orange-tinged oil. The thick paste is fed to the animals or combined with honey – a crude form of *amlou* – and eaten with bread for breakfast, and the oil is used daily by the Berber women in their cooking. In the rest of Morocco, the oil used to be very expensive and mainly used for its medicinal and cosmetic properties, such as easing arthritis, softening skin and smoothing wrinkles, but in recent years it has become more commonplace on the table, used in salads and tagines.

With increased research into its benefits, argan oil is now in high demand for beauty and food products around the world. Co-operatives have been set up in the villages for the women to continue to extract the kernels in the traditional manner and earn money for their skills, but the oil required for cosmetic laboratories simply needs to be cold-pressed from the kernels without any roasting, so that it is pale gold in colour, often referred to as 'silk oil'. Due to the increased demand, tourists need to be aware of goats being tethered in trees for photo opportunities and oil being sold by the roadside claiming to be cold-pressed argan but in fact mixed with inferior oils. The wild argan trees are now under the protection of UNESCO as they are rare and indigenous to Morocco.

Opposite top **Goats climbing an argan tree in Asilah to reach the fruit.**

Opposite bottom **A splendid display of fruit on an argan tree near Agadir.**

Below **Women working in co-operatives hand-crush the argan nuts to provide pure argan oil.**

Above **Goats out with their shepherds in the summer pastures above Tizi n Tamatert.**

Opposite top **A herd of camels in el Gouera at the edge of the Sahara. Camel milk is one of the delicacies offered to guests in Morocco.**

Opposite bottom **A honey and smen sandwich in the medina of Fes.**

Smen

Prepared from cow, sheep, goat or camel's milk, smen is butter that has been clarified, sometimes combined with herbs, and then stored in an earthenware jar to age. In the rural areas, the sealed jar is often left in a cool, dark place, or underground, for years. The longer the smen ages, the stronger the taste, so it can become very pungent and taste like strong cheese. It is a traditional speciality of the Berbers who enjoy it smeared on bread, stirred into coffee, or used as the primary cooking fat to enhance the flavour of couscous and to prepare the *k'dra* tagines. It is an acquired taste and modern, city households often opt for plain butter instead. You can substitute it with clarified butter that you prepare yourself by melting butter gently over a low heat and skimming the froth off the surface until you have a clear liquid which you can carefully pour into a container, leaving the milky layer at the bottom behind. Use this milky layer for greasing the *gdra* or the *tobsil dial louarqa*, special tins for cooking *b'stilla*, and store the clarified butter in a cool, dark place or in the fridge for weeks or months.

Lben

Drunk to quench the thirst on a hot day, lben is slightly acidic, fermented whey that is prepared in a *chkoua*, goatskin bottle, or a *khabia*, an earthenware jar, after the milk has been left to curdle in an earthenware *gdra*. The *chkoua* is hung from the branch of a tree and has to be swung back and forth until the splashing sound indicates that particles of fat have separated from the curdled milk. When the lben is traditionally prepared in a *khabia*, the curdled milk is constantly stirred with a wooden stick until the fat particles appear. Some households keep one *khabia* specifically for this and never rinse it so that the lben has a consistently soured taste. Once the milk has been strained into a jar, the fat is used to make butter, *zabda*, and the curds are combined with salt, pressed in a basket and left to dry to form a solid cream cheese, *jbane*. The strained whey that is in the jar is the precious lben.

Khlii

Khlii is a confit of meat made from *queddid*, strips of beef, lamb or mutton that have been marinated in a mixture of ground cumin and coriander, crushed garlic and vinegar and dried in the sun. The nomadic version of *queddid* is prepared with camel meat and is called *tichtar*. These sun-dried strips of meat could be described as Moroccan biltong or jerky but, rather than being chewed as a snack, they are used in

cooking and have one important destination – the preparation of khlii. Traditionally every household used to make *queddid* and khlii at least once a year. Even if the household couldn't afford much meat, khlii would be prepared with the leftover lamb or mutton from a religious feast, such as Aid el Adha, as before refrigeration this was the only way to preserve meat and it could be stored for the whole year in a clay pot.

The traditional method of preparing khlii requires hours and hours of simmering the *queddid* in water and suet to rehydrate it and render it soft and buttery. When it is left to cool, three layers form in the pot – the fat forms a solid layer on top to protect the confit of meat below, which sits on the sediment, the *agriss* – all of which have their culinary uses throughout the year. However, more modern methods involve steaming the sun-dried *queddid*, which is effective but yields a less flavoursome meat that then needs to be covered in oil to preserve it and doesn't produce the fat and the tasty *agriss* that Moroccans love. Although the tradition of making khlii at home is still alive in rural communities, many people now buy it ready-prepared at the markets to add to broths, tagines and couscous for that little bit of extra flavour.

Preserved lemons

Preserved lemons, *l'hamd markad*, are essential to the cooking of many tagines and to add a tangy, salty note to salads and kemia dishes. Generally they are prepared in the spring when the fruit is ripe and golden yellow. The native boussema and doqq lemons, which fall into the category of Marrakesh limonettas, are small to medium-sized with thin skins and a pointed apex, so they are often preserved whole in brine and both the rind and the flesh can be used. Some of the larger lemons are preserved in brine too, but the traditional method is to just use salt inserted into the flesh which then renders it inedible as it becomes too salty, so only the rind is used in dishes.

Dates

The date palm holds great significance in Morocco and in the Muslim faith. The nomadic Berbers rely heavily on dates as a main source of food so they have been at the foundation of their cooking for centuries and the leaves and fibres have provided them with thread, mattresses, lumber and rope, as well as many other household items and culinary uses. Many traditional Berber dishes include them, such as lamb tagines, couscous, and a variety of sweetmeats. Growing dates is a very labour-intensive process. It takes up to seven years to grow a date palm tree

Top **Preserved lemons alongside olives and pickles in the souk in Marrakesh.**

Bottom **A beautiful lemon tree laden with fruit in a garden in Fes.**

before it starts producing fruit, but then it will continually produce for the next 75 years. The palms need constant sun and dry conditions so the hot, arid desert valleys of southern Morocco, especially in the regions of Zagora, Ouarzazate, Errachidia and Erfoud, where the Date Festival is held (page 27), are the perfect locations for cultivating dates.

Morocco boasts over 100 different varieties of dates with 45 of those in the south of Morocco alone, the most popular being the Medjool, the Deglet Noor and the Halawi dates. Some of the finest dates come from the Zagora oasis in the south where stall-holders sell dozens of varieties, some red, yellow or green, including the sweet bouffeggou fruits and the small black bousthami. Overall, dates are important for the economy and Moroccans snack on them all the time, not just because they are delicious, but for their health benefits too. They are an excellent source of energy and contain a lot of antioxidants, believed to be good for the heart, the brain, and the digestion.

Medjool | Often referred to as 'the king of dates', the Medjool was once reserved only for Moroccan royalty and their guests. They are the most expensive of the date varieties because their cultivation is more labour-intensive. The date has a soft wrinkled, black coffee-coloured skin that gives way to a meaty, velvety and intensely sweet flesh with hints of wild honey and caramel. This is definitely a date of hospitality and welcome.

Halawi | This date is everything the Medjool is, but slightly smaller and less expensive, so it is often served as a dessert date or with couscous and to break the fast at Ramadan with a bowl of *harira*.

Deglet Noor | Originally from Algeria and also known as the 'Algerian Stuffed Date' in Morocco as they are the principal ones employed in stuffed date recipes and in tagines. Semi-dry with a firm texture and ranging in colour from dark red to amber, they are less succulent than the Medjool, but still sweet with a delicate flavour.

Almonds

Roasted almonds, almond butter, almond milk, almonds added to tagines and couscous, dates stuffed with almonds, pastries filled with almond paste scented with orange flower water – Moroccans go nuts for almonds! They are the second biggest crop in Morocco; olives are the first. Although native to Iran and the eastern Mediterranean, Morocco ranks fifth in the world in almond production. The traditional orchards are mainly located in the mountain areas, such as Tafraoute where the almond blossom festival is held, but the semi-intensive cultivation takes place in modern plantations in the provinces of Fes, Meknes, Béni-Mellal,

Top **Dates in the Draa Valley, the date basket of Morocco, where many varieties are grown and harvested.**

Bottom **Sweet-scented almond trees in bloom in the High Atlas region.**

Azilal, Marrakesh, Safi and Essaouira. And, if you are looking for a tasty breakfast or snack in any of these areas, just ask for homemade amlou with freshly baked bread or pancakes. Slightly runnier than peanut butter and sweetened with honey, it is a treat.

Bread

In the Muslim faith, bread is particularly sacred and should never be wasted. Moroccans will rescue bread lying in the street, or left unfinished on a table, as there is always a home for it whether it is given to the poor, to pets, or to livestock. And a cook will often bless the flour, water and yeast, and any other ingredients before making the bread dough. There are numerous breads in Morocco, some very regional, and most are semi-leavened with a crust apart from the distinct flat breads prepared on a griddle or metal sheet, such as ouarka (see below) and *m'semen*. In the rural areas almost every village shares a communal clay oven, the *ferran*, for cooking meat and stews, so the bread doughs are often stuck to the sides like a tandoori oven.

The bread served at most meals is called *khobz* but it is also known by its Berber names *kesra* and *agroum*. It can be made with white, wheat or a mixture of flours. Slightly thicker than a flat bread and round, it is baked in the oven so it has a crusty shell with a coarse interior, which makes it practical for the Moroccan custom of using hands to eat from a communal dish. Bread becomes a piece of useful, edible cutlery, as small pieces held between the thumb and first two fingers are dipped into sauces, soups and puréed salads, or employed as a scoop for juicy morsels and chunks of meat. When it comes to tagine eating, bread is essential for the utmost enjoyment of the sweet buttery sauces at the base of the dish. Rice doesn't play a big role in Morocco and couscous is traditionally served as a course on its own so, for Moroccans, a meal without bread would be unthinkable. It is integral to every meal.

Ouarka | The word ouarka means 'leaf' or 'sheet', which is what this paper-thin flat bread is, and it is used for many of the savoury and sweet pastries that Moroccans love and for the classic layered pie, *b'stilla*. It is difficult to make (although a basic recipe is given on page 74) and most Moroccans have the sense to go and buy ready-made sheets from a skilled ouarka-maker in the souk. The dough is really a thick batter and the ouarka-maker dips his or her hand into it, grabs some, almost wearing it like a glove, and then very quickly dabs it over a flat pan placed over a pot of simmering water. As it cooks, the ouarka-maker cuts around the edges and, as soon it turns white, peels it off the pan, places it on a surface and brushes it with a little oil to prevent it from drying out. The whole process is so skilled it takes less than a minute.

Top **The daily bread in a baker's window.**

Bottom **Baking flat breads in a wood-fired oven in Fes.**

Couscous

There are many different types of couscous in Morocco, some made with wheat flour, others with barley, maize or millet. In the rural areas, the village women still buy sacks of wheat, which they take to the local mill to be ground to semolina, and then laboriously prepare couscous every week by sprinkling the semolina flour with water and raking it with their fingers in a circular motion to form tiny balls. The balls are then rubbed by the palm of the hand against the side of the bowl and passed through a sieve to form a uniform size: *seffa* or *mefuf* is ultra-fine at 1mm in diameter and is mainly reserved for fillings and sweet dishes; *kesksou* (also *seksu* and *kuskusu*) is 2mm in diameter; and *mhammsa* is 3mm in diameter. The tiny granules are then spread out to dry in a *gsaa* before use. In modern households in the cities, many cooks prefer to avoid this labour-intensive process and buy sacks of ready-prepared couscous, which need to be steamed several times before eating. Outside Morocco and the rest of the Maghreb, the most commonly available packets of couscous are one step further as the granules are already precooked and only require soaking in water to swell, before being fluffed up and aerated with fingers and olive oil. (The recipes in this book employ this precooked version, which is available in supermarkets.)

The preparation of couscous varies from region to region and is dependent on the type of granules, but the principal method involves placing the dried granules in a *gsaa* and sprinkling them liberally with water. The moistened granules are then transferred to the metal *keskes*, a colander which is set snugly on top of a *gdra*, which contains water or a stew of meat or vegetables – the two utensils together are known in French as the two-tiered pot, the *couscoussier*, the term employed by the Pied-Noir communities, and the name that is used in international culinary circles. The steam between the *keskes* and the *gdra* is sealed with a piece of cloth, which is dipped in a mixture of flour and water. The couscous is then steamed, uncovered, until puffs of vapour emanate from the granules. The warm couscous is again returned to the *gsaa* and mixed with more water before being returned to the colander and steamed a second time until the granules become soft and plump. Finally it is flavoured with lashings of butter, olive oil, or smen, which are rubbed into the grains with the fingertips, and it is moistened with the broth from the stew.

This preparation plays such an important role in the culinary life of most Moroccans that it determines the status of a cook's ability. The word 'couscous' refers to the granules as well as the finished dish, which should be light and airy, almost floating above the plate and heavenly to touch and taste. If you manage to make a Moroccan swoon over your couscous, you will have achieved the greatest compliment of all.

Opposite, top left **A modern couscoussier to steam the couscous;** top right **the steamed couscous being tipped into a *gsaa*;** bottom left **rubbing oil into the grains to separate and aerate them;** bottom right **the stew that is cooked in the base of the couscoussier being tipped onto the couscous.**

Mint tea

A glass of mint tea, *atay bi nahna*, is offered wherever you go, in the morning, during the day, and at night. It is served as a welcome drink, it is offered while conducting business or bargaining in the souks, it is drunk to quench the thirst on a hot day, and it is always served as a digestive at the end of a meal. It is the essence of Moroccan hospitality.

Although the making and offering of tea is regarded as an institution in Morocco, it only arrived in North Africa in 1854, during the Crimean War, when British merchants were hindered by the blockade in the Baltic and had to seek new markets, such as Tangier, for their goods which included tea from China. Prior to this period, Moroccans had drunk simple infusions of wormwood, saffron, and herbs, including mint, which were offered to guests as a symbol of hospitality. Traditionally, when the leaders of different Berber tribes met to discuss a dispute, an elaborate tea ceremony was held using decorative samovars and glasses.

Nowadays, the ubiquitous sweet mint tea of Morocco is the national drink, apart from in the south of Morocco, particularly in the saffron-growing region around Taliouine, where saffron tea is offered as a mark of hospitality. In imperial circles and on refined occasions, a special infusion may be prepared with balls of amber but this is very rare.

The art of tea-making is steeped in ritual, but it is not complicated. In fact it is a charming process with a great deal of ceremony in the brewing and pouring. Traditionally, ornate samovars were used but, nowadays, these are generally reserved for elaborate tea ceremonies and feasts. Instead, a fine steel-plated, bulbous-shaped teapot is used and sugar is added to the pot rather than the glasses, so that the tea is served sweet. Sugar is generally chipped off a cone-shaped cane loaf and added liberally to the pot as the sweet-toothed Moroccans do not skimp on the sugar, which enhances the flavour of the mint and masks the bitterness of the green tea leaves. When in season, orange blossom, lemon verbena or geranium petals or leaves might be added to give the refreshing tea a floral lift.

To make the tea, the teapot is heated with boiling water first by swirling it around and then tipping it out. The green tea is added to the pot, followed by a large handful of fresh mint leaves on their stalks and sugar. The boiling water is poured in and stirred once to help dissolve the sugar and, once the mint leaves rise to the surface, the tea is left to infuse for 5 minutes. The tea is generally drunk from small, ornate glasses, often in little holders, and the teapot is held close to the glass and gradually raised higher and higher to create a sense of ceremony as well as a little froth on top of each glass. On festive occasions two teapots, one in each hand, will be held above the glass, raised with a skilful flourish to creates a thick froth on top. If the cuisine of Morocco is its 'perfumed soul' there are rituals to perform in the refreshment of it.

Top **Morocco's national drink: a glass of hot sweet mint tea.**

Bottom **Bundles of fresh mint for sale – most of it for mint tea!**

Basic recipes

There are a few basic ingredients, pastes and mixes worth having in your fridge or store cupboard as they form the base of so many dishes. Ras el hanout, harissa, chermoula and preserved lemons are just a few of these traditional ingredients.

Ouarka

This is a paper-thin flat bread, most commonly used for savoury and sweet pastries. It is quite difficult to make, so many Moroccans buy the ready-made sheets. Traditionally, the women are the best ouarka makers as they learn how to make it when they are young girls with nimble fingers. You can use bought filo pastry in the recipes as a good substitute. Makes roughly 12 sheets. Allow soaking time.

225g/8oz/1⅓ cups strong white flour	**175ml/6fl oz/¾ cup tepid water**
60g/2oz/⅓ cup fine semolina	**sunflower oil, for brushing**
15ml/1 tbsp olive oil	**kitchen paper, for separating the ouarka sheets**
15ml/1 tbsp wine vinegar	

Sift the white flour into a large bowl. Add the semolina, make a well in the middle and drop in the oil and vinegar. Gradually pour in the water, beating with a whisk, until you have a thick batter. Cover it and put it into the refrigerator for about 6 hours, or overnight.

Fill a wide, deep pot with water and bring to the boil. Reduce the heat, simmer gently and cover it with a flat plan or an inverted round baking tray. Wipe the surface lightly with a drop of oil, as you would for making crêpe.

Take the batter out of the refrigerator and beat it again, then, using a paintbrush or pastry brush, gently paint the batter thinly onto the surface of the oiled pan. Wait for the thin layer to turn white and the edges to curl, then gently peel it off the pan. (Your first one may be a flop, it often is, but the rest should be fine.)

Place it on a board, brush very lightly with oil and cover with a piece of kitchen paper or greaseproof paper. Repeat with the rest of the batter, remembering to brush each one with oil and separate them with a sheet of paper. This way they don't dry out and they don't stick together. If you're not using the sheets of ouarka immediately, you can keep them in a plastic bag in the fridge for a few days.

Ras el hanout

Beyond the souks of Morocco, you won't be able to make a genuine ras el hanout blend but you can conjure up your own magic using this recipe as a guide to add a touch of aromatic, warm poetry to your broths and tagines.

10ml/2 tsp cumin seeds	**10ml/2 tsp ground turmeric**
10ml/2 tsp coriander seeds	**5ml/1 tsp ground allspice**
10ml/2 tsp cardamom seeds	**5ml/1 tsp ground cloves**
5ml/1 tsp black peppercorns	**5ml/1 tsp ground mace**
5ml/1 tsp aniseeds	**10ml/2 tsp dried mint**
5ml/1 tsp nigella seeds	**5ml/1 tsp sea salt**
15ml/1 tbsp chilli powder	**2 dried lavender heads, crumbled with your fingers**
15ml/1 tbsp sweet paprika	**6 dried rosebuds, crumbled with your fingers**
10ml/2 tsp ground ginger	
10ml/2 tsp ground cinnamon	

Dry-roast the cumin, coriander and cardamom seeds in a skillet over a medium heat, until fragrant. While they are still warm, in a mortar and pestle grind the roasted seeds with the peppercorns, aniseeds and nigella seeds to form a coarse powder. Stir in all the ground spices, mint and salt and use your fingers to rub them together. Toss in the lavender and rose petals and tip the mix into a sealed container.

Tabil

This recipe calls for a hint of heat, rather than fiery heat.

30ml/2 tbsp coriander seeds	**or chilli powder**
30ml/2 tbsp caraway seeds	**5ml/1 tsp ground cardamom**
10ml/2 tsp fennel seeds	**5ml/1 tsp ground turmeric**
5ml/1 tsp black peppercorns	**5ml/1 tsp garlic powder**
5ml/1 tsp fine chilli flakes,	**sea salt**

Using a mortar and pestle, grind the coriander seeds with the caraway, fennel and black peppercorns to a coarse powder. Add the chilli, cardamom, turmeric and garlic with a sprinkling of salt. Mix well and keep in a sealed container.

ROSENWASSER
ROSVATTEN
PREMIUM
17 fl oz

Harissa

Makes roughly 4 tablespoons of harissa (a little goes a long way) but remember the heat is deceptive – it isn't instant on the tip of your tongue but comes a little later from the back of your mouth.

- **8 dried, long red chillies, soaked in water for 2–3 days**
- **4 garlic cloves, peeled**
- **5ml/1 tsp sea salt**
- **10ml/2 tsp cumin seeds**
- **10ml/2 tsp coriander seeds**
- **45ml/3 tbsp olive oil**

Drain the chillies, remove the stalks and squeeze out some of the seeds. Rip the chillies into two or three pieces and pop them into a mortar. Add the garlic and salt and pound them all together until you have an almost-smooth paste – this does take time but keep bashing to work the flesh in the chillies.

Dry-roast the cumin and coriander seeds in a skillet over a medium heat, until fragrant. Using a spice grinder or a separate mortar and pestle, grind the seeds to a powder. Gradually add the ground spice to the chilli paste, working it in with spoonfuls of olive oil.

Store the paste in a sterilized, sealed jar in the refrigerator. If you add a thin layer of olive oil to the top of it, it will keep for at least 6 months.

Homemade smen

If you would like to prepare a modern, flavoured smen, using your hands to squeeze out excess water rather than removing the milk solids, you can follow this recipe which falls somewhere between butter and a traditional smen, but can't be stored for too long.

- **450g/1lb/4 sticks unsalted butter, at room temperature**
- **115ml/4fl oz/scant ½ cup water**
- **15ml/1 tbsp sea salt**
- **15ml/1 tbsp dried oregano**

Soften the butter in a bowl. In a small pan, boil the water with the salt and oregano to reduce it a little, then strain it directly onto the butter. Stir the butter with a wooden spoon to make sure it is well blended and leave to cool.

Knead the butter with your hands to bind it, squeezing out any excess water. Drain well and spoon the butter into a hot, sterilized jar. Seal the jar and store it in a cool, dry place for at least 6 weeks.

Chermoula

This fresh-tasting spice paste can be used as a marinade, a sauce or dressing, just by adjusting the quantities. It should be fiery and zingy and lends a distinct flavour to many grilled fish and poultry dishes, and to some tagines. On special occasions, or in the south of Morocco, saffron is sometimes added to chermoula by soaking it first in a teaspoon or two of plain or scented water to draw out the colour and add to the flavour.

- **5ml/1 tsp cumin seeds**
- **3 garlic cloves, peeled and roughly chopped**
- **1 fresh red or green chilli, deseeded and roughly chopped**
- **sea salt**
- **small bunch of fresh coriander (cilantro), roughly chopped**
- **small bunch of fresh flat-leaf parsley, roughly chopped**
- **5ml/1 tsp sweet, or smoked, paprika**
- **juice of 1 lemon**
- **30–45ml/3–4 tbsp olive oil**
- **optional:**
- **fingerful of saffron threads**
- **orange blossom or rose water**

Dry-roast the cumin seeds in a skillet over a medium heat, until fragrant. Using a mortar and pestle, pound the garlic and chilli with a sprinkling of salt to form a coarse paste. Add the cumin seeds with the herbs and pound to a paste – it doesn't need to be smooth. Stir in the paprika and lemon juice and bind with the oil. Adjust the quantity of oil to the purpose of the paste – less oil for a thick condiment or rub-on marinade, more oil for a dressing.

If you want to add the saffron, soak it first in a splash of plain or scented water – literally a teaspoonful or two if possible. Once the colour has been drawn out, stir the threads and water into the chermoula.

Khlii eggs for two

Fes is said to be the 'Khlii Capital' and one of the most popular ways of enjoying it is in the Fassi breakfast of pan-fried khlii with eggs, served with bread and mint tea.

- **4 strips of khlii, cut into small pieces**
- **15ml/1 tbsp khlii fat**
- **4 eggs**
- **sea salt and freshly ground black pepper**

Place the strips of khlii in the base of a tagine or skillet. Add the fat and cook gently over a low heat until the fat melts. Using a spoon, create pockets in the khlii and crack an egg into each one. Cover with a lid, or aluminium foil, and cook gently until the whites have set. Season with a little salt and black pepper and serve immediately.

Preserved lemons

Of course, you can buy jars of ready-preserved lemons in Middle Eastern and African stores, as well as some supermarkets and specialist shops, but it is worth making your own following the traditional method. For 1 big jar:

- **10 organic, unwaxed lemons, preferably the small, thin-skinned Meyer variety**
- **150g/5oz/roughly ¾ cup sea salt**
- **juice of 3–4 lemons**

Wash and dry the whole lemons and slice the ends off each one. Stand each lemon on one end and make two vertical cuts three-quarters of the way through them, as if cutting them into quarters but keeping the base intact. Stuff a tablespoon of salt into each lemon and pack them into a large sterilized jar. Store the lemons in a cool place for 3–4 days to soften the skins.

Press the lemons down into the jar, so they are even more tightly packed. Pour the freshly-squeezed lemon juice over the salted lemons, until they are completely covered. Seal the jar and store it in a cool place for at least a month. Rinse the salt off the preserved lemons before using.

Dates with rose water and milk

My children (now adults) have never forgotten their delightful reception at Kasbah du Toubkhal in the Atlas Mountains. Aged four and seven they dismounted the mule that had transported them up the hill, and opened the big, heavy wooden door into the hidden garden of green herbs and pink roses where they were greeted with a splash of rose water to freshen their hands before being offered a succulent, plump date from an ornate wooden bowl. First they had to dip the date into a bowl of rose water, then into a bowl of milk before biting into the soft, velvety flesh, which filled their little mouths with its natural sweetness. This gesture of sharing and welcoming with two of Morocco's basic ingredients – dates and milk – was both delicious and memorable. For 4.

- **8 plump, pitted ready-to-eat dates**
- **30ml/2 tbsp rose water**
- **60ml/4 tbsp milk, at room temperature**
- **scented edible rose petals, for decorating**

To make this simple welcome gift special, arrange the dates on an ornate or silver dish or tray, and place two tiny bowls or cups – one of rose water, the other containing the milk – next to them. Decorate with fresh rose petals, if you like, and when you greet your guests explain that they need to dip the dates into the rose water and milk before biting into them.

Amlou

Traditionally, the Berber women in the southwest of Morocco would make amlou from the residue of the pressed argan oil. Sweetened with honey and bound with ground almonds, a little bit like crunchy peanut butter in texture, this thick nutty paste would be enjoyed with bread as the women sat around the village stove drinking delicately scented saffron tea. Nowadays, the women are busy cold-pressing the kernels for a refined oil, rather than roasting and stone-grinding the nuts to separate the oil, so the mass-produced amlou is smoother and lighter and not nearly so nutty to taste. Makes roughly 400ml/14fl oz.

- **250g/9oz/2 cups roasted almonds**
- **115ml/4fl oz/scant ½ cup argan oil**
- **60ml/4 tbsp honey**
- **sea salt**
- **ground cinnamon, for dusting**

Put the roasted almonds into a food blender and whizz until finely ground – don't over-grind as the mixture will turn to butter. Gradually, add the oil in a slow drizzle, stirring until blended and smooth – you can tip the ground almonds into a bowl and do this manually if you prefer. Gradually add the honey and season with salt to taste.

Tip the amlou into a bowl, dust with cinnamon and serve with freshly griddled flat breads.

Zitoun mchermel

Cracked green olives with harissa and preserved lemon: this could be described as a 'taste of Morocco' in a bowl. Offered to welcome a guest, snacked on at the olive stall in the souk, or as a *kemia* dish to whet the appetite for what's to come, this is great way to appreciate several of Morocco's key ingredients. This is enough for a bowl for 4–6.

- **350g/12oz/roughly 2½ cups cracked green olives, rinsed and drained**
- **30ml/2 tbsp olive oil**
- **juice of ½ lemon**
- **5–10ml/1–2 tsp harissa paste (the amount depends on how fiery you like your olives)**
- **rind of 1 small preserved lemon, finely chopped**
- **few sprigs of fresh coriander (cilantro), finely chopped (optional)**

Tip the olives into a bowl and toss in the oil and lemon juice. Add the harissa paste, making sure it lightly coats the olives. Toss in most of the preserved lemon and leave the olives to sit and absorb the flavours for at least 30 minutes. Garnish with the rest of the preserved lemon and a sprinkling of fresh coriander if you like, and enjoy with a refreshing drink.

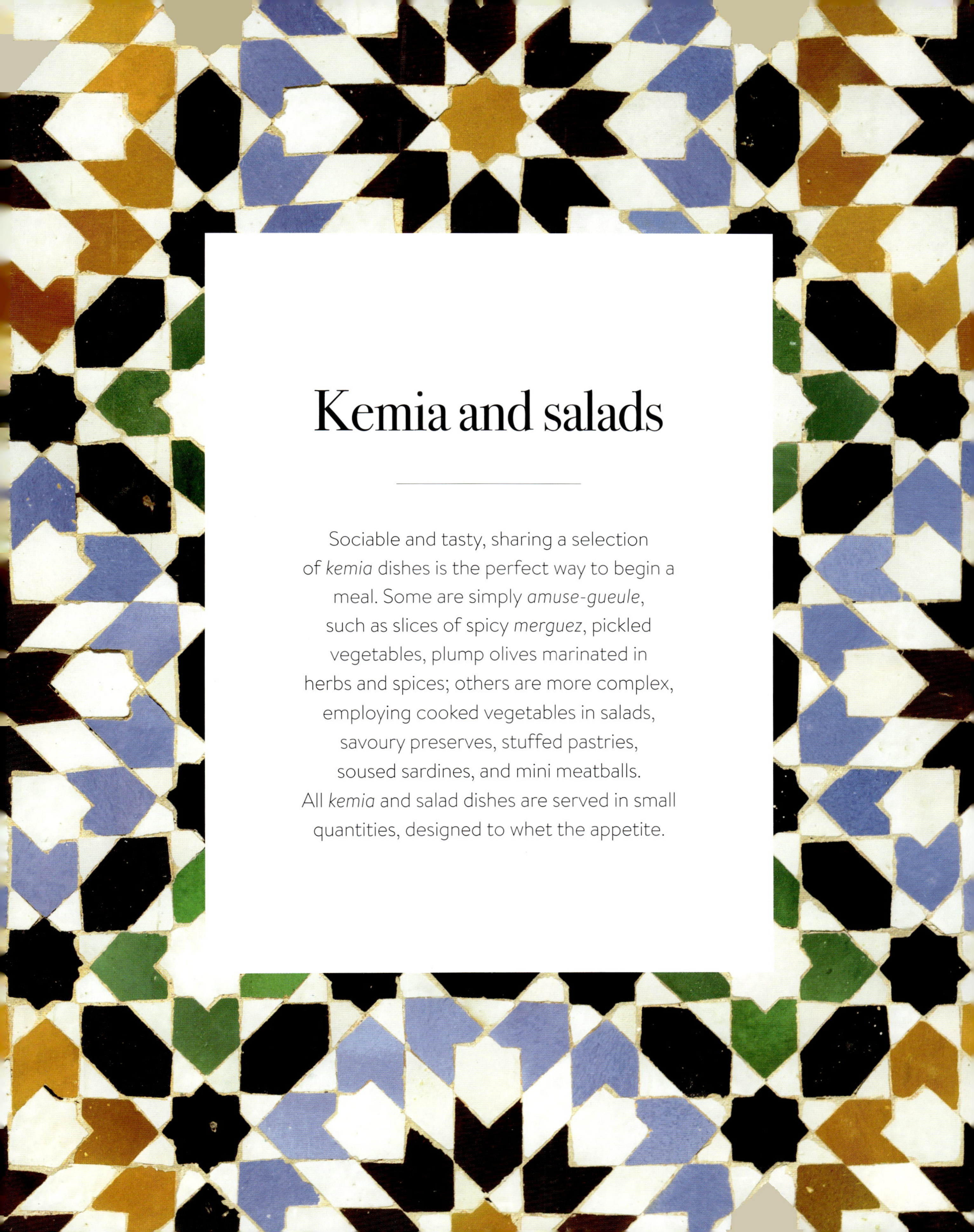

Kemia and salads

Sociable and tasty, sharing a selection of *kemia* dishes is the perfect way to begin a meal. Some are simply *amuse-gueule*, such as slices of spicy *merguez*, pickled vegetables, plump olives marinated in herbs and spices; others are more complex, employing cooked vegetables in salads, savoury preserves, stuffed pastries, soused sardines, and mini meatballs. All *kemia* and salad dishes are served in small quantities, designed to whet the appetite.

Matisha ma'asala

Matisha ma'asala is a lovely, thick tomato purée sweetened with honey and flavoured with cinnamon. It varies from cook to cook, as some like to simmer the tomatoes for over an hour to obtain a jam-like, sticky consistency. Topped with crunchy, toasted sesame seeds, it is best served at room temperature as a part of a *kemia* spread with bread to dip into it, but it can also be served as a sauce for grilled meat dishes.

Serves four

8 medium-sized on the vine tomatoes

30–45ml/2–3 tbsp olive oil

30ml/2 tbsp honey

10ml/2 tsp ground cinnamon

5ml/1 tsp ground ginger

sea salt and freshly ground black pepper

15ml/1 tbsp sesame seeds, toasted

Preheat the oven to 200°C/400°F/gas 6.

Place the tomatoes in an ovenproof dish, pour in the olive oil, and bake them in the oven for 20 minutes, or until soft and the skins have buckled. Remove them from the oven and leave until cool enough to handle so you can peel off the skins. Halve the skinned tomatoes to remove the seeds then chop the flesh to a pulp.

Put the pulped tomatoes into a heavy-based pan with a tablespoon of the roasting oil. Stir in the honey, cinnamon and ginger and cook very gently, stirring frequently, for about 20 minutes, until the mixture is thick. Season with salt and pepper, add more cinnamon if you like, and tip the mixture into a serving bowl. Leave it to cool, sprinkle the toasted sesame seeds over the top, and serve at room temperature with bread to dip into it.

Toasting sesame seeds

To dry-roast sesame seeds, place in a small, heavy frying pan over a medium heat, stirring around for a couple of minutes until they turn a golden brown.

Bissara dip with zaatar

This garlicky broad bean dip is enjoyed throughout Morocco. Sprinkled with fresh or dried thyme, zaatar, and toasted sesame seeds, it is a tasty appetizer served with flat bread. It is particularly popular in the cafés of Fes and Marrakesh, where Moroccans and tourists mingle over food.

Serves four

350g/12oz/2 cups dried broad (fava) beans, soaked overnight

4 garlic cloves, peeled

10ml/2 tsp cumin seeds

60–75ml/4–5 tbsp olive oil

sea salt

zaatar, fresh or dried thyme, to garnish

sesame seeds, toasted, to sprinkle (optional)

Drain the soaked beans, remove their wrinkly skins and place them in a large pan with the garlic and cumin seeds. Add enough water to cover the beans and bring to the boil. Boil for 10 minutes, then reduce the heat, cover the pan and simmer gently for about 1 hour, or until the beans are tender.

When cooked, drain the beans and, while they are still warm, pound or process them with the olive oil until the mixture forms a smooth dip. Season to taste with salt.

Serve warm or at room temperature, sprinkled with *zaatar* or thyme, and some toasted sesame seeds if you like. Alternatively, simply drizzle with a little olive oil.

Serrouda

Serrouda could be described as Morocco's hummus, but it is usually runnier than the Middle Eastern version, and is served warm. It is often enjoyed for breakfast as well as a starter to a meal. Loose and velvety in texture, it can be topped with melted butter, roasted nuts and seeds, or finely chopped onions, tomatoes and mint. In this recipe it is drizzled with roasted cumin seed butter.

Serves four

250g/9oz/1¾ cups dried chickpeas, soaked in water for 6 hours or overnight

4–6 plump garlic cloves, peeled

1 onion, peeled and halved

5ml/1 tsp bicarbonate of soda (baking soda)

30–45ml/2–3 tbsp olive oil

sea salt and freshly ground black pepper

5ml/1 tsp cumin seeds

25g/1oz/2 tbsp salted butter

hot or smoked paprika, for dusting

Rinse and drain the soaked chickpeas and tip them into a pan. Cover them with water – roughly 600ml/1 pint – add the garlic cloves, onion and bicarbonate of soda, and bring the water to the boil. Reduce the heat and simmer the chickpeas for about 2 hours, topping up the water if necessary, until they are soft.

Using a slotted spoon, lift the chickpeas and garlic cloves and onion out of the water and into a food processor. Blend with the olive oil until smooth, then blend again with 2–3 tablespoons of the cooking water so that the mixture becomes loose and velvety. Season well with salt and pepper.

While still warm, spoon the *serrouda* into a bowl. Dry-roast the cumin seeds in a small pan and when they begin to emit a nutty aroma, stir in the butter until it melts. Drizzle the melted cumin butter over the *serrouda* and finish with a dusting of paprika. Serve warm with chunks of crusty loaf or flat bread.

Zaalouk

This classic spicy aubergine and tomato salad is delicious served on its own with chunks of bread. You can bake the whole aubergines until they are soft and mild, or you can chargrill them for a smoky taste. For flavour, you can use fruity olive oil or nutty argan oil and serve this dish warm with toasted flat bread or chunks of crusty loaf.

Serves four

2 big aubergines (eggplants)

4 large tomatoes, skinned and chopped to a pulp

100ml/3½fl oz/generous ⅓ cup olive or argan oil

2–3 garlic cloves, crushed

5ml/1 tsp harissa (add more to taste if you like)

small bunch of fresh flat-leaf parsley, finely chopped

small bunch of fresh coriander (cilantro), finely chopped

juice of 1 lemon

sea salt and freshly ground black pepper

5ml/1 tsp cumin seeds, roasted and ground

Preheat the oven to 200°C/400°F/gas 6.

Place the aubergines on a baking tray and bake them in the oven for about 30 minutes, until soft when you press them with a finger. At the same time, place the tomatoes in an ovenproof dish, pour over half the olive or argan oil, and pop them in the oven to cook with the aubergines.

Remove both the aubergines and tomatoes from the oven and leave until cool enough to handle. Using a sharp knife, slit the aubergines open, scoop out the warm flesh, and chop it to a pulp. Skin the tomatoes, cut them in half to scoop out the seeds, and chop them to a pulp.

Heat the rest of the oil in a heavy-based pan and stir in the garlic, until it begins to colour. Add the tomatoes and harissa and cook over a medium heat for 5–8 minutes, until thick and pulpy. Add the aubergines along with the parsley and coriander, keeping a little back for garnish. Stir in the lemon juice and season with salt and pepper.

Tip the *zaalouk* into a serving bowl and serve warm or at room temperature with the herb garnish and a sprinkling of roasted cumin.

Chunky roasted cauliflower and courgette dip

This rustic dish can be served as chunky dip with flat bread, or as an accompaniment to meat. You can steam, grill or roast the cauliflower and courgette slices until they are soft enough to mash coarsely together with a fork.

Serves four to six

1 cauliflower, broken into florets

2 medium courgettes (zucchini), thickly sliced

10ml/2 tsp fennel seeds

45–60ml/3–4 tbsp olive oil

2–3 garlic cloves, crushed

juice of 1 lemon

small bunch of fresh flat-leaf parsley, finely chopped

sea salt and freshly ground black pepper

5ml/1 tsp paprika

Heat the oven to 200°C/400°F/gas 6.

Arrange the cauliflower florets and sliced courgette in a big oven dish or tray. Scatter the fennel seeds over the top, drizzle with the olive oil and pop them in the oven for 30–40 minutes, until lightly browned and tender to the fork.

While still warm, coarsely mash the cauliflower and courgette with a fork so that it is slightly chunky and tip it into a bowl with all the roasting oil. Beat in the crushed garlic, lemon juice and parsley, and season well with salt and pepper. Dust with paprika and serve with bread while still warm.

Grilled aubergine in honey and spices

Hot, spicy, sweet and fruity are classic flavours of Moroccan cooking and in this delicious dish, their combination sends you on a thrilling journey. Baby aubergines are very effective for this dish as you can slice them in half lengthways and hold them by their stalks.

Serves four

8 baby aubergines (eggplants), halved lengthways

30–45ml/2–3 tbsp olive oil, for frying

2–3 garlic cloves, crushed

5cm/2in piece of fresh root ginger, peeled and grated

5ml/1 tsp ground cumin

5ml/1 tsp harissa

45ml/3 tbsp honey

juice of 1 lemon

sea salt

Preheat the grill or a griddle. Brush each aubergine half with most of the olive oil and cook in a pan under the grill or in a griddle pan. Turn the slices so that they are lightly browned on both sides.

In a wide frying pan, fry the garlic in a little olive oil for a few seconds, then stir in the ginger, cumin, harissa, honey and lemon juice. Add enough water to cover the base of the pan and to thin the mixture, then lay the aubergine slices in the pan. Cook the aubergines gently for about 10 minutes, or until they have absorbed all the sauce.

Add a little extra water, if necessary, season to taste with salt, and serve at room temperature, with chunks of fresh bread to mop up the juices.

Alternative flavourings

Courgettes (zucchini) can also be cooked in this way. If you want to make a feature out of this sumptuous dish, serve it with other grilled vegetables and fruit, such as bell peppers, chillies, tomatoes, oranges, pineapple and mangoes.

Spicy plantain snacks

Sweet and crisp, deep-fried slices of plantain are not only a great street snack, but they also make excellent nibbles with drinks. Make sure the plantains are ripe – the skin should be brown and mottled – otherwise they tend to be woody rather than sweet and fruity. Be liberal with the spices as the starchy plantains are able to carry strong flavours.

Serves two to four as a snack

2 large ripe plantains

sunflower oil, for deep-frying

1 dried red chilli, roasted, deseeded and chopped

15–30ml/1–2 tbsp tabil (page 74)

coarse sea salt

To peel the plantains, cut off their ends with a sharp knife and make two to three incisions in the skin from end to end, then peel off the skin. Cut the plantains into thick slices.

Heat enough oil for deep-frying to 180°C/350°F, or until a cube of day-old bread browns in 30–45 seconds. Fry the plantain slices in batches until golden brown. Drain each batch on a double layer of kitchen paper.

While still warm, place them in a shallow bowl and sprinkle liberally with the dried chilli, tabil and salt. Toss them thoroughly and eat immediately.

Roasting the chilli

Place the chilli in a small, heavy frying pan and cook over a medium heat, stirring constantly, until the chilli darkens and gives off a peppery aroma.

Roasted red peppers with feta, capers and preserved lemon

Roasted red peppers, particularly the long, slim, horn-shaped type, feature widely across the Mediterranean region. However, it is the delightful burst of piquant fruit that gives these sumptuous roast peppers their typically Moroccan flavour. So versatile and juicy, they are quite delicious with kebabs and grilled meats as well as with other *kemia* dishes.

Serves four

4 fleshy, red bell peppers

200g/7oz feta cheese, crumbled

30–45ml/2–3 tbsp olive oil or argan oil

30ml/2 tbsp capers

peel of 1 preserved lemon, cut into small pieces

sea salt

Preheat the grill or broiler on the hottest setting. Roast the red peppers under the grill, turning frequently, until they soften and their skins begin to blacken. (Alternatively, spear the peppers, one at a time, on long metal skewers and turn them over a gas flame, or roast them in a very hot oven.) Place the peppers in a plastic bag, seal and leave them to stand for 15 minutes. Peel the peppers, remove the stalks and seeds, then slice the flesh and arrange on a plate.

Add the crumbled feta and pour over the olive or argan oil. Scatter the capers and preserved lemon over the top and sprinkle with a little salt, if required (this depends on whether the feta is salty or not). Serve with chunks of fresh bread to mop up the delicious, oil-rich juices.

Artichoke hearts with ginger, honey and preserved lemon

When globe artichokes are in season, they grace every Moroccan table as a first course or salad. The hearts are often poached in salted water until tender, chopped and tossed in olive oil with garlic, herbs and preserved lemon. For a more exciting appetizer, the artichokes are cooked here in a glorious spiced honey dressing. This dish also makes a perfect accompaniment for barbecued meat.

Serves four

30–45ml/2–3 tbsp olive oil
2 garlic cloves, crushed
scant 5ml/1 tsp ground ginger
pinch of saffron threads
juice of ½ lemon
15–30ml/1–2 tbsp honey
peel of 1 preserved lemon, finely sliced
8 artichoke hearts, quartered
150ml/¼ pint/scant ¾ cup water
sea salt

Heat the olive oil in a small heavy pan and stir in the garlic. Before the garlic begins to colour, stir in the ginger, saffron, lemon juice, honey and preserved lemon. Add the artichokes and toss them in the spices and honey. Pour in the water, add a little salt and heat until simmering.

Cover the pan and simmer for 10–15 minutes until the artichokes are tender, turning them occasionally. If the liquid has not reduced, take the lid off the pan and boil for about 2 minutes until reduced to a coating consistency. Serve warm or at room temperature.

Preparing globe artichokes

Remove the outer leaves and cut off the stems. Carefully separate the remaining leaves and use a teaspoon to scoop out the choke with all the hairy bits. Trim the hearts and immerse them in water mixed with a squeeze of lemon juice to prevent them from turning black. Frozen prepared hearts are available in some supermarkets and they can be used for this recipe.

Broad bean salad

Serves four

2kg/4½lb broad (fava) beans in the pod (450g/1lb pods equates to about 150g/5oz/1¼ cups shelled beans)

60–75ml/4–5 tbsp olive oil

juice of ½ lemon

2 garlic cloves, chopped

5ml/1 tsp ground cumin

10ml/2 tsp paprika

sea salt and freshly ground black pepper

small bunch of fresh coriander (cilantro), finely chopped

1 preserved lemon, chopped

handful of black olives, to garnish

Broad beans are popular in salads and rice dishes throughout the Middle East, North Africa and the Mediterranean region, but in Morocco the addition of preserved lemons gives them a distinctive taste.

To make the broad bean salad, bring a large pan of salted water to the boil. Meanwhile, pod the beans. Put the beans in the pan and boil for about 2 minutes, then drain and refresh the beans under cold running water. Drain well. Slip off and discard the thick outer skins to reveal the smooth, bright green beans underneath.

Put the beans in a heavy pan and add the olive oil, lemon juice, garlic, cumin and paprika. Cook the beans gently over a low heat for about 10 minutes, then season to taste with salt and pepper and leave to cool in the pan.

Tip the beans into a serving bowl, scraping all the juices from the pan. Toss in the fresh coriander and preserved lemon and garnish with the black olives.

Carrot salad

Serves four

450g/1lb carrots, cut into sticks

30–45ml/2–3 tbsp olive oil

juice of 1 lemon

2–3 garlic cloves, crushed

10ml/2 tsp sugar

sea salt and freshly ground black pepper

5–10ml/1–2 tsp cumin seeds, roasted

5ml/1 tsp ground cinnamon

5ml/1 tsp paprika

small bunch of fresh coriander (cilantro), finely chopped

small bunch of fresh mint, finely chopped

The refreshing carrot salad is often served as an appetizer but, if you prefer, serve it warm for supper with tangy, garlic-flavoured yogurt.

To make the carrot salad, steam the carrots over boiling water for about 15 minutes, or until tender. While they are still warm, toss the carrots in a serving bowl with the olive oil, lemon juice, garlic and sugar. Season to taste, then add the cumin seeds, cinnamon and paprika. Finally, toss in the fresh coriander and mint, and serve warm or at room temperature.

Roasting cumin seeds

Stir the cumin seeds gently in a heavy pan over a low heat until they change colour slightly and emit a warm, nutty aroma. Be careful not to burn them.

Feggous salad

Feggous is a seasonal muskmelon that looks like a bendy, ridged cucumber and is also known as an Armenian cucumber. As it is slightly drier than most cucumbers it is often combined with orange juice or orange blossom water, or both, in a simple salad. Served chilled, it is light and refreshing alongside other *kemia* dishes and usually finished with a sprinkling of fresh or dried oregano or thyme. You can substitute with an ordinary cucumber but salt the slices first to draw out some of the water content, then rinse and pat dry.

Serves four to six

2 feggous
juice of 1 orange
juice of ½ lemon
10ml/2 tsp orange flower water
5ml/1 tsp sugar
sea salt
fresh or dried oregano or thyme

Don't peel the feggous, just finely slice them and arrange the slices in a serving dish. Mix together the orange juice, lemon juice and the orange flower water with the sugar and pour it over the cucumber. Cover and chill for 1 hour, if you like, and serve with a sprinkling of salt and some oregano or thyme.

Beetroot salad with oranges

This salad can be made with bought vacuum-pack cooked beetroot or freshly steamed or boiled vegetables. The combination of sweet beetroot, zesty orange and warm cinnamon is both unusual and delicious, and this dish provides a lovely burst of colour in a summer buffet spread.

Serves four to six

675g/1½lb beetroot, steamed or boiled, then peeled

1 orange, peeled and sliced

30ml/2 tbsp orange flower water

15ml/1 tbsp sugar

5ml/1 tsp ground cinnamon

sea salt and freshly ground black pepper

Quarter the cooked beetroot, then slice the quarters. Arrange the beetroot on a plate with the orange slices or toss them together in a bowl. Gently heat the orange flower water with the sugar, stir in the cinnamon, and season to taste. Pour the sweet mixture over the beetroot and orange salad and chill for at least 1 hour before serving.

Cooking beetroot

To cook raw beetroot always leave the skin on and trim off only the tops of the leaf stalks. Cook in boiling water or steam over rapidly boiling water for 1–2 hours, depending on size. Small beetroot are tender in about 1 hour, medium roots take 1–1½ hours, and larger roots can take up to 2 hours.

Lentil salad with red onion and garlic

This delicious, garlicky lentil salad is frequently served as an accompaniment to kebabs in street cafés and restaurants, and as an appetizer at home. It can be served warm or cooled. If you feel like making a meal out of this dish, serve it with a generous spoonful of plain yogurt.

Serves four

175g/6oz/1 cup dried brown lentils

2 tomatoes, peeled and deseeded

45ml/3 tbsp olive oil

2 red onions, chopped

10ml/2 tsp ground turmeric

10ml/2 tsp ground cumin

900ml/1½ pints/3¾ cups vegetable stock or water

4 garlic cloves, crushed

small bunch of fresh coriander (cilantro), finely chopped

sea salt and freshly ground black pepper

lemon wedges, to serve

Rinse the lentils well, and drain. Chop the peeled and deseeded tomatoes. Heat 30ml/2 tbsp of the oil in a large pan and fry the onions until soft. Add the tomatoes, turmeric and cumin, then stir in the lentils. Pour in the stock or water and bring to the boil, then reduce the heat and simmer until the lentils are tender and almost all the liquid has been absorbed.

In a separate pan, fry the garlic in the remaining oil until brown and frizzled. Toss the garlic into the lentils with the fresh coriander and season to taste. Serve warm or at room temperature, with wedges of lemon for squeezing over.

Introducing different flavours

If you prefer, you can substitute the lentils with mung beans – they work just as well. When including this type of dish in a *kemia* spread, it is worth balancing it with a dip such as *zaalouk* and a fruity salad for the different textures.

Sautéed herb salad with chilli and preserved lemon

Firm-leafed fresh herbs, such as flat leaf parsley and mint tossed in a little olive oil and seasoned with salt, are fabulous to serve as a salad in a *kemia* spread, or go wonderfully with spicy kebabs or tagines. Lightly sautéed with garlic and served warm with yogurt, this dish is delightful even on its own.

Serves four

large bunch of fresh flat-leaf parsley

large bunch of fresh mint

large bunch of fresh coriander (cilantro)

bunch of rocket (arugula)

large bunch of spinach leaves (about 115g/4oz)

60–75ml/4–5 tbsp olive oil

2 garlic cloves, finely chopped

1 green or red chilli, deseeded and finely chopped

½ preserved lemon, finely chopped

sea salt and freshly ground black pepper

45–60ml/3–4 tbsp Greek (strained plain) yogurt, to serve

Roughly chop the herbs, rocket and spinach. Heat the olive oil in a wide, heavy pan. Stir in the garlic and chilli, and fry until they begin to colour. Toss in the herbs, rocket and spinach and cook gently, until they begin to soften and wilt. Add the preserved lemon and season to taste. Serve the salad warm with a dollop of yogurt.

Making garlic-flavoured yogurt

For additional flavour, crush a clove of garlic and stir it into the yogurt with salt and ground pepper to taste.

Fresh country salad

A bowl of freshly chopped seasonal vegetables is often brought to the table when you order *kemia* dishes or a tagine in a restaurant. And a fresh country salad will be one of the dishes included in a *diffa*, a celebratory meal.

Serves four to six

2 small red onions, chopped

1 bell pepper, red or green, deseeded and chopped

1 celery stick, chopped

2 green chillies, deseeded and finely sliced

2 garlic cloves, chopped

peel of 1 preserved lemon, finely sliced

90g/3½oz/¾ cup pitted green or black olives, chopped or sliced

30ml/2 tbsp olive oil

juice of 1 lemon

2.5ml/½ tsp ground cumin

sea salt and freshly ground black pepper

small bunch of fresh flat-leaf parsley, chopped

small bunch of fresh mint, chopped

5–10ml/1–2 tsp honey, for drizzling

Put all the chopped vegetables, preserved lemon and olives in a bowl. Toss in the olive oil and lemon juice with the ground cumin. Season with salt and pepper and add the parsley and mint. Drizzle with a little honey and serve.

Pan-fried baby squid with spices

You have to work quickly to prepare this dish, then serve it immediately, so that the squid is just cooked and tender. The flavours of turmeric, ginger and harissa are fabulous with the sweet honey and zesty lemon juice.

Serves four

8 baby squid, prepared, with tentacles (see also page 211)

5ml/1 tsp ground turmeric

15ml/1 tbsp smen or olive oil

2 garlic cloves, finely chopped

15g/½oz fresh root ginger, peeled and finely chopped

5–10ml/1–2 tsp honey

juice of 1 lemon

10ml/2 tsp harissa

sea salt

small bunch of fresh coriander (cilantro), roughly chopped, to serve

Pat dry the squid bodies, inside and out, and dry the tentacles. Sprinkle the squid and tentacles with the ground turmeric.

Heat the smen or olive oil in a large heavy frying pan and stir in the garlic and ginger. Just as the ginger and garlic begin to colour, add the squid and tentacles and fry quickly on both sides over a high heat. (Don't overcook the squid, otherwise it will become rubbery.)

Add the honey, lemon juice and harissa and stir to form a thick, spicy, caramelized sauce. Season with salt, sprinkle with the chopped coriander and serve immediately.

Hot spicy prawns with coriander

This is a quick and easy way of preparing prawns for a snack or appetizer. If you increase the quantities, it can be served as a main course. Scallops and mussels are also delicious cooked in this way or, alternatively, you can select a variety of mushrooms and add them to the pan with the sauce ingredients. Serve the prawns with bread to mop up the tasty juices.

Serves two to four

60ml/4 tbsp olive oil

2–3 garlic cloves, chopped

25g/1oz fresh root ginger, peeled and shredded

1 chilli, deseeded and chopped

5ml/1 tsp cumin seeds

5ml/1 tsp paprika

450g/1lb uncooked king prawns (jumbo shrimp), shelled

sea salt

bunch of fresh coriander (cilantro), chopped

1 lemon, cut into wedges, to serve

In a large, heavy frying pan, heat the oil with the garlic. Stir in the ginger, chilli and cumin seeds. Cook briefly, until the ingredients give off a lovely aroma, then add the paprika and toss in the prawns.

Fry the prawns over a fairly high heat, turning them frequently, for 3–5 minutes until just cooked. Season to taste with salt and add the coriander. Serve immediately, with lemon wedges for squeezing over the prawns.

Mini saffron fish cakes with chilled sweet cucumber and cinnamon salad

This scented cucumber salad makes a superbly refreshing accompaniment for the fish cakes. Both the fish cakes and salad include the sweet and spicy flavours that are so popular in Moroccan food. If you're in a rush and can't get fresh fish, canned tuna makes a good substitute.

Serves four

450g/1lb white fish fillets, such as sea bass, ling or haddock, skinned and cut into chunks

10ml/2 tsp harissa

rind of ½ preserved lemon, finely chopped

small bunch of fresh coriander (cilantro), finely chopped

1 egg

5ml/1 tsp honey

pinch of saffron threads, soaked in 5ml/1 tsp water

salt and ground black pepper

sunflower oil, for frying

For the salad

2 cucumbers, peeled and grated

juice of 1 orange

juice of ½ lemon

15–30ml/1–2 tbsp orange flower water

15–20ml/3–4 tsp sugar

2.5ml/½ tsp ground cinnamon

Make the salad in advance to allow time for chilling before serving. Place the cucumber in a strainer over a bowl and sprinkle with some salt. Leave to drain for about 10 minutes. Using your hands, squeeze out the excess liquid and place the cucumber in a bowl.

In a small jug, combine the orange and lemon juice, orange flower water and sugar and pour over the cucumber. Toss well, sprinkle with cinnamon and chill for at least 1 hour.

To make the fish cakes, put the fish in a food processor. Add the harissa, preserved lemon, coriander, egg, honey, saffron with its soaking water, and seasoning, and whizz until smooth. Divide the mixture into 16 portions. Wet your hands under cold water to prevent the mixture from sticking to them, then roll each portion into a ball and flatten in the palm of your hand.

Heat the oil in a large frying pan and fry the fish cakes in batches, until golden brown on each side. Drain the fish cakes on kitchen paper and keep hot until all the fish cakes are cooked. Serve immediately with the chilled cucumber salad.

Sautéed chicken livers with orange flower water and roasted hazelnuts

Sautéed offal, such as liver and kidney, is a popular appetizer, often cooked simply in olive oil and garlic and served with lemon to squeeze over. This dish of chicken livers makes a delicious, tangy appetizer on its own, served with a few salad leaves, or spooned on thin slices of toasted bread. In the restaurants of Casablanca, where the French influence still lingers, you will find variations of this dish using lamb's liver too.

Serves four

30–45ml/2–3 tbsp olive oil

2–3 garlic cloves, chopped

1 dried red chilli, chopped

5ml/1 tsp cumin seeds

450g/1lb chicken livers, trimmed and cut into bitesize chunks

5ml/1 tsp ground coriander

handful of roasted hazelnuts, roughly chopped

10–15ml/2–3 tsp orange flower water

½ preserved lemon, finely sliced or chopped

salt and ground black pepper

small bunch of fresh coriander (cilantro), chopped

fresh salad leaves, to serve

Heat the olive oil in a heavy frying pan and stir in the garlic, chilli and cumin seeds. Add the chicken livers and toss over the heat until they are browned on all sides. Reduce the heat a little and continue to cook for 3–5 minutes.

When the livers are almost cooked, add the ground coriander and hazelnuts. Stir in the orange flower water and preserved lemon. Season to taste with salt and black pepper and sprinkle with a little fresh coriander. Serve immediately with salad leaves.

Variation

Lamb's liver, trimmed and finely sliced, is also good cooked this way. The trick is to sear the outside so that the middle is almost pink and melts in the mouth. If you don't have orange flower water, try a little balsamic vinegar.

Broths and soups

Fragrant broths are daily fare, often packed with pulses and vegetables. Like *kemia*, soups are often served before the main meal to whet the appetite. Everyday meals in a household may consist of one main dish, possibly a tagine or couscous, to follow a light soup. However, soups may also be hearty enough to make a meal in themselves, served with lots of bread.

Cinnamon-scented chickpea and lentil soup with fennel and honey buns

Serves eight

30–45ml/2–3 tbsp smen or olive oil
2 onions, halved and sliced
2.5ml/½ tsp ground ginger
2.5ml/½ tsp ground turmeric
5ml/1 tsp ground cinnamon
pinch of saffron threads
2 x 400g/14oz cans of tomatoes
5–10ml/1–2 tsp caster (superfine) sugar
175g/6oz/1 cup brown lentils, picked over and rinsed
1.75 litres/3 pints/7½ cups meat or vegetable stock
200g/7oz/1 generous cup dried chickpeas, soaked overnight and boiled for 1–1½ hours until tender
200g/7oz/1 generous cup dried broad (fava) beans, soaked overnight and boiled for 1–1½ hours until tender
small bunch of fresh coriander (cilantro), chopped
small bunch of fresh flat leaf parsley, chopped
sea salt and freshly ground black pepper

For the buns

2.5ml/½ tsp dried yeast
300g/11oz/2 cups strong white bread flour, plus extra for dusting
salt
15–30ml/1–2 tbsp clear honey
5ml/1 tsp fennel seeds
250ml/9floz/generous 1 cup milk
1 egg yolk, mixed with a little milk

This thick pulse and vegetable soup, flavoured with ginger and cinnamon, varies from village to village and town to town. It is believed to have originated from a semolina gruel that the Berbers prepared to warm themselves during the cold winters in the Atlas Mountains. Over the centuries, it has been adapted and refined with spices and tomatoes from the New World.

Make the fennel and honey buns. Dissolve the yeast in about 15ml/1 tbsp lukewarm water. Sift the flour and a pinch of salt into a bowl. Make a well in the centre and add the dissolved yeast, honey and fennel seeds. Gradually pour in the milk, using your hands to work it into the flour along with the honey and yeast, until the mixture forms a dough – if the dough becomes too sticky to handle add more flour.

Turn the dough out on to a floured surface and knead well for about 10 minutes, until it is smooth and elastic. Flour the surface under the dough and cover it with a damp cloth, then leave the dough to rise until it has doubled in size.

Preheat the oven to 230°C/450°F/gas 8. Grease two baking sheets. Divide the dough into 12 balls. On a floured surface, flatten the balls of dough with the palm of your hand, then place them on a baking sheet. Brush the tops of the buns with egg yolk, then bake for about 15 minutes until they are risen slightly and sound hollow when tapped underneath. Transfer to a wire rack to cool.

To make the soup, heat the smen or olive oil in a stockpot or large pan. Add the onions and stir for about 15 minutes, or until they are soft. Add the ginger, turmeric, cinnamon and saffron, followed by the tomatoes and a little sugar. Stir in the lentils and pour in the stock or water. Bring the liquid to the boil, then reduce the heat, cover and simmer for about 25 minutes, or until the lentils are tender.

Stir in the cooked chickpeas and beans, bring back to the boil, then cover and simmer for a further 10–15 minutes. Stir in the fresh herbs and season the soup to taste. Serve piping hot, with the buns.

Chilled almond and garlic soup

The cold and chilled soups of North Africa are ancient in origin and were originally introduced to Morocco by the Arabs, possibly even the Romans. This particular milky white soup has travelled further with the Moors into Spain. Heavily laced with garlic, it is unusual but deliciously refreshing in hot weather, and makes a delightful, tangy first course.

Serves four

130g/4½oz/1 cup blanched almonds

3–4 slices of day-old white bread, crusts removed

4 garlic cloves, peeled

60ml/4 tbsp olive oil

about 1 litre/1¾ pints/4 cups iced water

30ml/2 tbsp white wine vinegar

sea salt

To garnish

a few sweet green grapes, halved and deseeded

a few flaked almonds

Place the blanched almonds in a food processor and blend to form a smooth paste. Add the bread, garlic, olive oil and half the water and process again until smooth. With the motor running, continue adding the rest of the water in a slow, steady stream until the mixture is smooth with the consistency of thin cream. Add vinegar and salt to taste. Chill for at least 1 hour, then serve garnished with the sliced grapes and almonds.

Velvety pumpkin soup with rice and cinnamon

Modern Moroccan streets and markets are full of colourful seasonal produce that inspire you to buy, go home and start cooking. The pumpkin season is particularly delightful, with the huge orange vegetables piled up on stalls and wooden carts. The sellers patiently peel and slice the pumpkins ready for making this delicious winter soup.

Serves four

about 1.1kg/2lb 7oz pumpkin

750ml/1¼ pints/3¼ cups chicken stock

750ml/1¼ pints/3¼ cups milk

10–15ml/2–3 tsp sugar

75g/3oz/½ cup cooked rice

sea salt and freshly ground black pepper

ground cinnamon, to serve

Remove any seeds or fibre from the pumpkin, cut off the peel and chop the flesh. Put the prepared pumpkin in a pan and add the stock, milk, sugar and seasoning. Bring to the boil, then reduce the heat and simmer for about 20 minutes, or until the pumpkin is tender. Drain the pumpkin, reserving the liquid, and purée it in a food processor, then return the purée with the liquid to the pan.

Bring the soup back to the boil again, throw in the rice and simmer for a few minutes, until the grains are reheated. Check the seasoning, dust with cinnamon and pour into bowls. Serve piping hot, with chunks of bread.

Chunky tomato and squash soup with ras el hanout and noodles

This full-flavoured *chorba* is the daily soup in many Moroccan households. The ras el hanout gives it a lovely, warming kick. You can purée the soup, if you prefer, but I like it just as it is, finished off with a swirl of yogurt or buttermilk and finely chopped coriander. Serve with chunks of fresh bread.

Serves four

45–60ml/3–4 tbsp olive oil

3–4 cloves

2 onions, chopped

1 butternut squash, peeled, deseeded and cut into small chunks

4 celery stalks, chopped

2 carrots, peeled and chopped

8 large, ripe tomatoes, skinned and roughly chopped

5–10ml/1–2 tsp sugar

15ml/1 tbsp tomato purée (paste)

5–10ml/1–2 tsp ras el hanout

2.5ml/½ tsp ground turmeric

1.7 litres/3 pints/7½ cups vegetable stock

a big bunch of fresh coriander (cilantro), chopped (reserve a few sprigs for garnish)

a handful of dried egg noodles, broken into pieces

sea salt and freshly ground black pepper

60–75ml/4–5 tbsp creamy yogurt, to serve

In a deep, heavy pan, heat the oil and add the cloves, onions, squash, celery and carrots. Fry until they begin to colour, then stir in the tomatoes and sugar. Cook the tomatoes until the water reduces and they begin to pulp.

Stir in the tomato purée, ras el hanout, turmeric and chopped coriander. Pour in the stock and bring the liquid to the boil. Reduce the heat and simmer for 30–40 minutes until the vegetables are very tender and the liquid has reduced a little.

To make a puréed soup, leave the liquid to cool slightly before processing in a food processor or blender, then pour back into the pan before adding the noodles. Alternatively, to make a chunky soup, simply add the noodles to the unblended soup and cook for a further 8–10 minutes, or until the noodles are soft.

Season the soup to taste and ladle it into bowls. Spoon a swirl of yogurt into each one, garnish with the extra coriander and serve with freshly baked Moroccan bread.

Fish broth with lemon and harissa

Along the northern coastal region of Morocco, in cities like Tangier, Tetouan, and Casablanca, you come across fish broths that echo the well-flavoured soupy stews of Mediterranean Spain and France. Served on their own with bread for dunking, or spooned over plain couscous, these plain or spicy broths, *chorba bil hout*, deliciously showcase the catch of the day.

Serves four

30–45ml/2–3 tbsp olive oil

1 onion, finely chopped

2 stalks celery, diced

2–3 garlic cloves, finely chopped

5–10ml/1–2 tsp harissa

small bunch of fresh flat-leaf parsley, finely chopped

1 litre/1¾ pints/4 cups fish stock or water

juice of 2 lemons

150ml/¼ pint/scant ¾ cup fino sherry or white wine

400g/14oz can of chopped tomatoes, drained of juice

sea salt and freshly ground black pepper

1kg/2¼lb fresh firm-fleshed fish, such as cod, haddock, ling, grouper, sea bass or snapper, cut into large chunks

500g/1¼lb shellfish, such as prawns (jumbo shrimp), clams and mussels, cleaned and in their shells (discard any mussels that do not close)

sea salt and freshly ground black pepper

small bunch of fresh coriander (cilantro) leaves, coarsely chopped

Heat the oil in a deep, heavy based pot and stir in the onion, celery and garlic, until it begins to colour. Add the harissa and parsley and pour in the fish stock. Bring the liquid to the boil, reduce the heat and simmer for 10 minutes to enable the flavours to mingle.

Add the lemon juice and fino sherry or wine, and stir in the tomatoes. Season to taste with salt and pepper. Gently stir in the fish chunks and shellfish and bring the liquid to the boil again. Reduce the heat and simmer for 3–4 minutes to make sure the fish is cooked through. (Discard any mussels that do not open.) Sprinkle the chopped coriander over the top and serve immediately with lots of bread, or with couscous.

Chicken, rice and saffron broth

This simple village broth can be packed with seasonal greens and served as a meal on its own, or kept simple to quench the thirst and serve with other light dishes in the hot weather. The chicken is cooked whole in the broth, torn into strips at the end, and refreshed with sweet, aromatic mint and lemon wedges to squeeze into it.

Serves four to six

1 small chicken

1 onion, quartered

1 lemon, quartered

bunch of fresh flat-leaf parsley stalks

5ml/1 tsp coriander seeds

1 cinnamon stick, broken

fingerful of saffron threads

sea salt and freshly ground black pepper

15ml/1 tbsp olive oil

2 onions, finely chopped

1–2 red chillies, deseeded and finely chopped

5ml/1 tsp cumin seeds

5ml/1 tsp fennel seeds

100g/3½oz/generous ½ cup long grain rice, rinsed and drained

bunch of fresh mint leaves, finely shredded

1 lemon, cut into wedges, to serve

Pop the whole chicken into a deep pot with the onion, lemon, parsley, coriander seeds, cinnamon stick, saffron threads and seasoning, and pour in enough water to cover it. Bring the liquid to the boil, reduce the heat, cover the pot and simmer for 1 hour, until the chicken is practically falling off the bone.

Lift the chicken out of the pot and leave it cool a little so you can handle it. Remove the skin and tear the tender flesh into strips.

Season the cooking liquid and strain it (don't pour away the liquid, it's the stock for your broth). Measure out roughly 1.7 litres/3 pints/7½ cups into a jug.

Heat the olive oil in the heavy-based pot and stir in the onions, chillies, cumin and fennel seeds, until fragrant. Pour in the strained stock and bring the liquid to the boil. Stir in the rice, reduce the heat and simmer for about 15 minutes. Add the strips of chicken and simmer for a further 5–10 minutes.

Check the seasoning, stir in half of the mint and ladle the broth into bowls. Garnish with the rest of the mint and serve with lemon quarters to squeeze over it.

Rfissa

Like the bean stew *loubia*, this is Moroccan comfort food. It is a dish of chicken, lentils and onions served on a bed of shredded *m'semen* over which a fragrant broth is poured. The dish can be made with other breads such as *trid* pastry, which is like a paper-thin crepe. When the dish is made with *trid*, it is also called *trid*; when the semolina pan-fried muffin-like bread *harcha* is used, the dish is called *rfissa medhoussa*. The origins of *rfissa* and *trid* can be traced back to the ancient Arab *tharid* and *fatteh* dishes, which would have come to Morocco with the Islamic occupation. It is often served as a communal dish during Ramadan.

Serves six to eight

100ml/3½fl oz/generous ⅓ cup olive oil

2–3 onions, sliced

large thumb-sized piece of fresh ginger, peeled and finely chopped

1 large chicken, left whole

15ml/1 tbsp sea salt

15ml/1 tbsp freshly ground black pepper

15ml/1 tbsp ras el hanout

large pinch of saffron threads

60ml/4 tbsp fenugreek seeds, soaked overnight and drained

small bunch of fresh coriander (cilantro), finely chopped (reserve some for garnishing)

small bunch of fresh flat-leaf parsley, finely chopped (reserve some for garnishing)

1.7 litres/3 pints/7½ cups water

175g/6oz/1 cup brown or green puy lentils, rinsed and drained

15ml/1 tbsp runny honey

5–10ml/1–2 tsp smen or butter

about 8 *m'semen* (page 157), cut into strips or shredded with your fingers

Heat the oil in a pot and stir in the onions and ginger for 3–4 minutes to soften. Add the chicken, seasoning and spices and most of the fresh herbs. Pour in the water – if it doesn't cover the chicken, add more until it does. Bring the water to the boil, reduce the heat and simmer for about an hour.

Lift the chicken out of the broth and place on a board to cool a little so that you can shred it with your fingers.

Meanwhile, strain the cooking broth into another pot and bring it to the boil. Toss in the lentils and simmer for 15–20 minutes, until tender.

Shred the chicken and keep warm. Stir the honey and smen into the lentil broth and season well to taste. Arrange the strips of *m'semen* on a serving dish, or in wide, individual bowls. Place the shredded chicken on top, ladle the lentils and fragrant broth over and around it, and garnish with the reserved fresh herbs.

Serve immediately and, if you like, you can ladle some of the lentil broth into small bowls or cups to serve with the *rfissa*.

Harira

Serves four to six

30–45ml/2–3 tbsp olive or argan oil

2 onions, chopped

2 celery stalks, trimmed and diced

2 small carrots, peeled and diced

2–3 garlic cloves, left whole and smashed

10ml/2 tsp cumin seeds

450g/1lb lean lamb or beef, cut into bite-sized cubes

10ml/2 tsp ground turmeric

10ml/2 tsp paprika

10ml/2 tsp ground cinnamon

5ml/1 tsp ground ginger

10ml/1 tsp sugar

2 bay leaves

30ml/2 tbsp tomato purée (paste)

1.2 litres/2 pints/5 cups lamb or chicken stock

2 x 400g/14oz cans of chopped tomatoes, drained of juice

400g/14oz can of chickpeas, drained and rinsed

400g/14oz can of haricot or cannellini beans, drained and rinsed

sea salt and freshly ground black pepper

small bunch of fresh flat-leaf parsley, coarsely chopped

small bunch of fresh coriander (cilantro), coarsely chopped

For the buerre manie

20ml/1½ tbsp softened butter or smen

15ml/1 tbsp plain (all-purpose) flour

Throughout Morocco, there are variations of this hearty broth prepared with lamb, chickpeas and lentils, or other pulses. It is one of the classic dishes served at religious feasts and, with a bowl of dates to accompany it, is traditionally served to break the fast during Islamic Ramadan and Jewish Yom Kippur. In traditional Berber households, *harira* is often eaten from earthenware bowls using rounded spoons carved from lemon wood. Falling somewhere between a broth and stew, *harira* can be thickened at the end with a 'buerre manie' which draws the flour into the liquid to give it a silky texture.

Heat the oil in the base of a deep, heavy-based pot. Stir in the onions, celery, and carrots and cook until the onions begin to colour. Add the smashed garlic and cumin seeds and toss in the lamb, cooking until lightly browned. Add the spices, sugar and bay leaves and stir in the tomato purée. Pour in the stock and bring the liquid to the boil. Reduce the heat, cover with a lid, and simmer for 1 hour, until the meat is tender.

Add the chopped tomatoes and chickpeas to the pot and cook gently for a further 30 minutes, until the soup is almost as thick as a stew. Top up with a little water if necessary, season with salt and pepper and toss in most of the parsley and coriander.

To finish the soup, combine the softened butter or smen with the flour to form a paste. Add it bit by bit to the broth, stirring all the time, so the liquid becomes smooth and silky. Ladle the broth into bowls, garnish with the remaining parsley and coriander and serve it piping hot with chunks of bread to dip in it.

Using dried pulses

If you have time to soak and cook the dried pulses instead of using a can, measure 75g/3oz/½ cup each of chickpeas and beans, soak for 6 hours or overnight, then rinse and drain, Tip them into a pot and cover with water and bring to the boil. Reduce the heat and simmer for about 2 hours, topping up the water if necessary, until soft. Drain and use as required.

Breads and savoury pastries

No broth (or tagine) would ever be served without bread. There are many varieties of semi-leavened and flat breads to use as a scoop, a mop or a pocket to fill, and some doughs are used to make savouries which are enjoyed as appetizers and as a snack in the street.

Beghrir

These pancakes are smooth on one side, bubbly on the other, and they melt in the mouth. Dripping with honey or drenched in sugar, they are often served for breakfast on cool, winter mornings in Morocco. They are also popular as a sweet snack in the streets.

Makes twenty to thirty

40g/1½oz fresh yeast

400g/14oz/2⅓ cups fine semolina

115g/4oz/generous ¾ cup plain (all-purpose) flour

5ml/1 tsp salt

3 eggs, beaten

300ml/½ pint/1¼ cups milk

900ml/1½ pints/3¾ cups water

olive or sunflower oil, for frying

75g/3oz/¾ stick butter

clear honey, to serve

Place the yeast in a small bowl and add 30ml/2 tbsp lukewarm water. Break up the yeast with a spoon and gradually press and stir it into the water until dissolved. Add a little extra water, if necessary, so that the yeast forms a thin, creamy paste. Cover the bowl and leave in a warm place for about 15 minutes, until frothy and bubbly.

Sift the semolina and flour with the salt into a large bowl. Make a well in the centre and drop in the eggs. Heat the milk and water together until just warm, then pour into the bowl, beating constantly. Pour in the yeast mixture and continue beating for 5 minutes. Cover the bowl with a cloth and leave the batter to rise in a warm place for at least 2 hours.

To cook the pancakes, heat a heavy frying pan and use a pad of kitchen paper to wipe it with a little oil. Pour a small cupful or ladleful of batter into the pan and spread evenly. Cook for about 2 minutes. Bubbles will form across the pancake and set in the batter. Lift out and wrap in a cloth to keep warm. Repeat with the remaining batter.

Melt the butter in a wide pan and dip the pancakes into it or, alternatively, pour the butter over them. Serve warm with clear honey.

Using dried yeast

If fresh yeast is not available, use 20g/¾oz easy-blend (rapid-rise) dried yeast. Mix this type of yeast with the semolina and flour before adding the liquids. Continue as in the main recipe.

Poppy seed harcha

These little semolina pan-fried breads are more scone- or muffin-like than most of the Moroccan flat breads. Slightly crunchy on the outside and softly textured inside, they can be prepared with milk or buttermilk and, similar to scones, they are delicious savoury or sweet, served with clotted cream or strained yogurt, and drizzled with honey.

Serves four

225g/8oz/1½ cups fine semolina

30ml/2 tbsp poppy seeds

30ml/2 tbsp golden caster or soft brown sugar

5ml/1 tsp baking powder

2.5ml/½ tsp salt

90g/3¼oz/scant 1 stick softened butter

100ml/3½fl oz/generous ⅓ cup milk

coarse semolina, for coating

olive or sunflower oil, for frying

Tip the fine semolina, poppy seeds, sugar, baking powder and salt into a bowl. Using your fingers, rub in the butter so that mixture becomes moist. Gradually add in the milk, using your hand to form a moist dough – you may need more or less milk.

Divide the dough into 8–10 balls. Cover with a cloth and leave the balls to rest for about 15 minutes.

Sprinkle the coarse semolina on the work surface. Roll each ball in the semolina and flatten them with the heel of your hand to form discs, roughly 1.5cm/½in thick.

Heat a heavy-based griddle or flat pan over a medium heat. Lightly oil the hot pan and cook the *harcha* in batches over a low heat for 4–5 minutes so that they cook all the way through. When golden in colour, flip them over and cook the other side for 4–5 minutes too.

Serve warm with honey, cream, cheese, jam, or *amlou* (page 78).

Kesra

This Moroccan bread is the perfect accompaniment for all kinds of savoury dishes. Chunks of the warm, crusty cornmeal loaves make wonderful scoops for tasty dips and are perfect for mopping up all the aromatic oils and cooking juices from salads and tagines.

Makes two round loaves

sunflower or vegetable oil

75g/3oz/½ cup cornmeal

2.5ml/½ tsp dried yeast

scant 5ml/1 tsp sugar

600ml/1 pint/2½ cups lukewarm water

450g/1lb/3½ cups strong white bread flour, plus extra for dusting

5ml/1 tsp sea salt

30ml/2 tbsp melted butter

aniseed, fennel or sesame seeds, to sprinkle

Lightly oil two baking sheets and dust them with 15ml/1 tbsp of the cornmeal. In a small bowl, dissolve the yeast and sugar in about 50ml/2fl oz/¼ cup of the lukewarm water.

Sift the flour, the remaining cornmeal and the salt into a bowl. Make a well in the centre and pour in the yeast mixture and the melted butter. Gradually add the remaining water, while using your hand to draw in the flour from the sides of the bowl and mix the ingredients into a dough. Add a little more flour if the dough becomes too sticky.

Knead the dough on a floured surface for about 10 minutes until smooth and elastic. Divide the dough in half and knead each piece into a ball. Flatten and stretch the balls of dough into circles, about 20cm/8in in diameter. Place on the baking sheets and sprinkle with seeds. Cover the loaves with damp cloths and leave in a warm place for about 1 hour, until doubled in size.

Preheat the oven to 220°C/425°F/gas 7. Pinch the tops of the loaves with your fingers or prick them with a fork. Bake for about 15 minutes, then reduce the oven temperature to 180°C/350°F/gas 4 and bake for a further 15 minutes, or until the loaves are crusty, golden and sound hollow when tapped underneath. Cool on a wire rack.

Shaping and flavouring the bread

The dough can be shaped in any way you prefer, or made into individual rolls. For ceremonial occasions, aniseed or fennel seeds are added to the dough to flavour the bread. To make a delicious breakfast bread, use half and half wholemeal (wholewheat) and white flours, and add a little honey to the dough with the lukewarm water.

Batbout

Batbout is a popular flat bread that is cooked on the stove in a flat pan or on a griddle and when it puffs up a hollow pocket forms in the middle, perfect for filling with grilled meat, fish and vegetables. *Batbout*, also known as *mkhamer* and *matlou* in different regions, can be made as small or large as you like but they need to be rolled quite thin so that they puff up when cooked. They also freeze well so it's worth making a large quantity.

Makes ten to twenty

10ml/2 tsp dried yeast

15ml/1 tbsp sugar

350g/12oz/2½ cups strong white bread flour

115g/4oz/generous ¾ cup wholemeal (wholewheat) flour

225g/8oz/1⅓ cups fine semolina, plus extra for dusting

10ml/2 tsp salt

45ml/3 tbsp olive oil

about 400ml/14fl oz/1¾ cups warm water

Cream the yeast in a bowl with 60ml/4 tbsp of the water and 5ml/1 tsp of the sugar, until it dissolves and becomes frothy.

Sift the two flours and semolina with the rest of the sugar and the salt into a large bowl. Make a well in the centre and pour in the oil, warm water and the creamed yeast. Using your hand, draw in the flour and knead the dough – add more water if you need it – until it is smooth and springy.

Take portions of the dough into your hands and knead them into smooth balls – these can be the size of plums or oranges, depending on how big you would like your flat breads to be. Arrange the balls on a lightly floured surface, leaving a gap between them, and cover with a clean dishtowel for 20 minutes.

Dust a work surface with fine semolina and roll out each ball into a thin round. Place the rounds onto a cotton sheet or several dish towels, cover with another sheet or more dish towels and leave them to prove and rise for about 1–2 hours, until light to touch and puffed up.

Heat a pan or griddle over a medium heat. Using a spatula, very carefully transfer two or three *batbout* to the hot pan – you don't want them to tear them in the process as that will prevent them from puffing up and forming a hollow pocket. Let them set for about 10 seconds then gently flip them over. Flip them several times until they are lightly browned and puffed. Transfer the cooked *batbout* to a rack and carry on cooking the rest of them in batches.

Mhemmer

Simple and delicious, perhaps with origins in Spain, this street-style spicy savoury snack is often served in the pocket of *batbout* or it is cut into fingers and dipped into a spice mix, or salt combined with dried chilli flakes. It can be cooked in a pan on top of the stove, or in the oven.

Serve four to six

6 medium-sized potatoes, halved with skins left on

8–10 eggs

10ml/2 tsp ground turmeric

10ml/2 tsp cumin seeds

5ml/1 tsp harissa

sea salt and freshly ground black pepper

2–3 spring onions (scallions), trimmed and finely sliced

small bunch of fresh flat-leaf parsley, finely chopped

small bunch of fresh mint, finely chopped

small bunch of fresh coriander (cilantro), roughly chopped

30ml/2 tbsp olive or argan oil

Put the potatoes into a pan with plenty of water and bring it to the boil. Add a pinch of salt and boil the potatoes until soft enough to mash. Drain and refresh under running cold water. Peel off the skins, or leave them on if you prefer, and mash the potatoes in a bowl.

Beat the eggs with the turmeric, cumin seeds and harissa. Season well with salt and pepper and beat the mixture into the mashed potato. Add the spring onions and fresh herbs.

Heat the oil in the base of a tagine, or a heavy-based frying pan, and tip in the potato mixture, making sure it spreads evenly in the pan. Cover and cook over a low flame for 10–15 minutes until the omelette is firm to touch. If you have a grill or oven you can finish it off by browning the top.

Divide the omelette into wedges or strips to serve in the hollow of *batbout* (previous page) with fresh country salad (page 110), *matisha ma'asala* (page 83), or pickled vegetables.

Roast chicken with cucumber and tomato salad in pitta pockets

Grillled or roasted chicken or lamb with salads, pickles or harissa, tucked into the pocket of *batbout* (page 146) is typical street fare. Pitta breads work just as well as a substitute.

Makes six

1 small cucumber, peeled and diced

3 tomatoes, peeled, deseeded and chopped

2 spring onions (scallions), chopped

30ml/2 tbsp olive oil

small bunch of fresh flat-leaf parsley, finely chopped

small bunch of fresh mint, finely chopped

½ preserved lemon, finely chopped

45–60ml/3–4 tbsp tahini

juice of 1 lemon

2 garlic cloves, crushed

sea salt and freshly ground black pepper

6 pitta breads or *batbout*

½ small roast chicken or 2 large roast chicken breasts, cut into strips

Place the cucumber in a strainer over a bowl, sprinkle with a little salt and leave for 10 minutes to drain. Rinse well and drain again, then place in a bowl with the tomatoes and spring onions. Stir in the olive oil, parsley, mint and preserved lemon. Season well.

In a small bowl, mix the tahini with the lemon juice, then thin the mixture down with a little water to the consistency of thick cream. Beat in the garlic and season.

Preheat the grill or broiler to hot. Lightly toast the pitta breads well away from the heat source until they puff up. (Alternatively, lightly toast the breads in a toaster.) Open the breads and stuff them liberally with the chicken strips and salad. Drizzle a generous amount of tahini sauce into each one and serve immediately.

Bruschetta with anchovies, quail's eggs and roasted cumin

Hard-boiled eggs are enjoyed as a snack or appetizer, dipped in salt and paprika, or in roasted cumin. Bite-size quail's eggs work well on these tasty bruschetta.

Serves four to six

1 Moroccan semi-leavened or similar thin loaf

2–3 garlic cloves

30–45ml/2–3 tbsp olive oil

1 red onion, halved and finely sliced

12 quail's eggs, boiled for about 4 minutes, shelled and halved

50g/2oz anchovy fillets

10–15ml/2–3 tsp cumin seeds, roasted and ground

small bunch of fresh flat-leaf parsley, roughly chopped

coarse sea salt

Preheat the grill on the hottest setting. Slice the loaf of bread horizontally in half and toast the cut side until golden. Smash the garlic cloves with the flat blade of a knife to remove their skins and crush the flesh slightly, and rub them over the toasted bread. Drizzle the olive oil over the bread and sprinkle with a little salt (not too much as the anchovies will be salty).

Cut each length of bread into four to six equal pieces. Pile the onion slices, quail's egg halves and anchovy fillets on the pieces of bread. Sprinkle liberally with the ground roasted cumin and chopped parsley and serve immediately while the bread is still warm.

Preparing anchovy fillets

Select anchovy fillets preserved in salt or oil. Soak anchovy fillets preserved in salt in a little milk for about 15 minutes to reduce the salty flavour, then drain (discarding the milk) and pat dry on kitchen paper. Drain fillets preserved in oil.

Roasting cumin seeds

To dry-roast seeds, place in a small, heavy frying pan over a medium heat, stirring around for a couple of minutes until they turn a golden brown. Grind in a pestle and mortar or small blender.

Chollo

Bread plays an important role in the daily enjoyment of food, but there are inevitably some loaves that are baked specifically for festive occasions. Spiced buns and plaited loaves, like these ones, are popular amongst both the Jewish and Muslim communities.

To make two loaves

5ml/1 tsp dried yeast

10ml/2 tsp sugar

450g/1lb/3½ cups strong plain (all-purpose) flour, plus extra for dusting

5ml/1 tsp salt

5ml/1 tsp aniseeds

10ml/2 tsp sesame seeds

50ml/3½ tbsp sunflower or olive oil

1 egg, lightly beaten

225ml/8fl oz/1 cup warm water

For glazing

1 egg, beaten

45ml/3 tbsp milk

10ml/2 tsp sesame seeds

Cream the yeast in a bowl with roughly 50ml/3½ tbsp lukewarm water and 1 teaspoon of the sugar, until it dissolves and becomes frothy.

Sift the flour with the salt into a large bowl and stir in the aniseeds and sesame seeds. Make a well in the centre of the flour and add the blended yeast, oil, egg, and the rest of the sugar. Pour in the warm water, drawing in the flour from the sides and using your hand to form a smooth dough.

Take the dough out of the bowl and knead it on a floured surface for about 10 minutes until light and elastic. Divide the dough into two balls and divide each ball into three. Knead and stretch the first set of into three ropes about 30cm/1ft long. Line the ropes side by side and plait them together. Pinch the ends together. Repeat with the other three lumps of dough.

Place both braided doughs on a floured baking tray. Cover with a damp dish towel and leave the loaves to prove for about 1 hour, until doubled in size.

Preheat the oven to 180°C/350°F/gas 4. To glaze, beat the egg with the milk in a bowl and brush it over the loaves. Sprinkle the tops with sesame seeds and place them in the oven for about 40 minutes, until they sound hollow when you tap the base. Transfer to a wire rack to cool a little and enjoy the bread with jam, honey, or savoury dishes.

M'semen

Hot off the griddle and dipped or drizzled in honey, *m'semen* are delicious for breakfast with a cup of strong coffee or aromatic mint tea. Square-shaped flat breads with an almost pancake-like texture, they can be enjoyed sweet, savoury or stuffed, and in some regions they are called *m'hajib* or *rghaif*. You can buy them from bakeries or street stalls, or make them at home.

Makes ten to twelve

450g/1lb/3½ cups strong white bread flour

60g/2oz/⅓ cup fine semolina

10ml/2 tsp sugar

10ml/2 tsp salt

5ml/1 tsp dried or instant yeast

approx. 300ml/½ pint/1¼ cups warm water

For folding and frying

250ml/9fl oz/1 cup vegetable oil

75g/3oz/½ cup fine semolina

25g/1oz/2 tbsp soft butter

Sift all the dry ingredients into a large bowl. Add the water and knead with your hand to form a smooth, elastic dough – add more water if you need to. Divide the dough into plum-sized portions and knead each one to form a smooth ball. Place the balls on an oiled tray and cover loosely with cling film or a clean dish towel. Leave for 20 minutes.

Meanwhile, clear a wide work-surface area for flattening and folding, and place bowls of vegetable oil, fine semolina and butter within easy reach. Oil the work-surface area and oil your hands.

Lift up a ball of dough, dip it into the bowl of oil and place it in the middle of your oiled work-surface. Using your oiled fingers, gently spread the dough into a paper-thin circle.

Dot the surface with bits of the softened butter and sprinkle with semolina. Fold the circle like a letter – one side into the middle and the remaining side over the top of it – so that you have a rectangle. Dot the top with some more butter, sprinkle with semolina and fold in the same way from the short end so that you create a square. Place the square on an oiled tray, cover with a clean dish towel and carry on with the rest of the dough balls.

Take the first square of dough and place it on the oiled work-surface. Using your oiled fingers, pat the square to flatten and stretch it so that it doubles in size. Repeat with the rest of the squares.

Place your griddle or flat pan over a medium heat. Depending on the size of your hot griddle, transfer 2–3 squares onto it and cook until crispy and golden on both sides. Lift the cooked *m'semen* onto a rack and repeat with the rest of the squares. As the *m'semen* are cooling, lift each one up by the edges and flex it by moving your hands backwards and forwards to release the layers within. Serve while still warm with butter and honey, jam or *amlou* (page 78).

Minced beef rghaif

Depending on where you are in the Maghreb, the ubiquitous square pan-fried flat breads called *m'semen* become known as *rghaif* when they have a savoury or sweet filling. In this recipe the *rghaif* are made in the same way as *m'semen* (on previous page), but a thin layer of spicy minced beef is added to each one at the flattening stage before folding.

Serves four to six

For the *m'semen*

450g/1lb/3½ cups strong white bread flour

60g/2oz/⅓ cup fine semolina, plus 75g/3oz/½ cup for folding

10ml/2 tsp sugar

10ml/2 tsp salt

5ml/1 tsp dried or instant yeast

approx. 300ml/½ pint/1¼ cups warm water

250ml/9fl oz/generous 1 cup vegetable oil, for folding and frying

For the filling

225g/8oz/1 cup minced (ground) beef

1 onion, finely chopped

2 garlic cloves, crushed

1 red or green chilli, deseeded and finely chopped

5ml/1 tsp ground cumin

5ml/1 tsp ground coriander

5ml/1 tsp paprika

bunch of fresh coriander (cilantro), finely chopped

bunch of fresh flat-leaf parsley, finely chopped

sea salt and freshly ground black pepper

Prepare the filling. Tip the minced beef into a bowl and add the rest of the filling ingredients. Using your hand, knead the mixture until slightly sticky and pasty. Cover and put aside.

Follow the recipe of the *m'semen* (page 157) to the stage of flattening the balls of dough into thin circles. For these stuffed *rghaif*, the circles don't need to quite so thin and, instead of dabbing them with butter, spread a thin layer of the meat paste over each one before folding. Sprinkle the first fold with semolina before folding the stuffed *rghaif* into squares. Be careful you don't overwork the dough or tear it, as you want the meat filling to remain in place.

Heat enough oil in a flat pan for shallow frying over a medium heat. Cook the *rghaif* in batches until crispy and golden on both sides. Add more oil if your pan becomes a bit dry. Lift the *rghaif* onto a rack and repeat with the rest of the squares. Serve hot with a salad or pickled vegetables.

B'stilla b'djej

I just love this pie! When it is good, it is seriously good and captures Morocco's culinary heart. Fragrant, aromatic and sweet, the crispy pastry, dusted with icing sugar and ground cinnamon, teases us with its savoury, saffron filling. The classic pie can be made with pigeon, squab or chicken – almonds or peanuts are often added, as well as the rind of bitter oranges or preserved lemons. It is traditionally cooked in an iron pan on top of the stove but you can bake it in the oven too. Often prepared as the first course for a *diffa*, a special celebratory meal, perhaps at a wedding or for the arrival of important guests, *b'stilla* should be sampled at least once on any visit to Morocco.

Serves four to six

30–45ml/2–3 tbsp olive oil

100g/3½oz/scant 1 stick butter

3 onions, halved lengthways, cut in half crossways and sliced with the grain

2 garlic cloves, finely chopped

90g/3½oz/scant ¾ cup blanched almonds, chopped

10ml/2 tsp ground cinnamon

5ml/1 tsp ground ginger

5ml/1 tsp teaspoon paprika

5ml/1 tsp ground coriander

3–4 skinless chicken fillets, cut into bite-size pieces

bunch of fresh flat-leaf parsley, finely chopped

big bunch of fresh coriander (cilantro), finely chopped

sea salt and freshly ground black pepper

7–8 sheets of ouarka or filo pastry

1 egg yolk

5–10ml/1–2 tsp ground cinnamon, for dusting

5–10ml/1–2 tsp icing (confectioners') sugar

Preheat the oven to 200°C/400°F/gas 6. In a heavy-based frying pan, heat the olive oil with a knob of the butter and stir in the onions. Fry over a medium heat for 5–6 minutes, until they begin to soften and colour. Stir in the garlic and almonds, cook until they begin to colour, then add the spices. Toss in the chicken and cook gently, until all the liquid in the pan has evaporated. Toss in the herbs, season with salt and pepper, and leave the chicken to cool.

Melt the rest of butter. Separate the sheets of ouarka or filo and keep them under a damp cloth. Brush a little butter in the base of an ovenproof dish – a round one produces an attractive pie – and cover with a sheet of pastry, allowing the sides to flop over the edge. Brush the sheet of pastry with butter and place another one on top. Repeat with another two layers.

Spread the chicken and onion mixture on top of the pastry and fold the edges over the filling, brushing them with butter too. Cover with the remaining sheets of pastry, brushing each one with butter, and tuck the overlapping edges under the pie, like making a bed, so that it is flat on top. To glaze, mix the egg yolk with a scant teaspoon of water and brush it over the top of the pie.

Place the pie in the oven and bake for about 25 minutes, until the pastry is crisp and golden. Dust the top with the cinnamon and icing sugar in a lattice pattern and serve immediately.

Picnic pie with egg, cashew nuts, ginger and coriander

This is a homely vegetarian version of the more elaborate and traditional *b'stilla* (see previous page). Any mixture of nuts and herbs can be used, but the cashew nuts make this recipe more unusual. Served with a fruity Moroccan salad, this pie makes a delightful meal or, on a lovely summer day, it is great to take on a picnic.

Serves six

30ml/2 tbsp olive oil

115g/4oz/1 stick butter

8 spring onions (scallions), trimmed and chopped

2 garlic cloves, chopped

25g/1oz fresh root ginger, peeled and chopped

225g/8oz/1¾ cups cashew nuts, roughly chopped

5–10ml/1–2 tsp ground cinnamon, plus extra to garnish

5ml/1 tsp paprika

2.5ml/½ tsp ground coriander, plus extra for dusting

sea salt and freshly ground black pepper

6 eggs, beaten

bunch of fresh flat-leaf parsley, finely chopped

large bunch of fresh coriander (cilantro), finely chopped

8 sheets of ouarka or filo pastry

Preheat the oven to 200°C/400°F/gas 6. Heat the olive oil with a little of the butter in a heavy pan and stir in the spring onions, garlic and ginger. Add the cashew nuts and cook for a few minutes, then stir in the cinnamon, paprika and ground coriander. Season well, then add the eggs. Cook, stirring constantly, until the eggs begin to scramble but remain moist. Remove the pan from the heat, add the parsley and fresh coriander, and leave to cool.

Melt the remaining butter. Separate the sheets of ouarka or filo and keep them under a slightly damp cloth. Brush the base of an ovenproof dish with a little of the melted butter and cover with a sheet of pastry, allowing the sides to flop over the rim. Brush the pastry with a little more of the melted butter and place another sheet of pastry on top. Repeat with another two sheets of pastry to make four layers.

Spread the cashew nut mixture on the pastry and fold the pastry edges over the filling. Cover with the remaining sheets of pastry, brushing each one with melted butter and tucking the edges under the pie, as though you were making a bed.

Brush the top of the pie with the remaining melted butter and bake for 25 minutes, or until the pastry is crisp and golden. Dust the top of the pie with a little extra ground cinnamon and then serve immediately.

Making individual pies

Instead of making a single large pie, you can make small, individual pies for a picnic or to serve at a party. Simply cut the pastry into strips or triangles, add a spoonful of the filling and fold them up into tight little parcels, making sure the edges are well sealed.

Fish and chermoula mini pies

These little savoury pies are made with ouarka, but filo pastry will work just as well. The filling is highly flavoured with chermoula, which can be made in advance and stored in the refrigerator for a few days. You can vary the filling by adding mussels or scallops, if you like.

Makes eight

500g/1¼lb firm white fish fillets

225g/8oz uncooked king prawns (jumbo shrimp)

sea salt

16 sheets of ouarka or filo pastry

60–75ml/4–5 tbsp sunflower oil

1 egg yolk, mixed with a few drops of water

For the chermoula

75ml/5 tbsp olive oil

juice of 1 lemon

5ml/1 tsp ground cumin

5–10ml/1–2 tsp paprika

2–3 garlic cloves, crushed

1 red chilli, deseeded and chopped

large bunch of fresh flat-leaf parsley, chopped

large bunch of fresh coriander (cilantro), chopped

Combine all the chermoula ingredients in a bowl and set aside.

Place the fish in a frying pan and add just enough water to cover the fillets. Season with a little salt and heat until just simmering, then cook gently for 3 minutes, or until the fish just begins to flake. Use a slotted spoon to remove the fish from the liquid and break it up, taking care to remove all bones.

Poach the prawns in the fish liquor for 10 minutes, until they turn pink, then drain and shell them. Gently toss the prawns and fish in the chermoula, cover and set aside for 1 hour.

Preheat the oven to 180°C/350°F/gas 4 and grease two baking sheets. To make the pies, open out the sheets of pastry but keep them under a damp cloth. Take two sheets of pastry: brush one sheet with oil and lay the second one on top, then brush it with a little oil. Place some of the fish mixture in the middle of the length of the sheet but to one side of its width. Fold the edge of the pastry over the filling, then fold the long side over to cover the filling completely. Wrap the ends of the pastry around the filling like a collar to make a neat package with the edges tucked in, then brush with egg yolk. Continue in the same way with the rest of the pastry and chermoula mixture, then bake the pies for about 20 minutes until golden brown.

Making triangular or open pies

Instead of neat parcels, the filo and filling can be folded into triangles, or shaped into open boats or slipper shapes.

Briouat

These little savoury pastries are filled with minced beef or lamb, spinach, and feta cheese with herbs; the fillings can be varied to suit individual tastes. Easy to make, they are usually shaped into cigars, squares, triangles and half moons.

Makes about thirty-two

8 sheets of ouarka or filo pastry

sunflower oil, for deep-frying

For the feta cheese filling

450g/1lb feta cheese

4 eggs

bunch each of fresh coriander (cilantro), fresh flat-leaf parsley and fresh mint, finely chopped

For the beef or lamb filling

15–30ml/1–2 tbsp olive oil

1 onion, finely chopped

30ml/2 tbsp pine nuts

5ml/1 tsp ras el hanout

225g/8oz/1 cup minced (ground) beef or lamb

sea salt and freshly ground black pepper

For the spinach filling

50g/2oz/½ stick butter

1 onion, finely chopped

275g/10oz/5 cups fresh spinach, cooked, drained and chopped

small bunch of fresh coriander (cilantro), finely chopped

pinch of grated nutmeg

sea salt and freshly ground black pepper

Prepare the fillings. To make the feta cheese filling, place the cheese in a bowl and mash with a fork, then beat in the eggs and the chopped herbs.

To make the meat filling, heat the olive oil in a heavy frying pan. Add the onion and pine nuts; cook, stirring, until coloured, then stir in the ras el hanout. Add the minced meat and cook for about 15 minutes, stirring, until browned. Season and cool.

To make the spinach filling, melt the butter in a small heavy pan. Add the onion and cook over a low heat for 15 minutes until softened. Stir in the spinach and coriander. Season with nutmeg, salt and pepper, then cool.

Lay a sheet of ouarka or filo pastry on a work surface. Cut the sheet widthways into four strips. Spoon a little filling mixture on the first strip, at the end nearest to you. Fold the corners of the pastry over the mixture to seal it, then roll up the pastry and filling away from you into a tight cigar. As you reach the end of the strip, brush the edges with a little water and continue to roll up the cigar to seal in the filling. Repeat, placing the finished cigars under a damp cloth.

Heat the sunflower oil for deep-frying to 180°C/350°F, or until a cube of day-old bread browns in 30–45 seconds. Add the cigars to the oil in batches and fry over a medium heat until golden brown. Drain on kitchen paper and serve warm.

Spring rolls with chicken, spring onions and almonds

Serves six

30ml/2 tbsp plain (all-purpose) flour

about 30ml/2 tbsp water

12 large spring roll wrappers

sunflower oil, for deep-frying

For the filling

1 small chicken

½ onion, finely chopped

3–4 garlic cloves, finely chopped

25g/1oz/2 tbsp butter

1 cinnamon stick

5ml/1 tsp ground ginger

5ml/1 tsp ras el hanout

pinch of saffron threads

small bunch of fresh flat-leaf parsley, chopped

small bunch of fresh coriander (cilantro), chopped

sea salt and freshly ground black pepper

6 eggs, beaten

10ml/2 tsp orange flower water

½ lemon

6–8 spring onions (scallions), thickly sliced

For the dipping mixture

115g/4oz/1 cup blanched almonds, lightly toasted and coarsely ground

30ml/2 tbsp icing (confectioners') sugar

5–10ml/1–2 tsp ground cinnamon

Another version of *briouat*, these pastries resemble spring rolls and offer a simple street-style version of the classic *b'stilla* (page 161). You could also serve them with a harissa dipping sauce instead of this traditional cinnamon and icing sugar mixture.

To make the filling, place the chicken in a large pan and cover with water. Add the onion, garlic, butter, cinnamon, ginger, ras el hanout, saffron, half the parsley and half the coriander. Bring to the boil, then reduce the heat, cover and simmer for about 1 hour, until the chicken is cooked through and tender.

Lift the chicken out of the pan and set aside to cool. Boil the cooking liquid until it is reduced to about 550ml/18fl oz/2½ cups. Season with salt and pepper and remove from the heat. Pour the beaten eggs into the hot stock, stirring until the egg has set, then drain through a fine strainer into a jug or bowl (keep the liquid!).

Cut the meat off the chicken and shred coarsely. Place in a bowl; add the egg stock with the remaining parsley and coriander, the orange flower water, lemon juice and spring onions. Mix well. In another bowl, combine the dipping ingredients.

In a bowl, mix together the flour with the water to form a paste. Place a spring roll wrapper on a work surface with one corner facing you. (Keep the others under a damp dish towel.) Sprinkle some almond dipping mixture over the wrapper. Place a tablespoon of the chicken mixture in a line 5cm/2in in from the corner. Fold the corner over the filling and roll it slightly. Fold in the sides so they overlap and enclose the filling. Roll up the spring roll tightly, holding the sides, then seal the end with a little flour paste. Repeat with the remaining wrappers and filling.

Heat the sunflower oil for deep-frying to 180°C/350°F, or until a cube of day-old bread browns in 30–45 seconds. Cook the spring rolls three or four at a time until crisp and golden. Drain on kitchen paper and serve immediately with the almond mixture for dipping.

Brik

These crispy filled pastries are a feature of the street food of the Maghreb. Delicious and adaptable, you will come across different ones in Morocco, Tunisia and Algeria but my favourite are the *brik* or *briouat* with tuna and egg. As the egg is designed to be runny within the pastry, there is an art to eating them by the holding the corners of the pastry as you bite into the middle. Pickled vegetables make a good accompaniment.

Makes four

15ml/1 tbsp olive oil

1 onion, finely chopped

6–8 anchovy fillets

200g/7oz can of tuna, rinsed and drained

5ml/1 tsp harissa

15ml/1 tbsp pickled capers, rinsed and drained

small bunch of fresh flat-leaf parsley, finely chopped

small bunch of fresh coriander (cilantro), finely chopped

25g/1oz/2 tbsp butter

4 sheets of ouarka or filo pastry

4 eggs

sunflower or olive oil, for deep-frying

Heat the olive oil in a frying pan and stir in the onion for 2 minutes to soften. Add the anchovies and fry until they melt into the oil. Turn off the heat and leave the mixture to cool.

Tip the onion mixture into a bowl and add the tuna. Break up the tuna with a fork and add the harissa, capers, parsley and coriander. Mix together well.

Melt the butter in a pan. Place a sheet of ouarka or filo on a clean work surface. Brush it lightly with the melted butter and place another sheet on top. Brush it with butter. Working quickly, do the same with the remaining two pastry sheets so that you have two sets of double-layered sheets. Using a sharp knife, cut both sets into two squares – approximately 20cm/8in – so that you have four squares. Place the squares in a row, with one of the corners pointing towards you so you can visualize folding them into triangles.

Again, working quickly, spoon a portion of the tuna mixture just off-centre in one corner of each square. Make a well in the tuna mixture and crack an egg into it. Fold the empty side of the filo over the filling, taking care not to move or burst the egg, and pinch the edges together with a little water to seal.

Heat enough oil for deep-frying in a heavy-based frying pan. Using a spatula, carefully lift up one of the folded triangles and slip it into the oil. Fry one or two at a time, until crisp and golden brown. Drain on kitchen paper and repeat with the other triangles. Serve immediately while the yolk is still runny.

Vegetables and pulses

Every souk and countryside market has stalls piled high with seasonal vegetables alongside the fruit and herbs – tomatoes, aubergines, courgettes, cauliflowers, carrots, leeks, artichokes, pumpkins and squash, fresh beans and dried. Vegetables and pulses are daily fare for many people, particularly the poorer households as meat is expensive. Cooked together in tagines and stews on the stove or in the communal oven, there are many dishes to choose from.

Tagine of artichoke hearts, potatoes, peas and saffron

When artichokes are in season, this succulent tagine is a favourite country dish made using other produce from the garden or fields as well. Fresh coriander, parsley and mint combine to complement the summery flavours of the vegetables while turmeric contributes its earthy warmth. Prepare the artichokes yourself by removing the outer leaves, cutting off the stems, and scooping out the choke and hairy bits with a teaspoon, or you can buy frozen prepared hearts.

Serves four to six

6 fresh artichoke hearts

juice of 1 lemon

30–45ml/2–3 tbsp olive oil

1 onion, chopped

675g/1½lb potatoes, peeled and quartered

small bunch of fresh flat-leaf parsley, chopped

small bunch of fresh coriander (cilantro), chopped

small bunch of fresh mint, chopped

pinch of saffron threads

5ml/1 tsp ground turmeric

about 350ml/12fl oz/1½ cups vegetable stock

finely chopped rind of ½ preserved lemon

250g/9oz/1½ cups peas (defrosted, if frozen)

sea salt and freshly ground black pepper

Poach the artichoke hearts very gently in plenty of simmering water with half the lemon juice, for 10–15 minutes until tender. Drain and refresh under cold running water, then drain again.

Heat the olive oil in a tagine or heavy pan. Add the chopped onion and cook over a low heat for about 15 minutes, or until softened but not browned. Add the potatoes, most of the parsley, the coriander, mint, the remaining lemon juice, and the saffron and turmeric to the pan. Pour in the vegetable stock, bring to the boil, then reduce the heat. Cover the pan and cook for about 15 minutes, or until the potatoes are almost tender.

Stir the preserved lemon, artichoke hearts and peas into the stew, and cook, uncovered, for a further 10 minutes. Season to taste, sprinkle with the remaining parsley, and serve with fresh bread or couscous.

Preparing artichokes

Once cut, the flesh of artichokes will blacken. To prevent this from happening, put the artichokes into acidulated water – you can use lemon juice or white wine vinegar.

Tagine of yam, carrots and prunes

The vegetables in this succulent, syrupy tagine should be slightly caramelized. They are at their best served with grilled meats, couscous or with lots of warm, crusty bread and a leafy, herb-filled salad. I first had this dish in a tiny hut in the Atlas Mountains. The air was cold and the food was warming – it was quite delicious. At home, I often make this wonderfully moreish dish with sweet potatoes, as yams are harder to find.

Serves four to six

45ml/3 tbsp olive oil

a little butter

25–30 pearl or button onions, blanched and peeled

900g/2lb yam or sweet potatoes, peeled and cut into bitesize chunks

2–3 carrots, cut into bitesize chunks

150g/5oz/generous 1 cup ready-to-eat pitted prunes

5ml/1 tsp ground cinnamon

2.5ml/½ tsp ground ginger

10ml/2 tsp clear honey

450ml/¾ pint/scant 2 cups vegetable stock

sea salt and freshly ground black pepper

small bunch of fresh coriander (cilantro), finely chopped

small bunch of mint, finely chopped

Preheat the oven to 200°C/400°F/gas 6. Heat the olive oil in a flameproof casserole with the butter and stir in the peeled onions. Cook for about 5 minutes until the onions are tender, then remove half of the onions from the pan and set aside.

Add the yam or sweet potatoes and carrots to the pan and cook until lightly browned. Stir in the prunes with the cinnamon, ginger and honey, then pour in the stock. Season well, cover the casserole and transfer to the oven for about 45 minutes.

Stir in the reserved onions and bake for a further 10 minutes. Gently stir in the fresh coriander and mint, and serve the tagine immediately.

Buying yams and sweet potatoes

The yam has a brown skin and cream-coloured flesh; the sweet potato has dark red or orange skin and orange flesh. Buy firm specimens that do not 'give' when pressed.

Tagine of butter beans, cherry tomatoes and olives

Serve this hearty butter bean dish with grills or roasts, particularly fish. It is substantial enough to be served on its own, with a leafy salad and fresh, crusty bread. In and around Tangier, where the Spanish influence remains quite strong, bean dishes like this often include a spicy sausage like chorizo. This would be added with the onion to lend its flavour to the whole dish.

Serves four

115g/4oz/⅔ cup dried butter (lima) beans, soaked overnight in cold water and drained

30–45ml/2–3 tbsp olive oil

1 onion, chopped

2–3 garlic cloves, crushed

25g/1oz fresh root ginger, peeled and chopped

pinch of saffron threads

16 cherry tomatoes

generous pinch of sugar

handful of fleshy black olives, pitted

5ml/1 tsp ground cinnamon

5ml/1 tsp paprika

sea salt and freshly ground black pepper

small bunch of fresh flat-leaf parsley, torn into pieces

Rinse the beans and place them in a large pan with plenty of water. Bring to the boil and boil for about 10 minutes, then reduce the heat and simmer gently for 1–1½ hours until tender. Drain the beans and refresh under cold water.

Heat the olive oil in a heavy pan. Add the onion, garlic and ginger, and cook for about 10 minutes, or until softened but not browned. Stir in the saffron threads, followed by the cherry tomatoes and a sprinkling of sugar.

As the tomatoes begin to soften, stir in the butter beans. When the tomatoes have heated through, stir in the olives, ground cinnamon and paprika. Season to taste and sprinkle over the parsley. Serve immediately.

Using canned beans

If you are in a hurry, you could use two 400g/14oz cans of butter beans for this tagine. Make sure you rinse the beans well before adding, as canned beans tend to be salty.

Baked vegetable tagine with harissa yogurt

This village tagine from the middle Atlas region of Morocco can be served as a side dish, or on its own with yogurt and chunks of crusty bread. Traditionally this dish is baked in a communal oven. At home you can use a heavy shallow casserole, or an earthenware baking dish.

Serves four to six

30–45ml/2–3 tbsp olive or argan oil

2 onions, halved and sliced with the grain

4 garlic cloves, chopped

1–2 red chillies, deseeded and chopped

10ml/2 tsp cumin seeds

10ml/2 tsp coriander seeds

10ml/2 tsp ground turmeric

6 potatoes, peeled and thickly sliced

2–3 carrots, peeled and thickly sliced

1 head of green, leafy cabbage, trimmed and thickly sliced

about 900ml/1½ pints/3¾ cups vegetable stock

225g/8oz/1⅓ cups peas (defrosted, if frozen)

bunch of fresh flat-leaf parsley, finely chopped

bunch of fresh mint, finely chopped

sea salt and freshly ground black pepper

4–6 large tomatoes, sliced

15g/½oz/1 tbsp butter, cut into small pieces

For the yogurt

500g/1¼lb/2¼ cups thick natural (plain) yogurt

2 garlic cloves, crushed

5–10ml/1–2 tsp harissa

sea salt and freshly ground black pepper

Preheat the oven to 180°C/350°F/gas 4. Heat the oil in a flameproof tagine or casserole. Add the onions and cook, stirring, for 2–3 minutes, until they begin to colour. Add the garlic, chillies, cumin seeds and coriander seeds, and cook, stirring, for 1–2 minutes.

Stir in the turmeric, potatoes, carrots and cabbage, then pour in the stock and mix the vegetables thoroughly with the spices and onions.

Put the lid on the tagine, or cover the dish with foil, and place it in the oven for about 25 minutes, or until the potatoes and carrots are tender but still retain a little bite.

Add the peas and most of the fresh parsley and mint, reserving a little for the garnish. Season with salt and pepper.

Arrange the tomato slices, overlapping each other, on top of the vegetables and sprinkle the pieces of butter over the top.

Place the tagine back into the oven, uncovered, for 15–20 minutes, until the tomatoes are lightly browned on top.

Meanwhile, beat the yogurt in a bowl with the garlic. Stir in the harissa, and season to taste with salt and pepper. Set aside until the tagine is ready.

Garnish the tagine with the rest of the parsley and mint, and serve with spoonfuls of the harissa yogurt and chunks of crusty bread.

Mixed bean and aubergine tagine with mint yogurt

In this Mediterranean tagine, the mixed beans and aubergine provide both texture and taste, which are enhanced by flavourful herbs and chillies. A mixture of courgettes and red and yellow peppers can be used instead of the aubergine, if you like.

Serves four

115g/4oz/⅔ cup dried red kidney beans, soaked overnight in cold water and drained

115g/4oz/⅔ cup dried black-eyed beans (peas) or cannellini beans, soaked overnight in cold water and drained

2 bay leaves

2 celery sticks, each cut into 4 batons

75ml/5 tbsp olive oil

1 aubergine (eggplant), about 350g/12oz, cut into chunks

1 onion, thinly shredded

3 garlic cloves, crushed

1–2 fresh red chillies, deseeded and finely chopped

30ml/2 tbsp tomato purée (paste)

5ml/1 tsp paprika

2 large tomatoes, roughly chopped

300ml/½ pint/1¼ cups vegetable stock

sea salt and freshly ground black pepper

15ml/1 tbsp each chopped fresh coriander (cilantro), mint and flat-leaf parsley

For the mint yogurt

150g/5oz/⅔ cup natural (plain) yogurt

30ml/2 tbsp chopped fresh mint

2 spring onions (scallions), chopped

Place the soaked and drained kidney beans in a large pan of unsalted boiling water. Bring back to the boil and boil rapidly for 10 minutes, then drain. Place the soaked and drained black-eyed or cannellini beans in a separate large pan of boiling unsalted water and boil rapidly for 10 minutes, then drain.

Place 600ml/1 pint/2½ cups of water in a large tagine or casserole, and add the beans, bay leaves and celery. Cover and place in an unheated oven. Set the oven to 190°C/375°F/gas 5. Cook for 1–1½ hours or until the beans are tender. Drain and set aside.

Heat 60ml/4 tbsp of the oil in a frying pan or flameproof tagine. Add the aubergine and cook, stirring, for 4–5 minutes, until browned. Remove from the pan and set aside.

Add the remaining oil to the frying pan or tagine, then add the onion. Cook, stirring, for 4–5 minutes, until softened. Add the garlic and chillies, and cook for a further 5 minutes, stirring frequently, until the onion is golden.

Reduce the oven temperature to 160°C/325°F/Gas 3. Add the tomato purée and paprika and cook, stirring, for 1–2 minutes. Add the tomatoes, browned aubergine, drained beans and stock. Season with salt and pepper.

Cover the tagine with the lid or, if using a frying pan, transfer the contents to a clay tagine or casserole. Place in the oven and cook for 1 hour.

Meanwhile, mix together the yogurt, mint and spring onions, and place in a small serving dish.

Toss the combined fresh coriander, mint and parsley through the aubergines and beans, season to taste and serve with the mint yogurt.

Okra and tomato tagine

Okra, also known as 'ladies' fingers', are a great favourite in the Maghreb and south into the heart of Africa. Once you cut into okra, they ooze a sticky substance, which renders them mucilaginous on cooking – not to everyone's taste – so keep them whole until the last minute, or cook them whole if you prefer.

Serves four

5–6 tomatoes

2 small onions

2 garlic cloves, crushed

1 fresh green chilli, deseeded

5ml/1 tsp paprika

small handful of fresh coriander (cilantro)

30ml/2 tbsp olive oil

350g/12oz okra, washed and patted dry

juice of 1 lemon

To peel the tomatoes, score a cross through the skins, then place them in boiling water for 30 seconds, and remove with a slotted spoon. Once cool enough to handle, peel off the skin – it should come away easily. Cut the tomatoes into quarters, and remove and discard the seeds. Roughly chop the flesh.

Roughly chop one of the onions and place it in a blender or food processor with the garlic, chilli, paprika, coriander and 60ml/4 tbsp water. Process to make a paste.

Thinly slice the second onion. Heat the sunflower oil in a flameproof tagine or heavy pan, add the sliced onion, and fry it for 5–6 minutes until golden brown. Transfer the onion to a plate and set it aside.

Reduce the heat, and place the onion and coriander paste into the tagine or pan. Cook the paste over a medium heat for 1–2 minutes, stirring frequently.

Cut the okra in half or keep whole and add them to a pan with the tomatoes, lemon juice and about 115ml/4fl oz/scant ½ cup water. Stir well to mix, then cover tightly with a lid, and simmer over a low heat for about 10 minutes, or until the okra is tender. Serve with the fried onion scattered on top.

Chickpea tagine

The preserved lemon in this recipe shows you that it comes from Morocco, where the distinctive yellow globes in glass jars glimmer like miniature suns in the markets. The flavour of preserved – or pickled – lemon is wonderful. Slightly salty, less tart than the fresh fruit, it adds a real zing to this chickpea tagine.

Serves four

150g/5oz/¾ cup dried chickpeas, soaked overnight, or 2 x 400g/14oz cans of chickpeas, rinsed and drained

30ml/2 tbsp sunflower oil

1 large onion, chopped

1 garlic clove, crushed (optional)

400g/14oz can of chopped tomatoes

5ml/1 tsp ground cumin

350ml/12fl oz/1½ cups vegetable stock

¼ preserved lemon

30ml/2 tbsp chopped fresh coriander (cilantro)

If using dried chickpeas, cook the soaked chickpeas in plenty of boiling water for 1–1½ hours, until tender. Drain well. Place the chickpeas in a bowl of cold water and rub them between your fingers to remove the skins.

Heat the oil in a flameproof tagine or casserole, add the onion and garlic, if using, and fry for 8–10 minutes, stirring often, until golden.

Add the chickpeas, tomatoes, cumin and stock, and stir well to combine. Bring to the boil, then reduce the heat and simmer, uncovered, for 30–40 minutes, until the chickpeas are very soft and most of the liquid has evaporated.

Rinse the preserved lemon under cold running water, and cut away the flesh and pith. Cut the peel into thin slivers, and stir it into the chickpea mixture together with most of the chopped fresh coriander.

Garnish with the rest of the fresh coriander, and serve immediately with chunks of crusty Moroccan bread.

Spicy carrot and chickpea tagine

This country-style tagine is purely vegetarian and typical of the poorer regions where meat is scarce. Pulses of all kinds and, in particular, chickpeas, provide the nourishing and filling content of these dishes. Serve with a dollop of yogurt and flat bread to mop up the flavour.

Serves four

150g/5oz/¾ cup dried chickpeas, soaked overnight, or 2 x 400g/14oz cans of chickpeas, rinsed and drained

45–60ml/3–4 tbsp olive oil

1 onion, finely chopped

3–4 garlic cloves, finely chopped

10ml/2 tsp ground turmeric

5–10ml/1–2 tsp cumin seeds

15ml/1 tsp ground cinnamon

5ml/1 tsp dried chilli flakes, cayenne, or chilli powder

2.5ml/½ tsp ground black pepper

15ml/1 tbsp honey

3–4 medium carrots, peeled and sliced on the diagonal

sea salt

15ml/1 tbsp rose flower water

bunch of fresh coriander (cilantro), finely chopped

If using dried chickpeas, cook the soaked chickpeas in plenty of boiling water for 1–1½ hours, until tender. Drain well. Place the chickpeas in a bowl of cold water and rub them between your fingers to remove the skins.

Heat the oil in the base of a tagine or heavy-based casserole pot. Stir in the onion and garlic until soft. Add the spices and honey and toss in the carrots. Pour in enough water to cover the carrots and cook gently, with the lid on, for 10–15 minutes.

Toss in the chickpeas. Check there is still enough liquid at the base of the tagine, cover with the lid, and cook gently for a further 5–10 minutes. Season with salt to taste, toss in the rose water and coriander, and serve.

Loubia

Robustly flavoured with garlic and harissa, this hearty bean stew is comfort food for many Moroccans. As meat is expensive, *loubia* is often prepared without it, but if there is any preserved meat, gueddid or khlii, in the house it will be tossed in for extra protein and flavour. This recipe is for a vegetarian version and is delicious eaten with chunks of bread to dip in the garlicky sauce.

Serves three to four

250g/9oz/1¾ cups dried haricot, borlotti or butter beans, soaked for 6 hours, or overnight, and drained

30ml/2 tbsp olive oil, butter or clarified butter

2 onions, finely chopped

6–8 garlic cloves, finely chopped

10ml/2 tsp cumin seeds

5–10ml/1–2 tsp sugar

10ml/2 tsp harissa

2 x 400g/14oz cans of plum tomatoes

sea salt

freshly ground black pepper

small bunch of fresh flat-leaf parsley, finely chopped

small bunch of fresh coriander (cilantro), finely chopped

Put the beans into a pot with plenty of water and bring to the boil. Reduce the heat and simmer for about 30 minutes until tender. Drain thoroughly.

Heat the oil or butter in the base of a tagine, or a heavy-based pot. Stir in the onions and garlic with the cumin seeds and sugar for 2–3 minutes, until they begin to colour. Add the harissa and toss in the beans, making sure they are coated in the onions and garlic. Stir in the tomatoes, breaking them up with a wooden spoon, cover with a lid and cook gently for about 30 minutes.

Season with salt and pepper and toss in most of the herbs. Garnish with the rest of the herbs and serve hot, with bread, or as a side dish.

Berber lentils with coriander

Simple and delicious, this nourishing village dish can be served on its own with bread, or as an accompaniment to grilled or roasted meat and poultry.

Serves three to four

25g/1oz/2 tbsp clarified butter or olive oil

1 onion, finely chopped

2 garlic cloves, finely chopped

5ml/1 tsp sugar

5ml/1 tsp cumin seeds

10ml/2 tsp ras el hanout

250g/9oz/2¼ cups brown or green lentils, rinsed and drained

600ml/1 pint/2½ cups water

sea salt and freshly ground black pepper

small bunch of fresh coriander (cilantro), roughly chopped

Heat the butter or oil in a heavy-based pan. Stir in the onion and garlic with the sugar and cumin seeds for 2–3 minutes. Stir in the ras el hanout and toss in the lentils, making sure they are thoroughly coated.

Pour in the water and bring it to the boil. Reduce the heat and simmer gently for about 35 minutes, until all the liquid has been absorbed but the lentils still have a bite to them. Season to taste and garnish with the coriander before serving.

Summer vegetable kebabs with harissa and yogurt dip

This simple and tasty vegetarian dish is delicious served with couscous and a fresh, crispy green salad. It also makes an excellent side dish to accompany meat-based main courses. In Morocco today, vegetable and fish kebabs are becoming increasingly popular in fashionable restaurants and households, where there is a tendency to move away from the traditional meat-based meals.

Serves four

2 aubergines (eggplants), part-peeled and cut into chunks

2 courgettes (zucchini), cut into chunks

2–3 red or green bell peppers, deseeded and cut into chunks

12–16 cherry tomatoes

4 small red onions, quartered

60ml/4 tbsp olive oil

juice of ½ lemon

1 garlic clove, crushed

5ml/1 tsp ground coriander

5ml/1 tsp ground cinnamon

10ml/2 tsp clear honey

5ml/1 tsp sea salt

For the harissa and yogurt dip

450g/1lb/2 cups Greek (strained plain) yogurt

30–60ml/2–4 tbsp harissa

small bunch of fresh coriander (cilantro), finely chopped

small bunch of fresh mint, finely chopped

sea salt and freshly ground black pepper

Preheat the grill or broiler on the hottest setting. Put all the vegetables in a bowl. Mix the olive oil, lemon juice, garlic, ground coriander, cinnamon, honey and salt and pour the mixture over the vegetables. Using your hands, turn the vegetables gently in the marinade, then thread them on to metal skewers. Cook the kebabs under the grill, turning them occasionally until the vegetables are nicely browned all over.

To make the dip, put the yogurt in a bowl and beat in the harissa, making it as fiery as you like by adding more harissa. Add most of the coriander and mint, reserving a little to garnish, and season well with salt and pepper. While they are still hot, slide the vegetables off the skewers and dip them into the yogurt dip before eating. Garnish with the reserved herbs. Serve, perhaps with couscous.

Preparing the vegetables

Make sure you cut the aubergines, courgettes and peppers into fairly even-size chunks, so they will all cook at the same rate.

Butternut squash with caramelized pink shallots

You can serve this dish as a vegetarian meal on its own, as a side dish or as a topping for couscous. When in season, substitute pumpkin for the squash. A dollop of yogurt flavoured with garlic or a spoonful of harissa goes very well with the squash and shallots. I often serve this dish with a herb-flavoured couscous and a green salad for supper.

Serves four

900g/2lb peeled butternut squash, cut into thick slices

120ml/4¼fl oz/½ cup water

45–60ml/3–4 tbsp olive oil

knob (pat) of butter

16–20 pink shallots, peeled

10–12 garlic cloves, peeled

115g/4oz/scant 1 cup blanched almonds

75g/3oz/½ cup raisins or sultanas (golden raisins), soaked in warm water for 15 minutes and drained

30–45ml/2–3 tbsp clear honey

10ml/2 tsp ground cinnamon

sea salt and freshly ground black pepper

lemon wedges, to serve (optional)

garlic-flavoured yogurt (page 109) or harissa-flavoured yogurt (page 195), to serve (optional)

Preheat the oven to 200°C/400°F/gas 6. Place the butternut squash in an ovenproof dish, add the water, cover and bake for about 45 minutes, until tender.

Meanwhile, heat the olive oil and butter in a large heavy pan. Stir in the shallots and cook until they begin to brown. Stir in the garlic and almonds. When the garlic and almonds begin to brown, add the raisins or sultanas. Continue to cook until the shallots and garlic begin to caramelize, then stir in the honey and cinnamon, adding a little water if the mixture becomes too dry. Season well with salt and pepper and remove from the heat.

Cover the squash with the shallot and garlic mixture and return to the oven, uncovered, for a further 15 minutes. Serve with lemon wedges for squeezing over the vegetables, and a dollop of yogurt.

Stir-fried carrots with mango and ginger

Ripe, sweet mango is divine with carrots and ginger in this spicy vegetable dish. The carrots are an excellent side dish for grilled meat or couscous, but I often serve them on their own with yogurt and a salad. The mango must be ripe, otherwise you will need to add a little honey to balance the flavours.

Serves four to six

15–30ml/1–2 tbsp smen or olive oil

1 onion, chopped

25g/1oz fresh root ginger, peeled and chopped

2–3 garlic cloves, chopped

1 dried red chilli, deseeded and chopped (optional)

5–6 carrots, sliced

30–45ml/2–3 tbsp shelled pistachio nuts, roasted

5ml/1 tsp ground cinnamon

5–10ml/1–2 tsp ras el hanout

1 small firm, ripe mango, peeled and roughly diced

small bunch of fresh coriander (cilantro), finely chopped

juice of ½ lemon

sea salt

Heat the smen or olive oil in a heavy frying pan. Stir in the onion, ginger, garlic and chilli if using, and fry for 1 minute. Add the carrots, tossing them in the pan to make sure that they are thoroughly mixed with the flavouring ingredients, and cook until they begin to brown.

Add the pistachio nuts, cinnamon and ras el hanout, then gently mix in the mango. Sprinkle with coriander, season with salt and pour over the lemon juice. Serve immediately.

Spiced pumpkin wedges

Warm spices are delicious with tender roasted pumpkin. Serve these sickle moons with any grilled, roasted or barbecued meat or poultry dish.

Serves four to six

1 medium pumpkin, halved lengthways, deseeded, and cut into 6–8 wedges

10ml/2 tsp coriander seeds

5ml/1 tsp cumin seeds

5ml/1 tsp fennel seeds

5–10ml/1–2 tsp ground cinnamon

2 dried red chillies, chopped

coarse salt

2 garlic cloves, peeled

30ml/2 tbsp olive oil

Preheat the oven to 200°C/400°F/gas 6. Prepare the pumpkin and cut into wedges. Grind the coriander, cumin and fennel seeds, cinnamon and chillies with a little coarse salt in a mortar and pestle. Add the garlic and a little of the olive oil and pound to form a paste.

Rub the spice mixture over the pumpkin segments and place them, skin-side down, in an ovenproof dish or roasting pan. Bake the spiced pumpkin for 35–40 minutes, or until tender. Serve hot.

Roasting pumpkin seeds

Save the seeds from the pumpkin and roast them lightly in a heavy frying pan with a little oil and salt to make a delicious, crunchy snack to serve with drinks.

Spinach with apple, pine nuts and cream

This sumptuous spinach dish is a lovely accompaniment for *meshwi*, grills and roasts.

Serves four to six

30–45ml/2–3 tbsp pine nuts (kernels)

30–45ml/2–3 tbsp olive oil

1 red onion, halved and sliced

1–2 dried red chillies, finely sliced

1 apple, peeled, cored and sliced

2 garlic cloves, crushed

5–10ml/1–2 tsp ground cumin, roasted

10ml/2 tsp clear honey

450g/1lb spinach, steamed and roughly chopped

60–75ml/4–5 tbsp double (heavy) cream

sea salt and ground black pepper

Roast the pine nuts in a dry, heavy frying pan until golden brown, then tip on to a plate. Pour the olive oil into the pan. Sauté the onion with the chilli until softened, then stir in the apple and garlic. Once the apple begins to colour, stir in most of the pine nuts, most of the roasted cumin and the honey.

Toss in the spinach and, once it has heated through, stir in most of the cream. Season to taste and remove from the heat.

Swirl the last of the cream on top, and sprinkle with the reserved pine nuts and roasted cumin. Serve immediately, straight from the pan.

Casablancan baked stuffed tomatoes

Stuffed vegetables are a great tradition of the 'Pied Noir' table and still a feature of Casablancan cuisine. These tomatoes stuffed with couscous and herbs are popular as a starter, or served on their own with a salad.

Serves six to eight

350g/12oz/2 cups medium or fine couscous

5ml/1 tsp salt

400ml/14fl oz/1¾ cups lukewarm water

15–30ml/1–2 tbsp sunflower oil

6–8 large tomatoes

30ml/2 tbsp olive oil

1 onion, finely chopped

1 carrot, peeled and finely diced

10ml/2 tsp honey

5–10ml/1–2 tsp ras el hanout

bunch of fresh flat-leaf parsley, finely chopped

bunch of coriander (cilantro), finely chopped

rind of 2 preserved lemons, finely chopped

sea salt and freshly ground black pepper

Preheat the oven to 180°C/350°F/gas 4. Put the couscous into a shallow bowl. Stir the salt into the lukewarm water until it dissolves and pour it over the couscous. Cover and leave the couscous to swell for about 10 minutes. Using your fingers, rub the sunflower oil into the couscous to separate the grains and air them.

Slice the top off each tomato and put aside. Using a spoon, scoop out the seeds and discard them. In a heavy-based pan, heat 1 tablespoon of the olive oil and stir in the onion and carrot with the honey until they begin to caramelize. Toss in the ras el hanout and leave to cool.

Tip the spicy mixture into the couscous and toss well. Add the fresh herbs and preserved lemon, and season.

Spoon the couscous into each tomato cavity and pop on the tomato lid. Place the filled tomatoes onto a baking dish, pour over the reserved olive oil, and bake in the oven for about 25 minutes. Serve hot or leave to cool and eat them at room temperature.

Seafood tagines and meshwi

Morocco has over 3500 kilometres of coastline, so fishing is an important industry for the country and fish is always bought fresh from the markets, not frozen. Sardines are perhaps the nation's favourite but other common fish include mackerel, sea bream, sea bass, tuna, whiting, sole and an abundance of shellfish in the daily catch. Small fish are often pan-fried or grilled in the street or as a starter to a meal, whereas larger fish are stuffed and baked or cooked in tagines.

Tagine of monkfish, potatoes, cherry tomatoes and olives

The fish for this tagine is marinated in chermoula, which gives it that unmistakable Moroccan flavour. It is a delightful dish at any time of year, served with lots of crusty bread to mop up the tasty juices, but it is especially good made with full-flavoured, new season potatoes and little sun-ripened cherry tomatoes. Serve with fresh, warm crusty bread to mop up the delicious juices.

Serves four

900g/2lb monkfish tail, cut into chunks

2 green bell peppers

15–20 small new potatoes, scrubbed, scraped or peeled

45–60ml/3–4 tbsp olive oil

4–5 garlic cloves, thinly sliced

15–20 cherry tomatoes

sea salt and freshly ground black pepper

90g/3¼oz/¾ cup kalamata or fleshy black olives

about 100ml/3½fl oz/generous⅓ cup water

For the chermoula

2 garlic cloves

5ml/1 tsp coarse sea salt

10ml/2 tsp ground cumin

5ml/1 tsp paprika

juice of 1 lemon

small bunch of fresh coriander (cilantro), roughly chopped

15ml/1 tbsp olive oil

Using a mortar and pestle to make the chermoula, pound the garlic with the salt to a smooth paste. Add the cumin, paprika, lemon juice and coriander, and gradually mix in the olive oil to emulsify the mixture slightly. Reserve a little chermoula for cooking, then rub the rest of the paste over the chunks of monkfish. Cover and leave to marinate for about 1 hour.

Preheat the grill or broiler on the hottest setting. Roast the peppers, turning frequently, until they soften and their skins begin to blacken. (Alternatively, spear the peppers on long metal skewers and turn them over a gas flame, or roast them in a very hot oven.) Place the peppers in a plastic bag, seal and leave to stand for 15 minutes. Peel the peppers, removing stalks and seeds, and cut the flesh intro strips.

Parboil the potatoes for about 10 minutes until slightly softened. Drain, refresh under cold water and drain again, then cut them in half lengthways. Heat the olive oil in a heavy pan and stir in the garlic. When the garlic begins to colour, add the tomatoes and cook until just softened. Add the pepper strips and the remaining chermoula, and season with salt and pepper.

Spread the potatoes over the base of a tagine, shallow pan or deep, ridged frying pan. Spoon three-quarters of the tomato and pepper mixture over and place the marinated fish chunks on top, with their marinade. Spoon the rest of the tomato and pepper mixture on top of the fish and add the olives. Drizzle a little extra olive oil over the dish and pour in the water. Heat until simmering, cover with a lid and steam over a medium heat for about 15 minutes, or until the fish is cooked through.

Moroccan fish tagine

For me, this spicy, aromatic dish proves just how exciting an ingredient fish can be. Serve it with couscous, which you can steam in the traditional way in a colander on top of the tagine.

Serves eight

1.3kg/3lb firm white fish fillets, such as monkfish or cod, skinned

90ml/6 tbsp harissa

60ml/4 tbsp olive oil

1 large aubergine (eggplant), cut into 1cm/½in cubes

2 courgettes (zucchini), cut into 1cm/½in cubes

4 onions, chopped

400g/14oz can of chopped tomatoes

400ml/14fl oz/1⅔ cups passata (bottled strained tomatoes)

200ml/7fl oz/scant 1 cup fish stock

1 preserved lemon, chopped

90g/3¼oz/¾ cup black olives

60ml/4 tbsp chopped fresh coriander (cilantro)

sea salt and freshly ground black pepper

couscous, to serve (page 296)

Cut the fish into 5cm/2in chunks, then place the chunks in a wide bowl and add 30ml/2 tbsp of the harissa. Toss to coat, then cover and chill for at least 1 hour.

Heat half the olive oil in the base of a flameproof tagine or shallow heavy pan. Add the aubergine cubes and fry for about 10 minutes, or until they are golden brown. Add the courgette cubes and fry for 2 minutes more. Remove the vegetables using a slotted spoon and set aside.

Add the remaining olive oil to the tagine or pan, then add the chopped onions and cook over a low heat for about 10 minutes, until golden brown. Stir in the remaining harissa and cook for 5 minutes more, stirring occasionally.

Put the courgette and aubergine back in the tagine, and stir to combine with the onions. Add the chopped tomatoes, passata and fish stock, and stir well. Bring to the boil, then lower the heat and simmer for about 20 minutes.

Add the marinated fish chunks, chopped preserved lemon and black olives to the pan, then stir gently so that you do not break up the delicate fish chunks. Cover the tagine with a lid and simmer over a low heat for about 15–20 minutes, or until the fish is cooked through.

Season to taste, then stir in the chopped fresh coriander. Serve immediately, accompanied by couscous, if you like.

Mixed seafood tagine

The distinctive mixture of spices and chillies used here is similar to a classic chermoula. Scorpion fish is the traditional choice for this dish, and red mullet or snapper makes a good, authentic alternative, but you can substitute other fish – try red bream, pomfret, porgy or even halved cod or hake steaks.

Serves four

60ml/4 tbsp olive oil

4 garlic cloves, sliced

1–2 green chillies, deseeded and chopped

large handful of fresh flat-leaf parsley, roughly chopped

5ml/1 tsp coriander seeds

2.5ml/½ tsp ground allspice

6 cardamom pods, split open

2.5ml/½ tsp ground turmeric

15ml/1 tbsp lemon juice

sea salt and freshly ground black pepper

350g/12oz scorpion fish, red mullet or red snapper fillets, cut into large chunks

225g/8oz squid, cleaned and cut into rings

1 onion, chopped

4 tomatoes, deseeded and chopped

300ml/½ pint/1¼ cups warm fish or vegetable stock

225g/8oz king prawns (jumbo shrimp)

15ml/1 tbsp chopped fresh coriander (cilantro)

lemon wedges, to serve

couscous, to serve (page 296)

Place the olive oil, garlic, chillies, parsley, coriander seeds, allspice and cardamom seeds in a mortar and pound to a smooth paste using a pestle. Stir in the ground turmeric and lemon juice, and season with salt and pepper.

Place the chunks of fish in a large bowl with the squid rings. Add the spice paste and toss together. Cover and leave the fish to marinate in the refrigerator for at least 2 hours, or longer, if time allows.

Place the chopped onion, deseeded and chopped tomatoes and stock in a tagine or casserole, and cover with a lid or aluminium foil. Place the tagine in an unheated oven, then set the temperature to 200°C/400°F/gas 6. Cook for 20 minutes.

Remove the fish from the marinade; set aside the squid and any excess marinade. Place the fish in the tagine with the vegetables. Cover and cook in the oven for 5 minutes more.

Add the prawns, squid rings and the remaining marinade to the tagine, and stir gently to combine, being careful not to break up the fish. Cover the tagine and return it to the oven again for 5–10 minutes, or until all the fish, prawns and squid are cooked through.

Taste the sauce and season with salt and pepper if necessary, then stir in the chopped fresh coriander. Serve immediately, accompanied by lemon wedges to squeeze over and couscous.

Preparing squid

Fresh squid should smell slightly sweet. Rinse and peel off the thin film of skin, then sever the head and trim the tentacles with a sharp knife. With your finger, pull out the backbone and reach down into the body pouch to remove the ink sac and any mushy bits. Rinse the empty pouch inside and out and pat try. Use the pouch and trimmed head for cooking (and tentacles if required); discard the rest.

Baked fish tagine with lime and tomato salad

Oven-baked tagines are very simple, often with the addition of a little bit of fruit or spice. This particular recipe is a delicious way of cooking red mullet as the flesh remains moist. Instead of red mullet, you can use sardines, mackerel, red snapper, grouper or sea bass, and you can replace the lime with slices of lemon or bitter orange.

Serves four

30ml/2 tbsp olive oil or argan oil

25g/1oz/2 tbsp butter

2–3 garlic cloves, finely sliced

4 red mullet, gutted and cleaned

sea salt and freshly ground black pepper

2–3 limes, finely sliced

5–10ml/1–2 tsp sumac

a few fresh coriander (cilantro) leaves, to garnish

For the salad

4–6 ripe tomatoes, halved and finely sliced

2 green chillies, deseeded and finely sliced

15–30ml/1–2 tbsp olive oil or argan oil

sea salt and freshly ground black pepper

Preheat the oven to 180°C/350°F/gas 4. Heat the oil and butter in a flameproof tagine or casserole, and stir in the garlic, until it begins to brown.

Remove from the heat, then place the fish in the tagine. Spoon some of the oil and garlic over the top, season with salt and pepper, and arrange lime slices over the top of each fish. Sprinkle over the sumac. Put the lid on the tagine, or cover with aluminium foil, and place it in the oven for 15 minutes.

Meanwhile, to make the salad, arrange the tomato slices in a shallow bowl. Sprinkle the chilli slices over the top, drizzle with a little oil, and season with salt and pepper. Set aside.

Remove the lid from the tagine and baste the fish with the cooking juices. Return the fish to the oven for 10 minutes. Garnish with some fresh coriander leaves, toss the tomato salad, and serve immediately.

Fish and potato tagine with saffron and preserved lemon

Classic and simple, variations of this tagine can be found everywhere in Morocco – at the coast, in the mountains, in countryside villages – as it works well with both saltwater and freshwater fish, such as carp and trout.

Serves four

500g/1¼lb new potatoes

pinch of saffron threads

150ml/¼ pint/scant ¾ cup warm water

juice of 2 lemons

45ml/3 tbsp olive oil

4–6 garlic cloves, peeled and smashed

4–6 medium tomatoes, finely sliced

1 preserved lemon, finely chopped

small bunch of fresh flat-leaf parsley, finely chopped

500g/1¼lb sea bass (or any firm-fleshed fish) fillets, cut into chunks

sea salt and ground black pepper

leafy green salad and couscous, to serve

Bring a pan of water to the boil. Add the potatoes and parboil them for 6–8 minutes, until just tender. Drain the potatoes, and refresh them in cold water. Peel off the skins, and cut them into 1cm/½in thick slices.

Prepare the saffron by dry-roasting the threads in a small frying pan for less than a minute until they emit a faint aroma. Using a mortar and pestle, grind to a powder. Stir in the warm water until the saffron dissolves, then add the lemon juice and 30ml/2 tbsp of the olive oil. Set aside.

Heat the remaining olive oil in a flameproof tagine or casserole, and stir in the garlic. Cook for 1–2 minutes, until the garlic begins to colour.

Turn the heat to low and line the garlicky base of the tagine with a layer of potatoes, followed by a layer of tomatoes. Sprinkle half the preserved lemon and parsley over the tomatoes.

Arrange the fish on top, skin-side up, then pour the saffron liquid over the fish. Season with salt and pepper. Arrange the rest of the tomatoes, preserved lemon, and parsley on top.

Place the lid on the tagine and cook over a medium heat for 15–20 minutes, until the fish is just cooked and the flavours have mingled. Serve immediately with plain, buttery couscous and a leafy salad.

Prawn tagine with ginger and harissa couscous

This tasty prawn tagine from Tangier echoes some of the Andalucian flavours from across the water in Spain. It makes a filling main course, but you can also serve the prawn tagine without the couscous as a starter with chunks of crusty bread to mop up the cooking juices.

Serves four

30ml/2 tbsp olive oil

2 onions, finely chopped

2 garlic cloves, finely chopped

50g/2oz fresh ginger, peeled and finely chopped

450g/1lb king prawns (jumbo shrimp), shells and heads removed

5–10ml/1–2 tsp sugar

5ml/1 tsp smoked paprika

400g/14oz can of tomatoes, drained

115ml/4fl oz/½ cup white wine or Fino sherry

sea salt and freshly ground black pepper

small bunch of fresh flat-leaf parsley, finely chopped, plus some whole leaves to garnish

For the couscous

350g/12oz/2 cups couscous

2.5ml/½ tsp salt

400ml/14fl oz/1¾ cups warm water

15–30ml/1–2 tbsp ghee, or olive oil with a knob of butter

10ml/2 tsp harissa

small bunch of fresh coriander (cilantro), finely chopped

First prepare the couscous. Place the couscous into an ovenproof dish. Stir the salt into the warm water and pour it over the couscous. Cover with a clean dish towel and leave it to absorb the water for 10–15 minutes.

Meanwhile, heat the olive oil in a flameproof tagine or casserole, and stir in the onions, garlic and ginger for 3–4 minutes, until they begin to colour.

Add the prawns, and cook until they turn opaque, then add the sugar, paprika, tomatoes and wine. Bring to a simmer, then cover with the lid, and cook over a gentle heat for 15 minutes.

Using a fork, rake through the couscous to separate the grains. Heat the ghee, or olive oil and butter, in the base of a tagine or wide shallow pan, and stir in the harissa paste. Add the couscous, and stir until well mixed. Stir in the fresh coriander.

Season of the tagine with salt and pepper, stir in the chopped parsley, and garnish with the leaves. Serve immediately with the harissa couscous.

Shellfish k'dra with lemon couscous

Serves six to eight

30–45ml/2–3 tbsp smen or clarified butter

10ml/2 tsp coriander seeds

10ml/2 tsp fennel seeds

2–3 red chillies, deseeded and finely chopped

5–10ml/1–2 tsp sugar

10ml/2 tsp ground turmeric

2 x 400g/14oz cans of tomatoes, drained of juice

300ml/½ pint/1¼ cups white wine

1.2 litres/2 pints/5 cups fish stock

4 garlic cloves, finely sliced

small bunch of fresh flat-leaf parsley, finely chopped

small bunch of fresh coriander (cilantro), finely chopped

sea salt and freshly ground black pepper

300g/11oz prawns (jumbo shrimp), shelled and deveined

300g/11oz mussels, thoroughly cleaned in cold water (discard any that do not close when tapped)

450g/1lb scallops, shelled and cleaned

For the lemon couscous

800g/1¾lb/4½ cups couscous

900ml/1½ pints/3¾ cups warm water

2.5ml/½ tsp salt

30ml/2 tbsp sunflower oil

1 preserved lemon, finely chopped

small bunch of fresh flat-leaf parsley, finely chopped

25g/1oz/2 tbsp butter

A shellfish *k'dra* is a lovely feature of the busy fishing ports in Tangier, Casablanca and Essaouira, where you can sit outdoors and enjoy the day's catch cooked in one big copper pot. In a traditional home, a shellfish *k'dra* would be prepared for a special occasion. Smen is the essential ingredient in a *k'dra*, but you can use clarified butter instead.

First prepare the couscous. Preheat the oven to 180°C/350°F/gas 4. Place the couscous in an ovenproof dish. Mix the warm water and salt, then pour over the couscous. Cover and leave for 10–15 minutes, until the couscous has swollen.

Meanwhile, heat the smen in a large copper or heavy pan. Add the coriander seeds, fennel seeds, chillies and sugar, and stir for 2 minutes until fragrant. Stir in the turmeric, then add the drained tomatoes with the wine and fish stock. Add the garlic and most of the herbs, reserving some for garnishing, and bring to the boil. Reduce the heat and simmer for 15 minutes.

Meanwhile, using your fingers, rub the sunflower oil into the couscous to separate the grains, then rub in the preserved lemon. Stir in the parsley. Cut the butter into pieces, and sprinkle over the top of the couscous, then cover with a dampened piece of baking parchment. Bake the couscous in the oven for 15–20 minutes to heat through.

Season the stock with salt and pepper and bring it to the boil again. Stir in the prawns, mussels and scallops, and cook over a medium heat for about 10 minutes, or until the shellfish is cooked through. Discard any mussels that have not opened.

Pile the couscous in a mound on a shallow serving dish. Hollow out the top of the dome and, using a slotted spoon, place most of the shellfish in the hollow and around the edge of the dish. Drizzle a little of the stock over the shellfish to keep it moist and pour the rest into a bowl to serve with it. Garnish with the reserved fresh parsley and coriander.

Red mullet with chermoula and preserved lemons

The coriander and chilli chermoula marinade gives this dish its distinct flavour. The olives and preserved lemon add a touch of excitement. On their own, these mullet make a delicious appetizer. Served with saffron couscous and a crisp, herb-filled salad, they are lovely as a main course. Choose larger fish if you wish.

Serves four

30–45ml/2–3 tbsp olive oil, plus extra for brushing

1 onion, chopped

1 carrot, chopped

½ preserved lemon, finely chopped

4 plum tomatoes, peeled and chopped

600ml/1 pint/2½ cups fish stock or water

3–4 new potatoes, peeled and cubed

4 small red mullet or snapper, gutted and filleted

handful of black olives, pitted and halved

sea salt and black pepper

small bunch of fresh coriander (cilantro), chopped

small bunch of fresh mint, chopped

For the chermoula

small bunch of fresh coriander (cilantro), finely chopped

2–3 garlic cloves, chopped

5–10ml/1–2 tsp ground cumin

pinch of saffron threads

60ml/4 tbsp olive oil

juice of 1 lemon

1 hot red chilli, deseeded and chopped

To make the chermoula, pound the ingredients in a mortar and pestle, or process them together in a food processor, then set aside.

Heat the olive oil in a pan. Add the onion and carrot and cook until softened but not browned. Stir in half the preserved lemon, along with 30ml/2 tbsp of the chermoula, the tomatoes and the stock or water. Bring to the boil, then reduce the heat, cover and simmer for about 30 minutes. Add the potatoes and simmer for a further 10 minutes, until they are tender.

Preheat the grill or broiler on the hottest setting and brush a baking sheet or grill pan with oil. Brush the fish fillets with olive oil and a little of the chermoula. Season with pepper, then place the fillets, skin-side up, on the sheet or pan and cook under the grill for 5–6 minutes.

Meanwhile, stir the olives, the remaining chermoula and preserved lemon into the vegetable sauce and check the seasoning. Serve the fish fillets in wide bowls, spoon the sauce over, and sprinkle liberally with chopped coriander and mint. Serve with lemon wedges for squeezing over if you like; couscous makes a good accompaniment.

Grilled fish in vine leaves with sweet and sour chilli dipping sauce

Serves four

about 30 preserved vine leaves

4–5 large white fish fillets, skinned, such as haddock, ling or monkfish

For the chermoula

small bunch of fresh coriander (cilantro), finely chopped

2–3 garlic cloves, chopped

5–10ml/1–2 tsp ground cumin

60ml/4 tbsp olive oil

juice of 1 lemon

sea salt

For the dipping sauce

50ml/2fl oz/¼ cup white wine vinegar or lemon juice

115g/4oz/generous ½ cup caster (superfine) sugar

15–30ml/1–2 tbsp water

pinch of saffron threads

1 onion, finely chopped

2 garlic cloves, finely chopped

2–3 spring onions (scallions), finely sliced

25g/1oz fresh root ginger, peeled and grated

2 hot red or green chillies, deseeded and finely sliced

small bunch of fresh coriander (cilantro), finely chopped

small bunch of fresh mint, finely chopped

Almost any kind of firm, white fish will do for these kebabs. The fish is first marinated in chermoula and then wrapped in vine leaves to seal in the flavours. The vine-leaf parcel becomes crisp when cooked to contrast with its succulent, aromatic contents. The piquant, sweet and sour dipping sauce complements these parcels perfectly.

To make the chermoula, pound the ingredients in a mortar and pestle, or process them together in a food processor, then set aside.

Rinse the vine leaves in a bowl, then soak them in cold water. Remove any bones from the fish and cut each fillet into about eight bitesize pieces. Coat the pieces of fish in the chermoula, cover and chill for 1 hour.

Meanwhile, prepare the dipping sauce. Heat the vinegar or lemon juice with the sugar and water until the sugar has dissolved. Bring to the boil and boil for about 1 minute, then leave to cool. Add the remaining ingredients and mix well to combine. Spoon the sauce into small individual bowls and set aside.

Drain the vine leaves and pat dry on kitchen paper. Lay a vine leaf flat on the work surface and place a piece of marinated fish in the centre. Fold the edges of the leaf over the fish, then wrap up the fish and leaf into a small parcel. Repeat with the remaining pieces of fish and vine leaves. Thread the parcels on to kebab skewers and brush with any leftover marinade.

Heat the grill or broiler on the hottest setting and cook the kebabs for 2–3 minutes on each side. Serve immediately, with the sweet and sour chilli sauce for dipping.

Spiced sardines with grapefruit and fennel salad

Sardines spiced with cumin and coriander are popular in the coastal regions of Morocco, both in restaurants and as street food. In Tangier, I ate them from a street stall, where they were cleaned and smeared with a spicy paste, dredged with flour and deep-fried, then sandwiched between two bits of bread with a handful of fresh coriander.

Serves four to six

12 fresh sardines, cleaned and gutted

coarse salt

1 onion, grated

60–90ml/4–6 tbsp olive oil

5ml/1 tsp ground cinnamon

10ml/2 tsp ground cumin, roasted

10ml/2 tsp ground coriander, roasted

5ml/1 tsp paprika

5ml/1 tsp ground black pepper

lemon wedges, to serve

For the salad

2 ruby grapefruits

5ml/1 tsp sea salt

1 fennel bulb

2–3 spring onions (scallions), finely sliced

2.5ml/½ tsp ground cumin, roasted

30–45ml/2–3 tbsp olive oil

Rinse the sardines and pat them dry on kitchen paper, then rub inside and out with a little coarse salt. In a bowl, mix the grated onion with the olive oil, cinnamon, cumin, coriander, paprika and black pepper. Make several slashes into the flesh of the sardines and smear the onion and spice mixture all over the fish, inside and out and into the gashes. Leave the sardines to stand for about 1 hour to allow the flavours of the spices to penetrate the flesh.

Meanwhile, prepare the salad. Peel the grapefruits with a knife, removing all the pith and peel in neat strips down the outside of the fruit. Cut between the membranes to remove the segments of fruit intact. Cut each grapefruit segment in half, place in a bowl and sprinkle with salt. Trim the fennel, cut it in half lengthways and slice finely. Add the fennel to the grapefruit with the spring onions, ground cumin and olive oil. Toss lightly.

Preheat the grill, broiler or barbecue. Cook the sardines for 3–4 minutes on each side, basting with any leftover marinade. Serve immediately, with lemon wedges for squeezing over and the refreshing grapefruit and fennel salad.

Griddled swordfish with roasted tomatoes and cinnamon

The sun-ripened tomatoes of Morocco are naturally full of flavour and sweetness, and when roasted with sugar and spices they simply melt in the mouth. As an accompaniment to chargrilled fish or poultry, they are sensational. These delectable tomatoes can also be stored in sealed containers in the refrigerator, ideal for impromptu barbecues.

Serves four

1kg/2¼lb large vine or plum tomatoes, peeled, halved and deseeded

5–10ml/1–2 tsp ground cinnamon

pinch of saffron threads

15ml/1 tbsp orange flower water

60ml/4 tbsp olive oil

45–60ml/3–4 tbsp sugar

4 swordfish steaks, about 225/8oz each

sea salt and freshly ground black pepper

rind of ½ preserved lemon, finely chopped

small bunch of fresh coriander (cilantro), finely chopped

handful of blanched almonds

knob (pat) of butter

Preheat the oven to 110°C/225°F/gas ¼. Place the tomatoes on a baking sheet. Sprinkle with the cinnamon, saffron and orange flower water. Trickle half the oil over, being sure to moisten every tomato half, and sprinkle with sugar. Place the tray in the bottom of the oven and cook the tomatoes for about 3 hours, then turn the oven off and leave them to cool.

Brush the remaining olive oil over the swordfish steaks and season with salt and pepper. Lightly oil a preheated cast-iron griddle and cook the steaks for 3–4 minutes on each side. Sprinkle the chopped preserved lemon and coriander over the steaks towards the end of the cooking time.

In a separate pan, fry the almonds in the butter until golden and sprinkle them over the tomatoes. Then serve the steaks immediately with the tomatoes.

Variations

If swordfish steaks are not available, tuna or shark steaks can be cooked in the same way with excellent results. Or, if you prefer, try the recipe with a lean sirloin or thinly cut fillet steak (beef tenderloin). The flavours lift the meat beautifully.

Seared tuna with ginger, chilli and watercress salad

Tuna steaks are wonderful seared and served slightly rare with a punchy sauce or salad. In this recipe the salad is served just warm, as a bed for the tender tuna. Add a dab of harissa as a condiment to create a dish that will transport you to the warmth of the North African coastline. If you can't get tuna, try using salmon steaks instead.

Serves four

30ml/2 tbsp olive oil, plus extra for greasing

5ml/1 tsp harissa

5ml/1 tsp clear honey

pinch of sea salt

4 tuna steaks, about 200g/7oz each

lemon wedges, to serve

For the salad

30ml/2 tbsp olive oil

a little butter

25g/1oz fresh root ginger, peeled and finely sliced

2 garlic cloves, finely sliced

2 green chillies, deseeded and finely sliced

6 spring onions (scallions), cut into bitesize pieces

2 large handfuls of watercress

juice of ½ lemon

sea salt and freshly ground black pepper

Mix the olive oil, harissa, honey and salt, and rub it over the tuna steaks. Heat a frying pan, grease it with a little oil and sear the tuna steaks for about 2 minutes on each side. They should still be pink on the inside.

Keep the tuna warm while you quickly prepare the salad: heat the olive oil and butter in a heavy pan. Add the ginger, garlic, chillies and spring onions, cook until the mixture begins to colour, then add the watercress. When the watercress begins to wilt, toss in the lemon juice and season well with salt and plenty of ground black pepper.

Tip the warm salad on to a serving dish or individual plates. Slice the tuna steaks and arrange on top of the salad. Serve immediately with lemon wedges for squeezing over.

Seared shellfish

Prawns (jumbo shrimp) and scallops can be cooked in the same way. The shellfish will just need to be cooked through briefly – too long and they will become rubbery.

Roasted shad stuffed with dates

Cooking fish with dates is a lovely Moroccan tradition and this dish was traditionally prepared with shad, which used to be abundant in the rivers and regarded as a real treat. Traditional Muslim and Jewish recipes still call for shad but as they are in decline, other fish like sea bream are often selected for this dish, which can be cooked in a tagine on the stove or in the oven. Cooking fish in this manner is often reserved for banquets and family celebrations where the whole fish is displayed on a dish surrounded by dates stuffed with almond paste.

Serves four

4 or 2 large fresh shad, gutted, cleaned and patted dry

sea salt and freshly ground black pepper

45ml/3 tbsp olive oil or 30ml/2 tbsp clarified or plain butter

1 onion, finely chopped

25g/1oz/2 tbsp finely chopped fresh ginger root

10–15ml/2–3 tsp ground cinnamon (reserve 5ml/1 tsp for dusting)

90g/3½/scant ¾ cup blanched almonds, finely chopped

100g/3½oz/generous ½ cup medium or short-grain rice, rinsed and drained

225g/8oz/1½ cups moist ready-to-eat dates, chopped

small bunch of fresh flat-leaf parsley, finely chopped

small bunch of fresh coriander (cilantro), finely chopped

1 orange, finely sliced

Preheat the oven to 180°C/350°F/gas 4. Line a baking dish with plenty of baking parchment or foil, so that the fish can be wrapped in it, and place the fish side by side on the foil. Season the cavities with salt and pepper.

Heat most of the oil or butter in a heavy-based pan. Stir in the onion and ginger and cook for 2–3 minutes until they begin to colour. Stir in the cinnamon and almonds, add the rice, and season with salt and pepper. Pour in just enough water to cover the rice and bring it to the boil. Reduce the heat and simmer, until all the water has been absorbed. Turn off the heat, cover the pan and leave the rice to steam for 10 minutes.

Toss in the dates, parsley and coriander and leave the mixture to cool before stuffing the fish. Spoon it into the cavities and brush the tops of the fish with the remaining oil or butter.

Place the orange slices around the fish, wrap up the parchment or foil to form a package, and place the dish in the oven for 15–20 minutes. Open the parchment or foil and bake for a further 5 minutes, to lightly brown the tops. Decorate the top with a thin line of cinnamon by rubbing it with your thumb and finger, and serve immediately.

Pan-fried sardine fillets with harissa and olive sauce

In the harbours and outside medinas in coastal towns like Essaouira, there are fish market stalls where you can have the fresh catch cooked on the spot for you. Fresh sardines, sea bream, mackerel and snapper are often grilled or pan-fried whereas the meaty flesh of monkfish and swordfish are perfect for threading onto skewers for kebabs. You can use any firm-fleshed fish for this dish, which is delicious served on its own, either on top of toasted flat bread or with bread to mop up the sauce.

Serves four

30–45ml/2–3 tbsp olive oil, for frying

4 large or 8 small sardine fillets, with the skin on, whole or butterflied if preferred

4 toasted flat breads (optional)

small bunch of fresh flat-leaf parsley, coarsely chopped

1 lemon, cut into wedges, to serve

For the sauce

30–45ml/2–3 tbsp olive oil

1 onion, chopped

2 garlic cloves, chopped

5ml/1 tsp harissa

5ml/1 tsp ground cinnamon

5ml/2 tsp sugar

400g/14 oz can of chopped tomatoes, drained of juice

90g/3½oz/¾ cup black or kalamata olives

sea salt and freshly ground black pepper

First make the sauce. Heat the oil in a heavy-based pan and stir in the onion and garlic for 2–3 minutes, until they begin to take on a little colour. Stir in the harissa, cinnamon and sugar and add the tomatoes. Cook for 4–5 minutes then toss in the olives and season to taste. Cover the pan to keep the sauce hot.

Heat the oil in a frying pan. Season the sardine fillets and place them skin-side down in the pan and fry for about 2 minutes, until golden brown, then flip them over and fry for another 1–2 minutes. Arrange the fillets on top of toasted flat breads, or on a plate, spoon the sauce over the top, sprinkle with parsley and serve with lemon wedges to squeeze over them.

Meat and poultry tagines and k'dras

Slow-cooked, sweet and tender lamb tagines with dried fruit and spices are perhaps the best known outside Morocco, but there are many other regional ones with beef, chicken, goat, pigeon, squab, quail and camel meat. Most tagines are cooked over a portable or fixed stove, but some are baked in the oven and, depending on the size of the tagine, you can cook a whole chicken, lamb shanks or beef on the bone as well as smaller cuts of meat.

Chicken tagine with green olives and preserved lemon

This classic tagine, *d'jaaj mchermel*, celebrates two of Morocco's most famous ingredients – cracked green olives and preserved lemons. Try this recipe when you are looking for a new way to cook a whole chicken, or chicken joints, as it is tangy and delicious.

Serves four

1.3kg/3lb chicken

3 garlic cloves, crushed

small bunch of fresh coriander (cilantro), finely chopped

juice of ½ lemon

5ml/1 tsp coarse salt

45–60ml/3–4 tbsp olive oil

1 large onion, grated

pinch of saffron threads

5ml/1 tsp ground ginger

5ml/1 tsp ground black pepper

1 cinnamon stick

175g/6oz/1¼ cups cracked green olives

2 preserved lemons, cut into slices

Place the chicken in a deep dish. Rub the garlic, coriander, lemon juice and salt into the body cavity of the chicken. Mix the olive oil with the grated onion, saffron, ginger and black pepper and rub this mixture over the outside of the chicken. Cover and leave to stand for about 30 minutes.

Transfer the chicken to a tagine or large, heavy flameproof casserole and pour the marinating juices over. Pour in enough water to come halfway up the chicken, add the cinnamon stick and bring the water to the boil. Reduce the heat, cover with a lid and simmer for about 1 hour, turning the chicken occasionally.

Preheat the oven to 150°C/300°F/gas 2. Using two slotted spoons, carefully lift the chicken out of the tagine or casserole and set aside on a plate, covered with foil. Turn up the heat and boil the cooking liquid for 5 minutes to reduce it.

Replace the chicken in the liquid and baste it thoroughly. Add the olives and preserved lemon and place the tagine or casserole in the oven for about 15 minutes. Serve the chicken immediately with couscous or your chosen accompaniments.

Tagine of poussins with dates and orange flower water

Dates and almonds are probably the most ancient culinary combination in Arab cuisines, married in sweet dishes or with lamb and chicken. For this type of tagine, the small birds can be cooked on top of the stove or in the oven. Quail, partridge, pheasant or pigeon can be used instead of poussins.

Serves four

25g/1oz fresh root ginger, peeled and roughly chopped

2 garlic cloves, peeled

60ml/4 tbsp olive oil

juice of 1 lemon

30–45ml/2–3 tbsp clear honey

sea salt and freshly ground black pepper

4 small poussins

350g/12oz/2¼ cups plump dates, pitted and ready-to-eat

5–10ml/1–2 tsp ground cinnamon

15ml/1 tbsp orange flower water

knob (pat) of butter

30–45ml/2–3 tbsp blanched sliced almonds

Using a mortar and pestle, crush the ginger with the garlic to form a paste. Mix the paste with the olive oil, lemon juice, honey and seasoning.

Place the poussins in a tagine or flameproof casserole and rub the paste all over them. Pour in a little water to cover the base of the dish and bring to the boil. Reduce the heat, cover and simmer for about 30 minutes, turning the poussins occasionally, until they are cooked through. Top up the water during cooking, if necessary.

Lift the poussins out of the tagine, transfer them to a plate, cover with foil and keep hot. Add the dates to the liquid in the tagine and stir in the cinnamon and orange flower water. Cook gently for about 10 minutes, or until the dates are soft and have absorbed the flavours of the sauce as well as some of the liquid.

Replace the poussins and cover the tagine to keep hot. Melt the butter in a separate pan and brown the almonds, then toss them over the poussins. Serve immediately.

Chicken tagine with apricots, rosemary, ginger and harissa

Fruity and spicy, with the delightful aroma of rosemary and sweetened ginger, this is the type of tagine best served with bread to mop up all the delectable syrupy juices. As an alternative to chicken thighs, you could adapt the recipe to use breasts of chicken, pigeon, turkey, pheasant or duck. Serve with crusty bread and a leafy green salad.

Serves four

15–30ml/1–2 tbsp clarified butter or argan oil

1 onion, finely chopped

15ml/1 tbsp finely chopped fresh rosemary, plus 2 sprigs

15–30ml/1–2 tbsp finely chopped preserved stem ginger

5–10ml/1–2 tsp harissa

8 skinless chicken thighs

175g/6oz/1¼ cup ready-to-eat dried apricots

juice of 1 lemon

1 lemon, cut into quarters

30ml/2 tbsp clear honey

sea salt and freshly ground black pepper

fresh green or purple basil leaves, to garnish

Heat the butter or oil in the base of a flameproof tagine or casserole, and add the onion. Cook, stirring, for 1–2 minutes to soften. Add the chopped rosemary and preserved stem ginger and cook for 1–2 minutes until fragrant, then stir in the harissa.

Add the chicken thighs, coating them in the onion mixture, and add the apricots with the sprigs of rosemary. Pour in enough water to cover the base of the tagine and come halfway up the chicken thighs. Pour in the lemon juice and slip in the lemon quarters. Drizzle the honey over the tagine, put on the lid, and cook the tagine over a gentle heat for about 45 minutes, adding more water if necessary.

Season the dish with salt and pepper, and garnish with the fresh basil leaves. Serve immediately, with chunks of crusty bread to dip into the syrupy cooking juices.

Chicken tagine with courgettes, lemon and mint

This is one of the lovely, light summery tagines I came across in the fertile agricultural region of the Mediterranean coast. You can adapt the tagine to the vegetables in season but it should always be tangy and flavoured with herbs.

Serves four to six

30ml/2 tbsp olive oil or argan oil

1 onion, finely chopped

2–3 garlic cloves, finely chopped

2 red chillies, deseeded and finely chopped

10ml/2 tsp coriander seeds

5ml/1 tsp cumin seeds

5ml/1 tsp dried mint

4 chicken breasts, cut into bitesize pieces

juice of 1 lemon

1 lemon, cut into 4–6 wedges

2 courgettes (zucchini), sliced thickly on the diagonal

4 tomatoes, peeled, deseeded and cut into chunks

small bunch of fresh flat-leaf parsley, roughly chopped

small bunch of fresh mint, roughly chopped

sea salt and freshly ground black pepper

Heat the oil in the base of a flameproof tagine or casserole, and stir in the onion, garlic, chillies, coriander and cumin seeds. Cook for 2–3 minutes. Add the dried mint and chicken, stirring to coat it in the onion and spices.

Add the lemon juice and lemon wedges, and pour in enough water to cover the base of the tagine. Bring the water to the boil, then put the lid on the tagine, turn the heat down to low, and simmer the chicken for 35 minutes.

Season the cooking juices with salt and pepper. Add the courgettes and tomatoes. Add the chopped fresh parsley and mint, and top up the water, if necessary. Put the lid back on and cook gently for 10–15 minutes, until the courgettes are cooked but still have a slight bite to them. Serve with couscous if you like.

Chicken tagine with roasted garlic and orange chermoula

I call this my 'Out There Tagine'. I created it for my friend, Alice Morrison, who lives in Imlil and has provided many of the location photos for this book. As she spends a lot of time living on bread, tea and dates 'out there' on desert expeditions, I thought she could do with a substantial and flavoursome tagine based on tradition but with a difference. Her Moroccan friends have loved it.

Serves four

8 chicken thighs

30ml/2 tbsp olive oil or butter

1 onion, sliced

1 small fennel bulb, sliced

few sprigs of fresh rosemary, finely chopped

10ml/2 tsp honey or muscovado sugar

900ml/1½ pints/3¾ cups chicken stock or water

400g/14 oz can of chickpeas, rinsed and drained

For the garlic paste

a handful of garlic cloves

10ml/2 tsp cumin seeds

10ml/2 tsp paprika or chilli flakes

10ml/2 tsp ground turmeric

For the chermoula

2 garlic cloves, peeled

5ml/1 tsp cumin seeds

pinch of sea salt

zest and juice of 2 oranges

juice of 1 lemon

1–2 fresh green chillies, finely chopped

5ml/1 tsp paprika

handful each of fresh flat-leaf parsley and coriander (cilantro), finely chopped

10ml/2 tsp orange flower water

For the vegetables

broccoli sprigs, baby carrots and asparagus, all trimmed and left whole

30–45ml/2–3 tbsp olive oil

salt and freshly ground black pepper

First make the garlic paste. Roast the garlic in a medium 180°C/350°F/gas 4 oven until soft and squishy. Pop them out of their skins and keep a few aside (you can now use the oven to roast the vegetables). Dry-roast the cumin seeds in a dry pan or skillet and then, using a mortar and pestle, pound them with the garlic to form a creamy paste. Beat in the paprika and turmeric.

In the base of a tagine, brown the chicken thighs in the olive oil or butter, then lift them out and put aside. Stir the onion, fennel and rosemary into the oil or butter in the base of the tagine for 2 minutes to soften. Stir in the garlic paste along with the honey and mix well. Put back the chicken thighs, making sure they are coated in the mixture. Pour in the stock, bring it to the boil, then reduce the heat and put on the lid and cook the chicken gently for about 40 minutes.

Season the tagine, checking for a balance of honey and heat, and toss in the chickpeas. Put the lid back on and cook for a further 40 minutes.

Meanwhile, lightly roast the vegetables in the olive oil in the medium oven for about 20 minutes or until tender. Season with salt and pepper and put aside.

Make the chermoula. Using a mortar and pestle, pound the garlic with the cumin seeds and a little salt. Pound in the orange zest, then stir in the orange and lemon juice. Stir in the fresh chilli, paprika and fresh herbs. Season to taste and stir in the orange flower water.

When the tagine is ready, arrange the reserved roasted garlic and the roasted vegetables over the top and drizzle everything generously with some of the chermoula. Serve the rest of the chermoula in a bowl to spoon over each plate, and enjoy the tagine with chunks of crusty bread.

Chicken k'dra with turnip and ras el hanout

This rustic dish, traditionally cooked in a copper pot, is designed to feed a big family or a group of people gathered together for a celebratory occasion. Serve with couscous or crusty bread.

Serves six to eight

30–45ml/2–3 tbsp smen or clarified butter

4 onions, finely chopped

4 garlic cloves, finely chopped

10ml/2 tsp cumin seeds

16 chicken thighs, skinned

10–15ml/2–3 tsp ras el hanout

10ml/2 tsp sugar

2 x 400g/14oz cans of chopped tomatoes

1.2 litres/2 pints/5 cups chicken stock

500g/1¼lb turnips, peeled and cut into bitesize chunks

sea salt and freshly ground black pepper

bunch of fresh coriander (cilantro), roughly chopped

bunch of fresh flat-leaf parsley, roughly chopped

15ml/1 tbsp butter

Heat the smen or butter over a medium heat in a large heavy, pan. Stir in the onions, garlic and cumin seeds, and cook for 2–3 minutes. Add the chicken thighs, stir to coat them in the onion mixture, then cook until lightly browned.

Add the ras el hanout, followed by the sugar and tomatoes, then pour in the stock. Bring the liquid to the boil, then reduce the heat, put on the lid, and cook gently for 45 minutes.

Add the turnip, and top up the liquid with a little water, if necessary. Cook for 15 minutes, or until the turnip is tender.

Season the k'dra with salt and pepper, and add half the fresh herbs. Melt the butter in a small pan, and drizzle it on to the surface of the k'dra. Garnish with the rest of the fresh coriander and parsley, and serve with a mound of couscous, or chunks of crusty bread to mop up the sauce.

Chicken k'dra with chickpeas and almonds

A k'dra is traditionally cooked with smen, which lends its own unique flavour to the dish, and for this recipe it is worth making your own to distinguish it from a tagine made with similar ingredients. The almonds in this recipe are pre-cooked until soft, adding an interesting texture and flavour as well.

Serves four

75g/3oz/½ cup blanched almonds

75g/3oz/½ cup dried chickpeas, soaked overnight and drained

4 part-boned skinless chicken breast portions

50g/2oz/¼ cup smen or clarified butter

2.5ml/½ tsp saffron threads

sea salt and freshly ground black pepper

2 onions, thinly sliced

900ml/1½ pints/3¾ cups chicken stock

1 small cinnamon stick

60ml/4 tbsp chopped fresh flat-leaf parsley, plus extra to garnish

lemon juice, to taste

Place the almonds in a pan of water and simmer for 1½–2 hours until fairly soft, then drain and set aside.

Meanwhile, cook the chickpeas in a pan of boiling water for 1–1½ hours until they are completely soft. Drain, then place in a bowl of cold water and rub with your fingers to remove the skins. Discard the skins and drain.

Place the chicken portions in a flameproof tagine or heavy pan, together with the smen or butter and half of the saffron, and season with salt and plenty of black pepper. Heat gently, stirring, until the smen or butter has melted. Add the onions and stock, bring to the boil and then add the chickpeas and cinnamon stick. Cover and cook very gently for 45–60 minutes.

Transfer the chicken to a serving plate and keep warm. Bring the sauce to the boil and simmer until reduced, stirring frequently. Add the almonds, parsley and the remaining saffron, and cook for 2–3 minutes.

Sharpen the sauce with a little lemon juice, then pour the sauce over the chicken. Serve, garnished with extra parsley.

Tagine of duck with chestnuts and pomegranate seeds

This is a lovely aromatic, winter dish, decorated with ruby-red pomegranate seeds – ideal for seasonal celebrations. Whole chestnuts are sometimes used in Arab-influenced dishes as a substitute for potatoes, as they are quite filling and can be found in abundance in the colder months. Serve with couscous.

Serves four

30g/1¼oz/2 tbsp ghee or clarified butter

2 onions, finely chopped

4 garlic cloves, finely chopped

25g/1oz fresh ginger, finely chopped

10ml/2 tsp cumin seeds

2–3 dried red chillies, left whole

4 duck legs

600ml/1 pint/2½ cups chicken stock

300g/11oz shelled chestnuts

30ml/2 tbsp honey

sea salt and freshly ground black pepper

seeds of 1 pomegranate, with the pith removed

small bunch of fresh mint, finely chopped

small bunch of fresh coriander (cilantro), finely chopped

Heat the ghee or butter in the base of a flameproof tagine or shallow heavy pan, and stir in the onions, garlic, ginger, and cumin seeds. Cook for 2–3 minutes, until they begin to colour.

Add the dried chillies and duck legs. Pour in the chicken stock and bring it to the boil. Reduce the heat, cover with a lid, and simmer gently for 25–30 minutes.

Add the chestnuts and honey, put the lid back on, and cook gently for a further 25–30 minutes, until the duck is very tender.

Season with salt and plenty of black pepper, and add most of the pomegranate seeds, fresh mint and fresh coriander, reserving some for the garnish. Cook for 5–10 minutes more.

Garnish with the reserved pomegranate seeds and herbs, and serve the tagine with couscous.

Duck tagine with saffron, caramelized pears and orange salad

Duck and pigeon tagines are popular in the cities of Fes and Marrakesh, and very often they are combined with fruit in the style of medieval Arab recipes.

Serves four

500g/1¼lb duck breasts

30ml/2 tbsp olive oil or argan oil

2 onions, finely chopped

25g/1oz fresh ginger, peeled and finely chopped

2–3 cinnamon sticks

a fingerful of saffron threads, soaked in 30ml/2 tbsp water

300ml/½ pint/1¼ cups chicken stock

150ml/¼ pint/scant ¾ cup white wine

30ml/2 tbsp butter

2 pears, peeled, quartered and cored

30ml/2 tbsp honey

30–45ml/2–3 tbsp orange flower water

sea salt and freshly ground black pepper

small bunch of fresh flat-leaf parsley, finely chopped

couscous, to serve

For the orange salad

2–3 oranges

15–30ml/1–2 tbsp orange flower water

1 green chilli, finely sliced

Slice the duck breasts into thick strips. Heat the oil in the base of a flameproof tagine or casserole, and stir in the onions and ginger. Cook for 2–3 minutes, until they begin to colour. Add the cinnamon sticks and duck, turning the duck to make sure it is coated in the ginger and onions.

Stir in the saffron and its soaking water, chicken stock and wine. Bring the liquid to the boil, then reduce the heat, put on the lid, and cook the duck over a low heat for 25–30 minutes.

Meanwhile, melt the butter in a heavy pan, then add the pears, and cook for 2–3 minutes. Add the honey, and continue to cook until the pears begin to caramelize.

Add the caramelized pears to the tagine along with the orange flower water. Season, then put the lid back on, and cook gently for 10–15 minutes, to allow the flavours to mingle.

To prepare the salad, peel the oranges with a small, sharp knife, removing the skin and pith. Cut the oranges horizontally into thin slices, remove any pips, and arrange them in a shallow serving dish. Sprinkle the orange flower water over them, and arrange the sliced chilli over the top.

When ready to serve, toss the salad. Garnish the tagine with the parsley, and serve with a mound of buttery couscous, and accompanied by the orange salad.

Mrouzia goat tagine

Mrouzia is one of the traditional dishes to make for Aid el Kebir when a whole sheep or goat is slaughtered and the meat is distributed amongst the family or community and some is given to the poor. Most of the meat on the bone will end up slow-roasted but some cuts will be used to make broths and tagines. This tagine is often intensely redolent with ras el hanout and sticky-sweet with raisins and honey but, in some regions, sour raisins are used to balance the sweetness as the original dish included vinegar. The quality of the ras el hanout can be so important to this tagine that some people will travel far to a particular spice merchant. In the past, *mrouzia* was made with the bits of meat left on the bones after the good cuts had been distributed and it was cooked with lots of fat so that it could be stored for a while, but modern versions often call for shoulder or shanks. This recipe employs goat meat and is served with lemon wedges for that sour kick. For the salad garnish, see page 110.

Serves four

1kg/2¼lb goat shoulder, cut into bite-sized chunks

15ml/1 tbsp olive oil

15ml1 tbsp ras el hanout, more if needed

25g/1oz/2 tbsp butter

1 onion, halved and thickly sliced

5ml/2 tsp cumin seeds

5ml/1 tsp ground ginger

pinch of saffron threads, soaked in 30ml/2 tbsp rose flower water

60ml/4 tbsp runny honey

225g/8oz/1¾ cups sweet or sour seedless raisins

sea salt and freshly ground black pepper

175g/6oz/1½ cups blanched almonds

1 lemon, quartered, to serve

Place the meat in a bowl with the olive oil and ras el hanout and, using your fingers, rub the mixture into the meat. Cover and put aside in a cool place for 2–4 hours.

Heat the butter in the base of a tagine and stir in the onion and cumin seeds for 2 minutes. Toss in the meat, lightly coating it in the onions, then add the ground ginger and saffron-rose water. Pour in enough water to cover the meat and bring it to the boil. Reduce the heat, put the lid on the tagine and simmer over a low heat for 2 hours, checking the liquid from time to time – you want it to reduce but not to go dry.

Meanwhile soak the raisins in warm water for an hour and drain. After the meat has simmered for 2 hours, add the honey. Add more ras el hanout at this stage, if you like, and season well with salt and lots of black pepper. Continue to cook the meat for 30 minutes, then add the raisins and cook gently until there is very little liquid left and it is sweet, spicy, sticky and silky.

Place the almonds in a hot oven, or fry them in a little butter, until they turn golden brown, then scatter them over the meat and serve immediately with wedges of lemon.

Tagine of spiced lamb kefta with lemon

The kefta, or meatballs, are poached gently with lemon and spices to make a dish that is surprisingly light. In Morocco today, this dish is found in the tiniest rural villages, in street stalls in the towns and cities, and in the finest restaurants of Casablanca, Fes and Marrakesh. Serve with a leafy salad and crusty bread.

Serves four

450g/1lb/2 cups finely minced (ground) lamb

3 large onions, grated

small bunch of fresh flat-leaf parsley, chopped

5–10ml/1–2 tsp ground cinnamon

5ml/1 tsp ground cumin

pinch of cayenne pepper

sea salt and freshly ground black pepper

40g/1½oz/3 tbsp butter

25g/1oz fresh root ginger, peeled and finely chopped

1 hot red chilli, deseeded and finely chopped

pinch of saffron threads

juice of 1 lemon

small bunch of fresh coriander (cilantro), finely chopped

300ml/½ pint/1¼ cups water

1 lemon, quartered

To make the kefta, pound the minced lamb in a bowl by using your hand to lift it up and slap it back down into the bowl. Knead in half the grated onions, the parsley, cinnamon, cumin and cayenne pepper. Season with salt and pepper, and continue pounding the mixture by hand for a few minutes, until well combined.

Break off small pieces of the mixture, and shape them into walnut-sized balls.

In a flameproof tagine or heavy lidded frying pan, melt the butter and add the remaining onion with the ginger, chilli and saffron. Stirring frequently, cook just until the onion begins to colour, then stir in the lemon juice and most of the coriander.

Pour in the water, season with salt and bring to the boil. Drop in the kefta, reduce the heat and cover the pan. Poach the kefta gently, turning them occasionally, for about 20 minutes.

Remove the lid from the tagine or pan, tuck the lemon quarters around the kefta and cook, uncovered, for a further 10 minutes, to reduce the liquid slightly.

Garnish the kefta with the rest of the chopped coriander. Serve hot, straight from the pan, accompanied by a leafy salad and with plenty of crusty fresh bread to mop up the delicious juices.

Tagine of lamb with prunes

This delicious tagine combines sweetness from prunes and honey, warmth from ginger and cinnamon, and a little crunch from toasted almonds. Serve with couscous, stirring in some finely chopped fresh coriander for extra flavour and colour.

Serves six

1kg/2¼lb lean boneless lamb, such as shoulder or neck fillet

25g/1oz/2 tbsp butter

15ml/1 tbsp sunflower oil

1 large onion, chopped

2 garlic cloves, chopped

2.5cm/1in piece of fresh root ginger, peeled and finely chopped

1 red bell pepper, deseeded and chopped

900ml/1½ pints/3¾ cups lamb stock or water

250g/9oz/1¾ cups ready-to-eat prunes

juice of 1 lemon

15ml/1 tbsp clear honey

1.5ml/¼ tsp saffron threads

1 cinnamon stick, broken in half

sea salt and freshly ground black pepper

50g/2oz/½ cup sliced almonds, toasted

For the couscous

450g/1lb/2½ cups medium couscous

25g/1oz/2 tbsp butter

30ml/2 tbsp chopped fresh coriander (cilantro)

Trim the lamb and cut it into 2.5cm/1in cubes. Heat the butter and oil in a large flameproof tagine or casserole until foaming. Add the onion, garlic and ginger, and cook, stirring occasionally, until the onion has softened but not coloured.

Add the lamb pieces and red pepper, and mix well. Pour in the lamb stock or water. Add the prunes, lemon juice, honey, saffron threads and cinnamon. Season with salt and pepper, and stir well.

Bring to the boil, then reduce the heat and cover the tagine or casserole with a lid. Simmer for 1½ –2 hours, stirring occasionally, until the meat is melt-in-the-mouth tender.

Place the couscous in a bowl and cover with salted water, stirring. Set aside for 10 minutes. Stir in the butter, and chopped fresh coriander.

Pile the couscous into a large, warmed serving dish or on to individual warmed bowls or plates.

Taste the stew for seasoning, and add more salt and pepper to taste, if necessary. Ladle the stew on to the couscous and scatter the toasted almond slices over the top.

Tagine of lamb with country salad

Morocco's hearty tagines are well known for their succulent meat cooked in a combination of honey and warm spices. This delicious recipe is for one of the most traditional and popular tagines, which is best served with a crunchy salad spiked with chilli to balance the sweetness of the main dish. Offer lots of fresh bread alongside for mopping up the thick, syrupy sauce.

Serves 6

1kg/2¼lb boneless shoulder of lamb, trimmed and cubed

30–45ml/2–3 tbsp vegetable oil

25g/1oz fresh root ginger, peeled and chopped

pinch of saffron threads

10ml/2 tsp ground cinnamon

1 onion, finely chopped

2–3 garlic cloves, chopped

sea salt and freshly ground black pepper

350g/12oz/2¼ cups pitted prunes, soaked for 1 hour

30ml/2 tbsp clear honey

For the salad

2 onions, chopped

1 red and 1 green bell pepper, deseeded and chopped

2–3 celery sticks, chopped

2–3 green chillies, deseeded and chopped

2 garlic cloves, chopped

30ml/2 tbsp olive oil

juice of ½ lemon

sea salt

small bunch of fresh flat-leaf parsley, chopped

a little fresh mint, chopped

Put the meat in a flameproof casserole or heavy pan. Add the oil, ginger, saffron, cinnamon, onion, garlic and seasoning, then pour in enough water to cover. Heat until just simmering, cover with a lid and simmer gently for about 2 hours, topping up the water if necessary, until the meat is very tender.

Drain the prunes and add them to the tagine. Stir in the honey and simmer for a further 30 minutes, or until the sauce has reduced.

To make the salad, mix the onions, pepper, celery, chillies and garlic in a bowl. Pour over the olive oil and lemon juice, and toss to coat. Season with salt and stir through the parsley and mint. Serve the hot lamb tagine with the chilli-laced salad, and crusty bread.

Tagine of baked lamb with chermoula, figs and honey

This traditional Berber dish is generally prepared for religious feasts and family celebrations. Often cooked as a whole lamb or goat over a camp fire, it can be adapted to a leg or shoulder that will fit into a wide tagine base or an earthenware baking dish. The meat is cooked slowly so that it is very tender. Serve with a salad, couscous or potatoes and steamed vegetables.

Serves four to eight

roughly 1.5kg/3¼lb leg or shoulder of lamb on the bone

90ml/6 tbsp chermoula

30ml/2 tbsp ghee or clarified butter

2 red onions, halved lengthways and sliced with the grain

300ml/½ pint/1¼ cups water

6 fresh figs, halved or quartered

25g/1oz/2 tbsp butter, cut into little pieces

30–45ml/2–3 tbsp orange flower water

30ml/2 tbsp clear honey

sea salt and freshly ground black pepper

small bunch of fresh flat-leaf parsley, roughly chopped

small bunch of fresh coriander (cilantro), roughly chopped

Preheat the oven to 180°C/350°F/gas 4. Using a small sharp knife, cut small incisions in the lamb and rub the chermoula all over the meat, working the mixture well into the incisions. Cover and marinate in the refrigerator for at least 6 hours, or overnight.

Heat the ghee in a wide flameproof tagine or casserole, and add the onions. Cook for 2–3 minutes, stirring, to soften.

Place the leg of lamb in the onions and brown it lightly on all sides. Pour in the water and mix it well with the onions and chermoula. Cover the tagine and place it in the oven for about 2 hours, basting from time to time.

Take the tagine out of the oven, place the figs around the lamb and dot them with the butter. Splash the orange flower water over the lamb, and drizzle the honey over the meat and figs. Season the lamb with salt and pepper and return the tagine, uncovered, to the oven for about 30 minutes, until the lamb is nicely browned and tender.

Let the lamb rest for about 10–15 minutes before serving, garnished with the parsley and coriander.

Tagine of beef with peas and saffron

This tagine is a popular supper dish, and can be made with beef or lamb. With a hint of floral saffron and the tang of lemon added towards the end of cooking, this rich, gingery beef with brown olives is one of the delights of Fes and Marrakesh. Serve with bread or plain couscous.

Serves six

1.2kg/2½lb chuck steak or braising steak, trimmed and cubed

30ml/2 tbsp olive oil

1 onion, chopped

25g/1oz fresh root ginger, peeled and chopped

5ml/1 tsp ground ginger

pinch of cayenne pepper

pinch of saffron threads

sea salt and freshly ground black pepper

1.2kg/2½lb peas, fresh and shelled, or frozen

2 tomatoes, peeled and chopped

1 preserved lemon, chopped

a handful of brown kalamata olives

Put the cubed chuck or braising steak in a tagine, flameproof casserole or heavy pan with the olive oil, chopped onion, fresh and ground ginger, cayenne and saffron, and season with salt and pepper.

Pour in enough water to cover the meat completely and bring to the boil. Then reduce the heat and cover and simmer for about 1½ hours, or until the meat is very tender. Cook for a little longer if necessary.

Add the peas, tomatoes, preserved lemon and olives. Stir well and cook, uncovered, for about 10 minutes, or until the peas are tender and the sauce has reduced. Check the seasoning and serve.

Beef tagine with sweet potatoes

Fes is credited with Morocco's finest tagines. This is a particularly good one, the sweet potatoes and warm spices providing a mellow contrast to the robust flavour of the beef.

Serves four

675–900g/1½–2lb braising or stewing beef

30ml/2 tbsp sunflower oil

a good pinch of ground turmeric

sea salt and freshly ground black pepper

1 large onion, chopped

1 fresh red or green chilli, deseeded and finely chopped

7.5ml/1½ tsp paprika

a good pinch of cayenne pepper

2.5ml/½ tsp ground cumin

450g/1lb sweet potatoes

15ml/1 tbsp chopped fresh flat-leaf parsley

15ml/1 tbsp chopped fresh coriander (cilantro)

15g/½oz/1 tbsp butter

Trim the meat of excess fat, and cut it into 2cm/¾in cubes. Heat the oil in a flameproof tagine or casserole, and fry the meat, with the turmeric and seasoning, over a medium heat for 3–4 minutes until the meat is evenly browned, stirring frequently.

Cover the pan tightly with a lid and cook for 15 minutes over a fairly gentle heat, without lifting the lid. Meanwhile, preheat the oven to 180°C/350°F/gas 4.

Add the onion, chilli, paprika, cayenne pepper and cumin to the pan together with just enough water to cover the meat. Cover tightly and cook in the oven for 1–1½ hours, until the meat is very tender, checking occasionally and adding a little extra water, if necessary, to keep the stew fairly moist.

Meanwhile, peel the sweet potatoes and slice them straight into a bowl of salted water to avoid discolouring. Transfer to a pan, bring to the boil, then simmer for 2–3 minutes. Drain.

Stir most of the herbs into the meat, adding a little extra water if it appears dry. Arrange the potato slices over the meat and dot with the butter. Cover and cook in the oven for 10 minutes more, until the potatoes are tender.

Increase the oven temperature to 200°C/400°F/gas 6 or preheat the grill or broiler to its hottest setting. Remove the lid and cook in the oven or under the grill for 5–10 minutes, until the sweet potatoes are golden. Serve, garnished with the rest of the herbs.

Merguez and black-eyed bean tagine

Bean stews made with spicy cured sausage, or other preserved meats, are popular in Morocco. You can use black-eyed beans, or any other beans or chickpeas, and accompany it with a salad of hot green peppers and parsley, or pickled vegetables.

Serves four to six

175g/6oz/1 cup dried black-eyed beans (peas), soaked in cold water overnight

30ml/2 tbsp ghee or 15ml/1 tbsp each olive oil and butter

1 large onion, cut in half lengthways and sliced along the grain

2–3 garlic cloves, roughly chopped and bruised with the flat side of a knife

5ml/1 tsp cumin seeds

5–10ml/1–2 tsp coriander seeds

5ml/1 tsp fennel seeds

5–10ml/1–2 tsp sugar or clear honey

1 spicy merguez, about 25cm/10in long, sliced

150ml/¼ pint/scant ¾ cup white wine

400g/14oz can of tomatoes

bunch of fresh flat-leaf parsley, roughly chopped

sea salt and freshly ground black pepper

Drain the soaked black-eyed beans, transfer them to a pan and fill the pan with plenty of cold water. Bring to the boil and boil for 1 minute, then lower the heat and partially cover the pan with a lid. Simmer the beans for about 25 minutes, or until they are tender but retain a little bite. Drain the beans, then rinse well under cold running water and remove any loose skins.

Preheat the oven to 180°C/350°F/gas 4. Melt the ghee in a flameproof tagine or casserole. Stir in the onion, garlic and spices, and fry until the onion begins to colour. Stir in the sugar or honey, add in the spicy sausage, and cook until it begins to brown.

Add the beans, followed by the wine, and stir. Bring to the boil to cook off the alcohol, then lower the heat and add the tomatoes. Stir in half the parsley, and season with salt and pepper.

Cover with a lid and bake for about 40 minutes. Before serving, adjust the seasoning to taste and sprinkle with the remaining parsley.

Meat and poultry meshwi

People gathered around smoking grills, lured by the aroma of meat and poultry being cooked around the souks and countryside markets, is a scene from daily life. Small cuts of meat are often grilled this way whereas large cuts or whole beasts, usually reserved for religious and celebratory festivals, are slow-cooked in the communal or pit oven. Morocco has a meat-loving and sharing culinary culture so, when a whole beast is roasted to mark an occasion, some of it is given to the poor.

Fiery chicken wings with blood oranges

This is a great recipe for the barbecue – it is quick and easy, and best eaten with the fingers. The juicy oranges are there to suck after experiencing an explosion of fiery spices on the tongue. The oranges can be cooked separately or threaded alternately with the chicken wings on skewers. Cherry tomatoes can be used as well, as it is the burst of juice that makes this dish so delicious.

Serves four

60ml/4 tbsp fiery harissa
30ml/2 tbsp olive oil
sea salt
16–20 chicken wings
4 blood oranges, quartered
icing (confectioners') sugar
small bunch of fresh coriander (cilantro), roughly torn

Put the harissa in a small bowl with the olive oil and mix to form a loose paste. Add a little salt and stir to combine. Brush this mixture over the chicken wings so that they are well coated. Cook the wings on a hot barbecue or under a hot grill or broiler, for 5 minutes on each side.

Once the wings begin to cook, dip the orange quarters lightly in icing sugar and grill them for a few minutes, until they are slightly burnt but not black and charred. Serve the chicken wings immediately with the oranges, garnished with fresh coriander.

Pan-fried quail with ginger and grapes

This is a delicious method of cooking quail. Sweet grapes and buttery juices are especially good with lots of zesty ginger. This dish has quite a sophisticated air about it and often features on the menus of the more expensive restaurants in Fes and Casablanca. A Moroccan friend prepared it for me using pigeon and it was so good I came home and made it with quail. Serve with bread to mop up the juices.

Serves four

30–45ml/2–3 tbsp vegetable oil

50g/2oz/¼ cup butter

8 quail, prepared

25g/1oz fresh root ginger, peeled and grated

sea salt and freshly ground black pepper

3 garlic cloves, crushed

450g/1lb/3 cups seedless white grapes

Heat 30ml/2 tbsp of the oil and most of the butter in a large heavy frying pan. Add the quail and brown on both sides for 8 minutes. Add the ginger and season, then stir in the garlic. Cook until it begins to colour, then take off the heat.

In a separate pan, cook the grapes, covered, in the remaining oil and butter for a few minutes. Sprinkle with salt and cook for 20 minutes, or until soft.

Add the grapes to the quail. Put back on the heat and cook for 10–15 minutes. Serve from the pan.

Roast duck legs with quince, ginger, honey and cinnamon

The quince is a fruit of the ancient world, recorded in recipes from the Roman and Arab empires that launched invasions on vast tracts of the Middle East and North Africa. These scented fruit that resemble large, hard pears often feature with lamb or rich poultry, as in this typically Moroccan recipe. When cooking, quinces fill the air with their heady scent and impart a fruity honey flavour to the dish.

Serves four

4 duck legs

30ml/2 tbsp olive oil

sea salt and freshly ground black pepper

2 quinces

600ml/1 pint/2½ cups water

juice of 2 lemons

a little butter

25g/1oz fresh root ginger, peeled and grated

10ml/2 tsp ground cinnamon

30ml/2 tbsp clear honey

small bunch of fresh coriander (cilantro), chopped

Preheat the oven to 230°C/450°F/gas 8. Rub the duck legs with half the olive oil, season with salt and pepper, and place on a rack in a roasting pan. Roast in the oven for about 30 minutes until the skin is crisp and golden.

Meanwhile, quarter, core and peel the quinces. Bring the water to the boil in a pan with a spoon of lemon juice. Add the quince quarters and simmer for about 15 minutes until tender. Drain and refresh, then cut each quince quarter into slices.

Heat the remaining olive oil and butter in a frying pan and fry the quince slices until brown. Remove from the pan, place in a dish and keep warm.

Take the duck out of the oven and pour 30ml/2 tbsp of the duck fat into the pan in which the fruit was cooked. Stir in the ginger and cook for 1 minute, then add the cinnamon, honey and the remaining lemon juice. Pour in 30–45ml/2–3 tbsp water and stir until it bubbles up to make a small amount of sauce, then remove from the heat.

Arrange the duck legs and quince slices on a plate and spoon the sauce over them. Sprinkle with coriander and serve immediately.

Kouah

These simple lamb's liver kebabs are popular in the souks and outdoor markets, often right beside the butchering of the animals. Other bits of offal get cooked in the same way. Threaded onto sticks the liver is grilled quickly, then sprinkled with salt and cumin and finely chopped parsley.

Serves four

500g/1¼lb fresh lamb's liver, trimmed and cut into bite-sized pieces

sea salt

5ml/1 tsp ground cumin

small bunch of fresh flat-leaf parsley, finely chopped

lemon wedges, for squeezing

Thread the liver onto skewers. Place the skewers over the charcoal grill for 1–2 minutes each side. Sprinkle with the salt, cumin and parsley and serve with lemon wedges to squeeze over them.

Dafina

Traditionally, *dafina*, also known as *skhena* in Morocco, is a Sephardic stew that would be slow-cooked overnight on a Friday in a clay pot buried in the coals of the communal oven to be eaten the following day for the Sabbath lunch. A basic *dafina* is usually prepared with a shin of beef or a breast or shoulder of lamb, and a sliced cow's foot or marrow bones can be added to enrich and thicken the stew. Chickpeas, potatoes and eggs are usually added to the pot in Morocco. In Jewish tradition eggs symbolize life and rebirth and are ritually served first with the whole potatoes, which represent a harmonious world. Each Jewish community has its own way of serving *dafina* but it is often accompanied by leftover couscous.

Serves four to six

1kg/2¼lb beef or lamb, cut into large pieces

2 marrow bones (optional)

225g/8oz/1¼ cups dried chickpeas, soaked overnight and drained

500g/1¼lb new or baby potatoes, peeled and left whole

6 small onions, peeled and left whole

12 garlic cloves, peeled and left whole

6 pitted dates, halved

2 cinnamon sticks

10ml/2 tsp cumin seeds

10ml/2 tsp paprika

15ml/1 tbsp ground turmeric

6 eggs

15ml/1 tbsp honey

15ml/1 tbsp olive, argan or vegetable oil

sea salt and freshly ground black pepper

Put the meat in large heavy-based pot with the bones, if using. Cover with plenty of water and bring it to the boil. Remove any scum that collects on the surface of the water.

Add the chickpeas, potatoes, onions, garlic, dates and spices to the pot. Make sure there is plenty of water to completely cover everything. Carefully slip in the eggs (whole in their shells), drizzle the honey and oil over the top, and season with salt and a generous grinding of black pepper. Put the lid on the pot and gently simmer for 3–4 hours, or place the pot in a very low oven overnight.

Before serving, check the seasoning. Remove the eggs from the stew, shell them and return them to the thick broth. The eggs will have turned brown during the slow cooking and the yolks will be very creamy. Serve the *dafina* with couscous, rice or bread.

Tangia

Tangia is both the name of the earthenware amphora cooking vessel and the resulting slow-cooked, confit-style meat dish. It is thought to originate with the craftsmen and traders around the city souks who would chip in for the meat on a Thursday and take it to the communal oven where it would cook slowly in the ashes overnight to be enjoyed at Friday lunchtime when the shops are closed. It is probably the only dish that is traditionally cooked by men and is particularly associated with Marrakesh where it is reputed to be the city's signature dish. Don't skimp on the preserved lemon as it is an integral part of the overall taste. To prepare the dish at home, you can slow-cook it in a very low oven.

Serves six to eight

1kg/2¼lb fatty lamb or mutton, cut into chunks

rind of 1 preserved lemon, finely sliced

8 garlic cloves, peeled and smashed

15ml/1 tbsp smen or clarified butter

10ml/2 tsp ground cumin

10ml/2 tsp paprika

large pinch of saffron threads, crumbled and soaked in a tablespoon of warm water to draw out the colour

15ml/1 tbsp olive oil

sea salt and freshly ground black pepper

flat bread and pickled vegetables (page 290), to serve

Place all the ingredients in a heavy-based earthenware or cast-iron pot and cover with 600ml/1 pint/2½ cups water. Put the lid on the pot and place it in a very low oven for 4–6 hours, until the meat is so tender you can pull it apart with your fingers. Check the seasoning before serving and enjoy it with freshly toasted flat bread and Moroccan pickles.

Roast leg of lamb with dates and almonds

Whole roasted lamb or goat cooked outdoors over a charcoal fire in a specially prepared pit is a traditional celebration dish for feasts. The lamb is carefully tended and basted with butter and spices until it tastes quite amazing. At home, this similar, more modest version can be prepared with a well-marinated leg of lamb. Serve with couscous and a well-flavoured vegetable tagine.

Serves six to eight

2.25kg/5lb leg of lamb
4 garlic cloves, peeled
5ml/1 tsp coarse salt
10ml/2 tsp ground coriander
10ml/2 tsp ground cumin
10ml/2 tsp paprika
5ml/1 tsp ground black pepper
2.5ml/½ tsp cayenne pepper
175g/6oz/1½ stick butter
115g/4oz/scant 1 cup ready-to-eat pitted dates
30ml/2 tbsp blanched almonds
4 lemons, quartered

Use a small sharp knife to make small, deep incisions all over the leg of lamb. With a mortar and pestle, crush the garlic with the salt to a paste, then add the ground coriander, cumin, paprika, black pepper and cayenne.

Pound the butter in a bowl and beat in the garlic and spice paste. Smear the spicy butter all over the leg of lamb, and into the incisions, and leave to marinate for 3–4 hours.

Preheat the oven to 220°C/425°F/gas 7. Place the lamb in a roasting pan and roast for about 20 minutes. Turn the lamb and baste with the spicy cooking juices and cook for 15 minutes. Turn and baste again, reduce the heat to 180°C/350°F/gas 4 and roast for a further 2 hours, basting occasionally.

Scatter the dates and almonds over and around the lamb and cook for 30 minutes, or until the meat is very tender. Serve hot with lemon quarters for squeezing over the aromatic meat.

Making a date and almond paste

Alternatively, you could pound the dates and almonds to a coarse paste and smear the mixture over the lamb to give it a sticky coating.

Mechoui

Although the Arabic word *mechoui/meshwi* refers to grilled meats, in Morocco *mechoui* is also the name of a traditional festive dish of an entire lamb or kid, rubbed all over with a blend of smen, cumin, black pepper and garlic, and roasted slowly over embers in a pit dug in the ground until the meat is so tender it can be torn off with fingers and shared amongst a community, or a large family. It is generally prepared in this way for holy days, such as Aid el Adha, to celebrate the near-sacrifice of Isaac, and it is one of the dishes cooked for the Jewish *hilloula* and the Berber *moussem*, which are both festive celebrations to mark a religious or significant event, such as a marriage or the death of a saint. Around the souks, the *mechoui* stalls sell cuts of the plain roasted meat, which people buy to dip in salt and cumin. When cooking a joint of smen-coated lamb in a communal or kitchen oven, Moroccan cooks might add seasonal fruit, such as fresh figs, plums, apricots or quince to the dish.

Serves six to eight

roughly 2.25kg/5lb leg of lamb

200ml/7fl oz/scant 1 cup water

30–45ml/2–3 tbsp runny honey

about 6 fresh figs, plums or apricots, halved and pitted (optional)

sea salt and freshly ground black pepper

fresh coriander (cilantro) leaves, roughly chopped, for garnishing

For the marinade

4 garlic cloves, chopped

60g/2oz fresh ginger, chopped

1 red chilli, deseeded and chopped

pinch of sea salt

small bunch of fresh coriander (cilantro), chopped

small bunch of fresh flat-leaf parsley, chopped

5–10ml/1–2 tsp ground cumin

5–10ml/1–2 tsp ground coriander

45ml/3 tbsp smen, softened butter or olive oil

First make the marinade. Using a mortar and pestle, pound the garlic, ginger and chilli with salt to form a coarse paste. Add the fresh coriander and parsley, pound to a paste, and stir in the ground cumin and coriander. In a bowl, beat the paste into the smen, until thoroughly mixed. Cut small incisions in the shoulder of lamb with a sharp knife and rub the spicy smen all over the meat, making sure it goes into the incisions. Cover and marinate in the refrigerator for at least 6 hours, or overnight.

Preheat the oven to 200°C/400°F/gas 4. Place the leg of lamb in a roasting dish, pour the water around it, and pop it in the oven. Roast for roughly 1 hour 15 minutes, basting from time to time, until it is nicely browned. Spoon the honey over the meat and, if adding fresh figs, plums or apricots, place them around the meat, and return the dish to the oven for a further 15 minutes.

Place the roasted lamb and fruit on a serving dish and leave it to sit for about 15 minutes. Meanwhile, bubble up the juices in the roasting dish, season with salt and pepper, and pour it over the roasted lamb. Sprinkle with coriander and serve.

Bus-station kefta with egg and tomato

Egg and tomato dishes are very popular in bus and train stations and in ports along the Mediterranean coast. Travellers waiting for connecting transport services tuck into dishes like this to sustain themselves during long journeys. The dish is always eaten out of the pan in which it is cooked. It would make a great informal brunch or supper dish.

Serves four

225g/8oz/1 cup finely minced (ground) lamb

1 onion, finely chopped

50g/2oz fresh breadcrumbs

5 eggs

5ml/1 tsp ground cinnamon

small bunch of fresh flat-leaf parsley, finely chopped

sea salt and freshly ground black pepper

30ml/2 tbsp olive oil

a little butter

400g/14oz can of chopped tomatoes

10ml/2 tsp sugar

5ml/1 tsp ras el hanout

small bunch of fresh coriander (cilantro), roughly chopped

crusty bread, to serve

In a bowl, knead the minced lamb with the onion, breadcrumbs, one egg, cinnamon, parsley and salt and pepper until well mixed. Lift the mixture in your hand and slap it down into the bowl several times. Take a small amount of mixture and shape it into a small ball about the size of a walnut. Repeat with the remaining mixture to make about 12 balls.

Heat the olive oil with the butter in a large heavy frying pan. Fry the meatballs until nicely browned, turning them occasionally so they cook evenly. Stir in the tomatoes, sugar, ras el hanout and most of the coriander. Bring to the boil, cook for a few minutes to reduce the liquid, and roll the balls in the sauce. Season to taste with salt and pepper.

Make room for the remaining four eggs in the pan and crack them into spaces between the meatballs. Cover the pan, reduce the heat and cook for about 3 minutes or until the eggs are just set. Sprinkle with the remaining coriander and serve in the pan, with chunks of bread to use as scoops.

Merguez

These chargrilled spicy sausages are very popular throughout the Maghreb and vary according to the spices of each region. Generally, the sausages are grilled at street stalls and served with bread as a snack, or they are added to grain and pulse dishes.

Serves four

250g/8oz/1 cup minced (ground) beef

100g/3½oz/scant ½ cup minced (ground) beef fat

2 garlic cloves, crushed

5ml/1 tsp ground cumin

5ml/1 tsp ground coriander

5ml/1 tsp ground paprika

5ml/1 tsp chilli flakes, chilli powder or cayenne pepper

5ml/1 tsp dried thyme

30–45ml/2–3 tbsp cold water

sea salt and freshly ground black pepper

sausage casings

flat bread and pickled vegetables, to serve

Put the minced beef and fat into a bowl. Add the garlic, spices and thyme and, using your hand, knead together thoroughly. Moisten the mixture with a little water and season with salt and pepper. Cover the bowl and chill in the refrigerator for 2–3 hours.

Fill a piping bag with the sausage mixture and squeeze it into the sausage casings, tying and twisting as you go. Hang the sausages to dry in an airy warm place for at least 24 hours.

Prepare a charcoal, or conventional, grill or broiler and cook the sausages for 2–3 minutes on each side, until nicely browned and cooked through. Serve hot or at room temperature with Moroccan pickles and bread.

Making pickled vegetables

Crunchy pickles make a delicious accompaniment and are easy to make. Simply combine whole or chopped raw vegetables with white wine vinegar mixed with a little salt and leave to soak for about 3 weeks. The most popular pickled vegetables enjoyed in Morocco are green tomatoes, hot peppers, white cabbage and garlic.

Spicy minced beef kebabs with hot chickpea purée

Try this dish for a summer barbecue. Make the kebabs as fiery as you like by adding more cayenne pepper. The smooth, soothing chickpea purée adds a sumptuous touch. You need metal skewers with wide blades for these kebabs to hold the pounded meat in place so that it resembles a sheath on a sword when serving. The whole sheath can be pushed off the skewer. Serve with salad and bread.

Serves six

500g/1¼lb/2¼ cups finely minced (ground) beef

1 onion, grated

10ml/2 tsp ground cumin

10ml/2 tsp ground coriander

10ml/2 tsp paprika

5ml/1 tsp cayenne pepper

5ml/1 tsp salt

small bunch of fresh flat-leaf parsley, finely chopped

small bunch of fresh coriander (cilantro), finely chopped

For the chickpea purée

225g/8oz/1¼ cups dried chickpeas, soaked overnight in cold water and drained

50ml/2fl oz/¼ cup olive oil

juice of 1 lemon

2 garlic cloves, crushed

5ml/1 tsp cumin seeds

30ml/2 tbsp light tahini

60ml/4 tbsp thick Greek (strained plain) yogurt

sea salt and freshly ground black pepper

40g/1½oz/3 tbsp butter, melted

Cook the soaked chickpeas for the purée in a pan of boiling water for 1–1½ hours until they are soft. Drain, then place in a bowl of cold water and rub with your fingers to remove the skins. Discard the skins and drain.

Meanwhile, mix the minced beef with the onion, cumin, ground coriander, paprika, cayenne, salt and chopped fresh herbs. Knead the mixture well, then pound it until smooth in a mortar with a pestle or in a food processor. Place in a dish, cover and leave to stand for 1 hour.

Preheat the oven to 200°C/400°F/Gas 6. To make the chickpea purée, process the chickpeas in a food processor with the olive oil, lemon juice, garlic, cumin seeds, tahini and yogurt. Season, tip into an ovenproof dish, cover with foil and heat through for 20 minutes.

Divide the meat mixture into 6 portions and mould each on to a metal skewer, so that the meat resembles a fat sausage. Heat the grill or broiler on the hottest setting and cook the kebabs for 4–5 minutes on each side.

Melt the butter and pour it over the hot chickpea purée. Serve the kebabs with the hot chickpea purée.

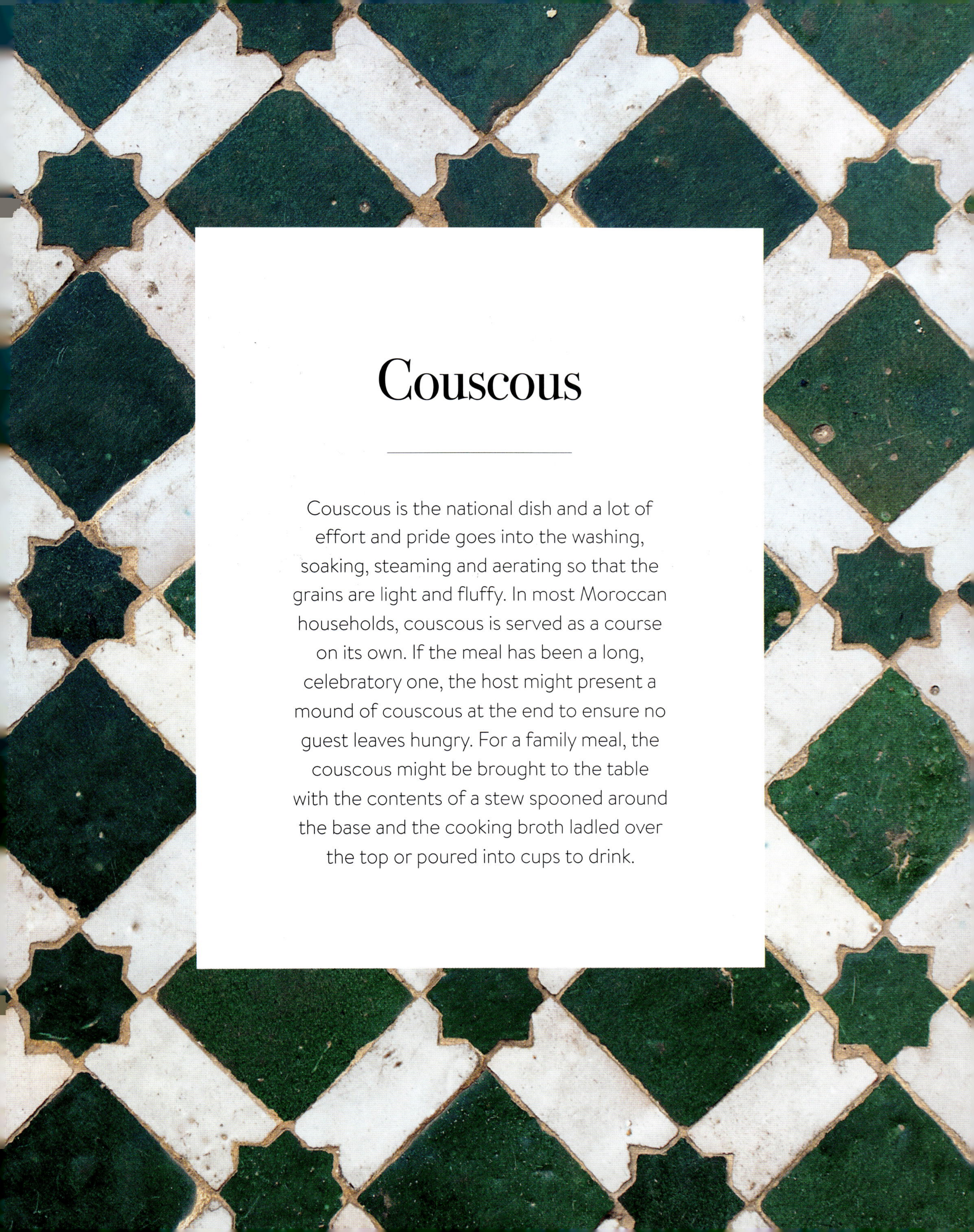

Couscous

Couscous is the national dish and a lot of effort and pride goes into the washing, soaking, steaming and aerating so that the grains are light and fluffy. In most Moroccan households, couscous is served as a course on its own. If the meal has been a long, celebratory one, the host might present a mound of couscous at the end to ensure no guest leaves hungry. For a family meal, the couscous might be brought to the table with the contents of a stew spooned around the base and the cooking broth ladled over the top or poured into cups to drink.

Plain, buttery couscous

Couscous is held in such high esteem that religious feasts and celebratory feasts would be unthinkable without it. Traditionally, it is piled high in a mound, and served as a dish on its own after a tagine, or roasted meat. The parboiled couscous available outside Morocco is extremely easy to prepare, making it a practical accompaniment for many dishes.

Serves four to six

350g/12 oz/2 cups medium couscous, rinsed and drained

5ml/1 tsp salt

400ml/14fl oz/1¾ cups warm water

30ml/2 tbsp sunflower or olive oil

25g/1oz/2 tbsp butter, broken into little pieces

For the topping

15ml/1 tbsp butter

100g/3½oz/¾ cup blanched almonds

dusting of ground cinnamon (optional)

Preheat the oven to 180°C/350°F/gas 4. Tip the couscous into an ovenproof dish. Stir the salt into the warm water and pour it over the couscous. Leave the couscous to absorb the water for about 10 minutes.

Using your fingers, gently rub the oil into the grains to break up the lumps by lifting them into the air and letting them fall. This way you air the grains and make sure they are separated. Scatter the butter over the surface and cover with a piece of foil, or wet greaseproof paper. Place the dish in the oven for about 15 minutes to heat through.

Meanwhile, prepare the almonds for the top. Melt the butter in a heavy-based pan and stir in the almonds over a medium heat until they begin to turn golden. Drain the almonds on kitchen paper.

Take the couscous out of the oven and fluff up the grains with a fork. Serve it from the dish, or tip it onto a plate piled high in a pyramid, dusted with a little cinnamon and the almonds scattered over the top.

Green couscous with a spring broth

This is a lovely spring or summer dish as it is prepared with the young green vegetables in season, such as fresh broad beans and peas, artichokes, asparagus, rocket leaves, spring onions, and baby courgettes. You can serve it as a course on its own, or as an accompaniment to many tagines and grilled meat dishes.

Serves four to six

For the broth

1.2 litres/2 pints/5 cups vegetable, or chicken, stock

350g/12oz/3 cups fresh broad (fava) beans, shelled

200g/7oz/1 cup fresh peas, shelled

12 spring onions (scallions), trimmed and sliced thickly

6 baby courgettes (zucchini), sliced thickly

4–6 artichoke bottoms, cut into quarters (see page 99)

sea salt and freshly ground black pepper

bunch of fresh flat-leaf parsley, finely chopped

bunch of fresh coriander (cilantro), finely chopped

bunch of fresh mint, finely chopped

For the couscous

500g/1¼lb/3 cups medium couscous, rinsed and drained

5ml/1 tsp sea salt

600ml/1 pint/2½ cups warm water

15–30ml/1–2 tbsp olive oil

15ml/1 tbsp butter

Preheat the oven to 300°C/400°F/gas 6. First prepare the vegetable broth. Pour the stock into a heavy-based pan and bring it to the boil. Drop in the broad beans, peas, spring onions, courgettes and artichoke bottoms and cook for 5–10 minutes, until tender. Season the broth with salt and pepper and stir in most of the herbs – reserve some for garnishing.

Tip the couscous into an ovenproof dish. Stir the salt into the warm water and pour it over the couscous. Leave the couscous to absorb the water for about 10 minutes. Using your fingers, rub the oil into the grains to break up the lumps and air them. Scatter the butter over the surface and cover with a piece of foil or wet greaseproof paper. Place the dish in the oven for about 15 minutes to heat through.

Remove the couscous from the oven and tip it onto a serving plate. Using a slotted spoon, lift the vegetables out of the broth and arrange them around, or over, the couscous mound. Moisten with a little broth and garnish with the reserved herbs. Ladle the rest of the broth into small cups or bowls to drink while enjoying the couscous.

Couscous with dried fruit and nuts

In Morocco this dish of steamed couscous with dried fruit and nuts, topped with sugar and cinnamon, is served during special celebrations. It is often presented as a course on its own, just before the dessert. At home though, it is delicious served with spicy tagines or grilled or roasted meat and poultry dishes. Try it as a side dish at your next barbecue.

Serves six

500g/1¼lb/3 cups medium couscous, rinsed and drained

600ml/1 pint/2½ cups warm water

5ml/1 tsp sea salt

pinch of saffron threads

45ml/3 tbsp sunflower oil

30ml/2 tbsp olive oil

a little smen or butter

115g/4oz/scant 1 cup dried apricots, cut into slivers

75g/3oz/½ cup pitted dates, chopped

75g/3oz/½ cup seedless raisins

115g/4oz/scant 1 cup blanched slivered almonds

75g/3oz/½ cup pistachio nuts

10ml/2 tsp ground cinnamon

45ml/3 tbsp sugar

Preheat the oven to 180°C/350°F/gas 4. Put the couscous in a bowl. Mix the warm water with the salt and the saffron, and stir into the couscous. Leave to stand for 10 minutes, or until the grains are tender. Add the sunflower oil and, using your fingers, rub it through the grains.

In a heavy pan, heat the olive oil and smen or butter and stir in the apricots, dates, raisins, most of the almonds (reserve some for garnish) and pistachio nuts.

Cook until the raisins plump up, then tip the nuts and fruit into the couscous and toss together. Tip the couscous into an ovenproof dish and cover with foil. Place in the oven for about 20 minutes, until heated through.

Toast the reserved slivered almonds. Pile the hot couscous in a mound on a large serving dish and sprinkle with the cinnamon and sugar – these are usually sprinkled in stripes down the mound. Scatter the toasted almonds over the top and serve hot.

Casablancan couscous with roasted summer vegetables

This dish is based on the classic couscous recipe for a stew containing seven vegetables. The number seven is believed to bring good luck, so you can use vegetables of your choice as long as they add up to seven in type. I like to serve this dish with a dollop of thick and creamy yogurt but, if you wish, you can also serve it with a spoonful of fiery harissa as a condiment.

Serves six

3 red onions, peeled and quartered

2–3 courgettes (zucchini), halved lengthways and cut across into 2–3 pieces

2–3 red, green or yellow bell peppers, deseeded and quartered

2 aubergines (eggplants), cut into 6–8 long segments

2–3 leeks, trimmed and cut into long strips

2–3 sweet potatoes, peeled, halved lengthways and cut into long strips

4–6 tomatoes, quartered

6 garlic cloves, crushed

25g/1oz fresh root ginger, sliced

a few fresh rosemary sprigs

about 150ml/¼ pint/scant ¾ cup olive oil

10ml/2 tsp sugar or clear honey

sea salt and freshly ground black pepper

For the couscous

500g/1¼lb/3 cups medium couscous, rinsed and drained

5ml/1 tsp salt

600ml/1 pint/2½ cups warm water

45ml/3 tbsp sunflower oil

about 25g/1oz/2 tbsp butter, diced

Preheat the oven to 200°C/400°F/gas 6. Arrange all the vegetables in a roasting pan. Tuck the garlic, ginger and rosemary around the vegetables. Pour lots of olive oil over the vegetables, sprinkle with the sugar or honey, salt and pepper, and roast for about 1½ hours until they are extremely tender and slightly caramelized. The cooking time will depend on the size of the vegetable pieces. Turn them in the oil occasionally.

When the vegetables are nearly ready, put the couscous in a bowl. Stir the salt into the warm water, then pour it over the couscous, stirring to make sure it is absorbed evenly. Leave to stand for 10 minutes to plump up then, using your fingers, rub the sunflower oil into the grains to air them and break up any lumps. Tip the couscous into an ovenproof dish, arrange the butter over the top, cover with foil and heat in the oven for about 20 minutes.

To serve, use your fingers to work the melted butter into the grains of couscous and fluff it up, then pile it on a large dish and shape into a mound with a little pit at the top. Spoon some vegetables into the pit and arrange the rest around the dish. Pour the oil from the pan over the couscous or serve separately. Serve immediately with yogurt, or harissa if you prefer, and bread for mopping up the juices.

Spicy couscous with aromatic shellfish broth

Serves four to six

For the couscous

500g/1¼lb/3 cups medium couscous, rinsed and drained

5ml/1 tsp salt

600ml/1 pint/2½ cups warm water

45ml/3 tbsp sunflower oil

5–10ml/1–2 tsp harissa

25g/1oz/2 tbsp butter, diced

For the shellfish broth

500g/1¼lb mussels in their shells, scrubbed with beards removed (discard any that open)

500g/1¼lb uncooked prawns (jumbo shrimp) in their shells

juice of 1 lemon

50g/2oz/2 tbsp butter

2 shallots, finely chopped

5ml/1 tsp coriander seeds, roasted and ground

5ml/1 tsp cumin seeds, roasted and ground

2.5ml/½ tsp ground turmeric

2.5ml/½ tsp cayenne pepper

5–10ml/1–2 tsp plain (all-purpose) flour

600ml/1 pint/2½ cups fish stock

120ml/4½fl oz/½ cup double (heavy) cream

sea salt and freshly ground black pepper

small bunch of fresh coriander (cilantro), finely chopped

Some couscous dishes include a soup-like stew, which is ladled over the cooked couscous and mopped up with lots of bread. In this recipe, mussels and prawns have been used but you could use any shellfish, either shelled or still in their shells. This is the type of dish you can enjoy on a warm evening along the coast by Casablanca or Tangier.

Preheat the oven to 180°C/350°F/gas 4. Place the couscous in a bowl. Stir the salt into the warm water, then pour the liquid over the couscous, stirring. Set aside for 10 minutes.

Stir the sunflower oil into the harissa to make a paste, then, using your fingers, rub it into the couscous and break up any lumps. Tip into an ovenproof dish, arrange the butter over, cover with kitchen foil and heat in the oven for about 20 minutes.

Meanwhile, put the mussels and prawns in a pan, add the lemon juice and 50ml/2fl oz/¼ cup water, cover and cook for 3–4 minutes, shaking the pan, until the mussels have opened. Drain the shellfish, reserving the liquor, and shell about two-thirds of the mussels and prawns. Discard any closed mussels.

Heat the butter in a large pan. Cook the shallots for 5 minutes, or until softened. Add the spices and fry for 1 minute. Off the heat, stir in the flour, the fish stock and shellfish cooking liquor. Place back on the heat and bring to the boil, stirring. Add the cream and simmer, stirring occasionally, for about 10 minutes. Season with salt and pepper, add the shellfish and most of the fresh coriander. Heat through, then sprinkle with the remaining coriander.

Fluff up the couscous with a fork or your fingers, working in the melted butter. To serve, pass round the couscous and ladle the shellfish and broth over the top.

Roasting spices

Toss the spices in a heavy pan over a high heat until they begin to change colour and give off a nutty aroma, then immediately tip them into a bowl.

Couscous with lamb cutlets, harissa and fennel

Throughout the Middle East and North Africa, every butcher prepares thin lamb cutlets for grilling or frying – ask your butcher to do the same for this dish. This style of couscous dish is often served with sour pickles, such as cabbage or hot peppers.

Serves four

45ml/3 tbsp olive oil

2 onions, quartered

4 garlic cloves, chopped

30–45ml/2–3 tbsp tomato purée (paste)

10ml/2 tsp harissa

600ml/1 pint/2½ cups water

4 fennel bulbs, stalks removed and quartered (feathery fronds reserved)

50g/2oz/½ stick butter

8 thin lamb cutlets (US rib chops)

sea salt and freshly ground black pepper

For the couscous

350g/12oz/2 cups medium couscous, rinsed and drained

2.5ml/½ tsp salt

400ml/14fl oz/1¾ cups warm water

30ml/2 tbsp sunflower oil

knob (pat) of butter, diced

Heat the olive oil in a heavy pan, add the onions and garlic and cook for 15 minutes, until softened. Mix the tomato purée with the harissa and dilute with a little water. Pour it into the onion pan with the pint of water. Bring to the boil and add the fennel. Reduce the heat, cover and cook for about 10 minutes, or until tender.

Meanwhile, prepare the couscous. Stir the salt into the warm water. Place the couscous in a bowl and cover with the water, stirring. Set aside for 10 minutes. Using your fingers, rub the sunflower oil into the couscous.

Use a slotted spoon to lift the onions and fennel from the cooking liquid and transfer to a covered dish; keep warm. Bring the liquid to the boil to reduce it.

Melt the butter in a heavy frying pan, add the cutlets to the pan and brown them on both sides. Add the cutlets to the reduced liquid and simmer for 15 minutes, or until tender.

Meanwhile, preheat the oven to 180°C/350°F/gas 4. Tip the couscous into an ovenproof dish and arrange the diced butter over the top. Chop the fennel fronds and sprinkle over the couscous. Cover with kitchen foil and heat in the oven for about 20 minutes.

Put the vegetables back in the pan with the lamb and heat through. Fluff up the couscous then mound it on to a serving dish. Place the cutlets around the edge and spoon the vegetables over. Moisten with the cooking liquid and serve.

Cinnamon couscous with beef tfaia

Regarded as a grand tagine, beef *tfaia* is usually on the menu of restaurants in Fes, Marrakesh and Meknes. Traditionally it would be made in a couscoussier with the meat cooking in the bottom compartment, creating the steam for the couscous above. However, the parboiled couscous can be prepared separately and the whole dish combined at the end. The *tfaia* is a sweet cinnamon and saffron mixture of onions and raisins that is spooned on top of the stew. This mixture can be cooked as part of the dish, or served separately on top of the beef.

Serves four

500g/1¼lb lean beef

1 onion, finely chopped

2–3 garlic cloves, finely chopped

5ml/1 tsp ground coriander

5ml/1 tsp ground cumin

4–6 cardamom pods

pinch of saffron threads

sea salt and ground black pepper

For the couscous

350g/12oz/2 cups medium couscous, rinsed and drained

2.5ml/½ tsp salt

400ml/14fl oz/1¾ cups warm water

15–30ml/1–2 tbsp sunflower oil

15g/½oz/1 tbsp butter

5–10ml/1–2 tsp ground cinnamon

For the *tfaia*

15ml/1 tbsp olive oil

15ml/1 tbsp butter

2–3 onions, thinly sliced

30ml/2 tbsp sultanas (golden raisins)

2–3 cinnamon sticks

5ml/1 tsp saffron threads, soaked in 2–3 tbsp warm water

30ml/2 tbsp honey

sea salt and ground black pepper

Preheat the oven to 180°C/350°F/gas 4. Slice the meat into strips. Place it in a flameproof tagine or casserole with the onion, garlic and spices. Pour in just enough water to cover the meat. Bring it to the boil, then reduce the heat, cover with the lid, and simmer for 40 minutes, or until very tender.

Place the couscous in an ovenproof dish. Stir the salt into the warm water, and pour it over the couscous. Cover, then leave the couscous to absorb the water for 10–15 minutes.

Using your fingers, rub the oil into the couscous to separate the grains, lifting them into the air to aerate them. Sprinkle the butter over the top. Place a piece of dampened baking parchment over the top of the couscous and cook in the oven for 15–20 minutes to heat through.

Meanwhile, for the *tfaia*, heat the oil with the butter in a heavy pan, and add the onions. Cook for 3–4 minutes, stirring, until the onions begin to soften. Add the sultanas, cinnamon sticks, saffron and soaking water, honey and seasoning. Reduce the heat, cover with a lid, and cook gently for 15 minutes.

Transfer the couscous to a serving dish, piling it in a mound. Sprinkle with cinnamon. Create a well in the top, lift the meat into it and spoon the *tfaia* over the top. Season the meat's cooking liquid and serve with the dish.

Sweet treats, preserves and tea

The most common way to end a meal is with a simple platter of fresh seasonal fruit but Moroccans enjoy sweet treats and puddings at other times of day and, in particular, at religious and celebratory feasts and festivals. Dried fruit and nuts, honey and cinnamon feature in many pastries and sweetmeats, whereas larger fresh fruits like pears and quinces are often poached with sugar and preserved. All sweet treats are enjoyed with coffee or the national drink, mint tea.

Watermelon and spiced orange granitas with grilled fruits

These refreshing granitas are glorious in the summer, and particularly welcome as a dessert to follow a spicy tagine. Contrast them with grilled fruits such as pineapple, mango and banana. Make the granitas the day before they are required. If you close your eyes while eating, the flavours will transport you to a beach under the hot Moroccan sun.

Serves six to eight

1 pineapple

1 mango

2 bananas

45–60ml/3–4 tbsp icing (confectioners') sugar

For the watermelon granita

1kg/2¼lb watermelon, seeds removed

250g/9oz/1½ cups caster (superfine) sugar

150ml/¼ pint/scant ¾ cup water

juice of ½ lemon

15ml/1 tbsp orange flower water

2.5ml/½ tsp ground cinnamon

For the spiced orange granita

900ml/1½ pints/3¾ cups water

350g/12oz/2 cups caster (superfine) sugar

5–6 cloves

5ml/1 tsp ground ginger

2.5ml/½ tsp ground cinnamon

600ml/1 pint/2½ cups fresh orange juice

15ml/1 tbsp orange flower water

To make the watermelon granita, purée the watermelon flesh in a blender. Put the sugar and water in a pan and stir until dissolved. Bring to the boil, simmer for 5 minutes, then cool.

Stir in the lemon juice, orange flower water and cinnamon, then beat in the watermelon purée. Pour the mixture into a bowl, and place in the freezer. Stir every 15 minutes for 2 hours and then at intervals for another hour, so that the mixture freezes but is slushy.

To make the spiced orange granita, heat the water and sugar together in a pan with the cloves, stirring until the sugar has dissolved, then bring to the boil and boil for about 5 minutes. Leave to cool and stir in the ginger, cinnamon, orange juice and orange flower water.

Remove the cloves, then pour the mixture into a bowl, cover and place in the freezer. Freeze as for the watermelon granita.

To serve, peel, core and slice the pineapple. Peel the mango, and cut the flesh off the stone (pit) in thick slices. Peel and halve the bananas. Preheat the grill or broiler on the hottest setting. Arrange the fruit on a baking sheet. Sprinkle with icing sugar and grill for 3–4 minutes until slightly softened and lightly browned. Arrange the fruit on a serving platter and scoop the granitas into dishes. Serve immediately.

Minted pomegranate yogurt with grapefruit salad

In North Africa, the juicy, ruby seeds of ripe pomegranates are often added to plain, steaming couscous. In this Moroccan dessert the seeds add texture, flavour and colour to an equally simple dish. You can eat the yogurt for breakfast or during the day for a healthy snack but it makes a fabulous topping for a delicately scented citrus fruit salad.

Serves three to four

300g/10oz/1½ cups Greek (strained plain) yogurt

2–3 ripe pomegranates

small bunch of fresh mint, finely chopped, plus a few leaves to garnish

honey or sugar, to taste (optional)

For the grapefruit salad

2 red grapefruit

2 pink grapefruit

1 white grapefruit

15–30ml/1–2 tbsp orange flower water

honey or sugar, to taste (optional)

Put the yogurt in a bowl and beat well. Cut open the pomegranates and scoop out the seeds, removing all the bitter pith. Fold the pomegranate seeds and chopped mint into the yogurt. Sweeten with a little honey or sugar, if it needs it, then chill until ready to serve.

Peel the red, pink and white grapefruits, cutting off all the pith. Cut between the membranes to remove the segments, holding the fruit over a bowl to catch the juices.

Discard the membranes and mix the fruit segments with the reserved juices. Sprinkle with the orange flower water and add a little honey or sugar, if using. Stir gently.

Decorate the chilled yogurt with a scattering of mint and serve with the grapefruit salad.

Variations

Alternatively, you can use a mixture of oranges and blood oranges, interspersed with thin segments of lemon. Lime segments work well with the grapefruit, and mandarins or tangerines could be used too. As the idea is to create a refreshing, scented salad; juicy melons and kiwi fruit would also be ideal.

Poached pears in scented honey syrup

Fruit has been poached in honey since ancient times. The Romans did it, as did the Persians, Arabs, Moors and Ottomans. The Moroccans continue the tradition today, adding a little orange rind or aniseed, or even lavender to give a subtle flavouring. Delicate and pretty to look at, these scented pears provide an exquisite finishing touch to a Moroccan meal.

Serves four

45ml/3 tbsp clear honey
juice of 1 lemon
250ml/9fl oz/generous 1 cup water
pinch of saffron threads
1 cinnamon stick
1–2 dried lavender heads
4 firm pears

Heat the honey and lemon juice in a heavy pan that will hold the pears snugly. Stir over a gentle heat until the honey has dissolved. Add the water, saffron threads, cinnamon stick and flowers from 1–2 lavender heads. Bring the mixture to the boil, then reduce the heat and simmer for 5 minutes.

Peel the pears, leaving the stalks attached. Add the pears to the pan and simmer for 20 minutes, turning and basting at regular intervals, until they are tender. Leave the pears to cool in the syrup and serve at room temperature.

Almond and pistachio ice creams

Creamy green pistachio ice cream and snowy almond ice cream are legendary ancient culinary delights of the Arabian Empire, adopted from the Persians. These refreshing modern versions are equally cooling in the heat of the day and provide a memorable finale for a Moroccan meal. All ice creams can be made and whisked by hand but, for a really smooth texture, you need to rely on the modern ice cream machine.

Serves six to eight

For the almond ice cream

150g/5oz/1¼ cups blanched almonds, finely ground

300ml/½ pint/1¼ cups milk

300ml/½ pint/1¼ cups double (heavy) cream

4 egg yolks

175g/6oz/generous ¾ cup caster (superfine) sugar

30–45ml/2–3 tbsp orange flower water

2–3 drops almond essence (extract)

For the pistachio ice cream

150g/5oz/1¼ cups blanched pistachio nuts, finely ground

300ml/½ pint/1¼ cups milk

300ml/½ pint/1¼ cups double (heavy) cream

4 egg yolks

175g/6oz/generous ¾ cup sugar

30–45ml/2–3 tbsp rose flower water

green food colouring (optional)

To make the almond ice cream, put the almonds in a pan with the milk and cream, and bring to the boil. In a large bowl, beat the egg yolks with the sugar, then pour in the hot milk and cream, beating all the time. Pour the mixture back into the pan and stir over a low heat until it thickens slightly. Take care not to overheat the custard as, if it approaches simmering point, it will curdle.

Stir in the orange flower water and almond essence, and leave the mixture to cool. Pour the cold mixture into a bowl or freezer container and chill, then freeze. Whisk the mixture thoroughly after about 1 hour, when it should be icy around the edges. Continue to freeze the ice cream, whisking two or three times, until it is smooth and very thick. Then return it to the freezer and leave for several hours or overnight. Alternatively, churn the mixture in an ice cream maker.

Make the pistachio ice cream in the same way as the almond ice cream, using the pistachio nuts instead of the almonds and rose water instead of the orange flower water and almond essence. Add a little green food colouring to the pistachio ice cream, if you like.

Remove both batches of ice cream from the freezer 10–15 minutes before serving and allow to soften slightly.

Jabane

A variety of soft and hard nougats, made with sesame seeds, sunflower seeds, peanuts, almonds, pistachios and pumpkin seeds, are sold in the streets and in the souks. However, this soft, fluffy nougat, which employs mastic for its chewy twang and mild, resinous flavour, is traditionally served in Jewish households to celebrate the end of Passover. Throughout Morocco, *jabane* is hugely popular but this soft version has the texture of the semi-set raw meringue mixture which the traditional *jabane*-seller skilfully winds around a long stick and then peels off bits to give to excited children – a bit like candyfloss.

Serves eight to ten

300g/11oz/2¼ cups shelled, unsalted pistachios

300ml/½ pint/1¾ cups water

900g/2lb/4¾ cups caster (superfine) sugar (reserve 1 teaspoon)

small piece of mastic, the size of a small coin

juice of 2 lemons

whites of 4 large eggs

Roast the pistachios in a skillet or frying pan, or toast them in a medium oven on a baking tray, until they emit a lovely nutty aroma. Using a mortar and pestle, or an electric blender, crush the roasted pistachios coarsely. Put to one side.

Pour the water into a heavy-based pan and add the sugar. Bring the mixture to the boil, stirring all the time, until the sugar has dissolved. Reduce the heat and simmer gently for about 10 minutes, until the syrup coats the back of the wooden spoon – the syrup should be thick and transparent.

Using a small mortar and pestle, grind the mastic with the reserved teaspoon of sugar and add it with the lemon juice to the syrup. Take the pan off the heat and cool the syrup down by beating it continuously, until warm to touch.

Whisk the egg whites in a bowl until thick and frothy and then fold them, one spoonful at a time, into the warm syrup. Place the pan over a low heat and stir for 5 minutes. Keeping a little back for garnish, gradually add the crushed pistachios, making sure they are well dispersed throughout the mixture.

Spoon the mixture into individual serving bowls and leave to cool a little. Garnish with a sprinkling of ground pistachios and serve while still warm, or at room temperature.

Burnt mulhalbia with rose-petal jam

This classic milk pudding, which features throughout the Middle East and North Africa, is flavoured with orange flower water but you can use rose water or vanilla. The Moroccan version is usually decorated with ground almonds and cinnamon, but, for a change, here the top is caramelized and finished with a little rose petal jam. You can make rose petal jam with the scented petals from your garden, but the jam is also available in most Middle Eastern and North African stores.

Serves four to six

50g/2oz/⅓ cup rice flour

900ml/1½ pints/3¾ cups milk

115g/4oz/⅔ cup caster (superfine) sugar, plus 30–45ml/2–3 tbsp, for sprinkling

15ml/1 tbsp orange flower water

30–45ml/2–3 tbsp rose petal jam, to serve

In a bowl, combine the rice flour with a little of the milk to form a thin paste. Pour the remaining milk into a pan. Add the sugar and bring it to the boil, stirring all the time.

Reduce the heat and stir a spoonful or two of the hot milk into the rice flour paste, then pour the paste into the pan. Bring the mixture to the boil, stirring continuously. Add the orange flower water, then reduce the heat and simmer gently for 20–25 minutes, stirring occasionally, until the mixture becomes quite thick. Pour the mixture into flameproof serving bowls and leave to cool, allowing a skin to form on top.

Preheat the grill or broiler on the hottest setting. Sprinkle each dessert liberally with caster sugar and place under the grill until the sugar melts and browns, taking care to remove the dessert before the sugar burns. Cool and then chill. Serve topped with a little warmed rose petal jam.

Saffron and cardamom crème caramel

Chilled creamy custards, milk puddings and rice puddings are wonderful –the Persians invented some of them, the Arabs loved them and the Ottomans refined them. Some are deeply traditional; others have a modern twist. You can serve the puddings with *ghoriba* if you like.

Serves four to six

600ml/1 pint/2½ cups milk

115g/4oz/⅔ cup sugar, plus 60ml/4 tbsp for caramel

pinch of saffron threads

2.5ml/½ tsp cardamom seeds

15–30ml/1–2 tbsp rose flower water

4 eggs, lightly beaten

60ml/4 tbsp boiling water

***ghoriba*, to serve (optional)**

Preheat the oven to 180°C/350°F/gas 4. Heat the milk, sugar, saffron and cardamom in a pan until the milk is just about to boil. Set aside to cool. Add the rose water, then gradually pour the mixture into the eggs, beating all the time. Set aside.

To make the caramel, heat the 60ml/4 tbsp sugar in a small heavy pan until melted and dark brown. Stir in the boiling water, holding the pan at arm's length as the caramel will spit. Let it bubble before tipping it into individual crème caramel dishes, dividing equally. Swirl the dishes to coat the base and sides evenly. Leave to cool.

Pour the custard into the dishes and stand them in a roasting pan. Pour in cold water to two-thirds of the way up the dishes. Bake in the oven for about 1 hour, or until the custard has set. Cool, then chill for several hours or overnight.

To serve, run a knife around the edges of the dishes and invert onto plates. Serve immediately.

Ghoriba

These buttery cookies can be plain or scented with flower water, rolled in toasted sesame seeds (see page 343) or baked smooth with a single blanched almond in the top as here. They go beautifully with the crème caramels, or just with a glass of tea.

M'hanncha

The snake, or *m'hanncha* as it is known in Arabic, is the most famous sweet dish in Morocco. This coiled pastry looks impressive and tastes divine. The crisp, buttery pastry is filled with almond paste that has been scented with cinnamon and orange flower water. Serve *m'hanncha* as a dessert or as an afternoon snack with mint tea. Pieces are broken off and the coil gets smaller.

Serves eight to ten

115g/4oz/1 cup blanched almonds

115g/4oz/1 stick butter, softened, plus extra for cooking nuts and buttering pastry

300g/11oz/2¼ cups ground almonds

50g/2oz/½ cup icing (confectioners') sugar, plus extra for topping

115g/4oz/⅔ cup caster (superfine) sugar

5–10ml/1–2 tsp ground cinnamon, plus extra for topping

15ml/1 tbsp orange flower water

3–4 sheets of ouarka or filo pastry

1 egg yolk

Fry the blanched almonds in a little (about 1½ tablespoons) butter until golden brown, then pound them using a pestle and mortar until they resemble coarse breadcrumbs. Place the nuts in a bowl and mix in the main quantity of butter, ground almonds, icing sugar, caster sugar, cinnamon and orange flower water. Use your hands to form the mixture into a smooth paste. Cover and chill in the refrigerator for about 30 minutes.

Preheat the oven to 180°C/350°F/gas 4. Open out the sheets of pastry, keeping them in a pile so they do not dry out, and brush the top one with a little melted butter.

Take lumps of the almond paste and roll them into fingers. Place them end to end along the long edge of the top sheet of pastry, then roll the pastry up into a tube the thickness of your thumb, tucking in the ends to stop the filling oozing out. Repeat with the other sheets, until all the filling is used up.

Grease a large round baking pan or the widest baking sheet you can find. Lift one of the pastry rolls in both hands and gently push it together from both ends, like an accordion, to relax the pastry before coiling it in the centre of the pan or baking sheet. Do the same with the other rolls, joining the ends to enlarge the circle to form a tight coil like a snake.

Mix the egg yolk with a little water and brush this over the pastry, then bake for 30–35 minutes, until crisp and lightly browned. Top the freshly cooked pastry with a liberal sprinkling of icing sugar, and add lines of cinnamon like the spokes of a wheel. Serve at room temperature.

Silky milk b'stilla with cinnamon

Although the classic *b'stilla* dishes are thought to have Andalucian origins, this sweet version probably owes its elegance and silky milk sauce to the Ottomans. Also known as *ktefa*, it is both a celebratory and sophisticated dessert.

Serves four

115g/4oz/1 cup blanched almonds

4 sheets of ouarka or filo pastry

50g/2oz/¼ cup butter

For the milk sauce

400ml/14fl oz/1¾ cup milk

90g/3½oz/¾ cup caster (superfine) sugar

1 cinnamon stick

30ml/2 tbsp orange flower or rose flower water

15ml/1 tbsp cornflour (cornstarch)

For dusting

15ml/1 tbsp icing (confectioners') sugar

5ml/1 tsp ground cinnamon

Preheat the oven to 180°C/200°F/gas 6. Spread the almonds on a baking tray and pop them in the oven to roast for about 10 minutes, until they are golden brown. Leave them to cool a little, then tip onto a sheet of greaseproof paper, or a clean dish towel, and crush them with a rolling pin into coarse pieces.

Place the ouarka or filo sheets on a work surface and cover them with a clean dish towel so they don't dry out. Place one of the sheets on the surface and use an inverted cup or bowl to cut around so that you get as many circles from each sheet as you can – depending on the size of bowl, you might have as many as 8 circles. Keep the circles under the dish towel as you cut out the others.

Line several baking trays with greaseproof paper. Melt the butter in a pot. Brush one circle lightly with butter, place another on top, brush it with butter too and place it on the baking tray. Continue with the remaining circles – you may have to do this in batches depending on your oven space. Place the trays in the oven for 4–5 minutes, until the pastries are crisp and golden brown. Leave to cool on a rack.

Meanwhile, make the milk sauce. Bring the milk to scalding point in a heavy-based pan. Add the sugar, cinnamon stick and scented water, stirring until the sugar dissolves. Simmer gently for 2–3 minutes. In a cup, slake the cornflour with 2 tablespoons of milk to form a thick paste. Stir a tablespoon of the hot milk into the slaked cornflour and then tip it into the pan, stirring all the time, until the milk begins to thicken. Remove the cinnamon stick.

To assemble the *b'stilla*, lay out individual plates and place a pastry circle on each one, ladle some of the milk sauce over the top, followed by a sprinkling of toasted almonds, then place another pastry on top. Continue stacking in this way until you have used everything up – you should have roughly 4 layers for each *b'stilla*. Dust the top layers with icing sugar and cinnamon and serve immediately while the milk sauce is still warm.

Apricot parcels with honey glaze

These parcels can be made with dried apricots poached in syrup and then stuffed, but I prefer to use fresh fruit as it lends a juicy tartness to the otherwise sweet dish, which the dried fruit does not possess. Roll or twist the parcels into any shape or size, just make sure you leave them open, so that the fruit and pastry benefit from the honey glaze. Serve with cream, crème fraîche, or a spoonful of yogurt.

Makes twelve

200g/7oz/1¾ cups blanched almonds, ground

115g/4oz/⅔ cup caster (superfine) sugar

30–45ml/2–3 tbsp orange flower or rose flower water

3–4 sheets of ouarka or filo pastry

12 fresh apricots, slit and pitted

30ml/2 tbsp clear honey

Preheat the oven to 180°C/350°F/gas 4. Using your hands, a blender or food processor, bind the ground almonds, sugar and flower water to a soft paste.

Place the ouarka or filo sheets on a work surface and cover them with a clean dish towel so they don't dry out. Place one of the sheets on the surface and use an inverted cup or bowl to cut out 12 circles (or cut into squares). Keep the circles or squares under the dish towel as you cut out the others.

Take small walnut-size lumps of the paste and roll them into balls. Press a ball of paste into each slit apricot and gently squeeze the fruit closed. Place a stuffed apricot on a circle or square of pastry, fold up the sides to secure the fruit and twist the ends to form an open boat. Repeat with the remaining apricots and pastry pieces.

Place the pastry parcels in a shallow ovenproof dish and drizzle the honey over them. Bake for 20–25 minutes, until the pastry is crisp and the fruit has browned on top. Serve hot or cold.

Seffa

Sweet couscous is traditional and popular as a celebratory dish and for serving at religious festivals. It is also enjoyed as a nourishing breakfast, served warm or at room temperature, with a drizzle of honey or buttermilk.

Serves four to six

175g/6oz/1½ cups white raisins or sultanas

300ml/½ pint/1¼ cups warm tea, made with green or black leaves

450g/1lb/2½ cups fine couscous, rinsed and drained

600ml/1 pint/2½ cups boiling water

pinch of sea salt

15–30ml/1–2 tbsp sunflower oil

15–30ml/1–2 tbsp cane sugar

15–30ml/1–2 tbsp orange flower water

15ml/1 tbsp ground cinnamon

25g/1oz/2 tbsp butter

30g/2 tbsp shelled, unsalted pistachios

30ml/2 tbsp icing (confectioners') sugar

30–45ml/2–3 tbsp runny honey

double (heavy) cream, or buttermilk, for pouring (optional)

Put the raisins in a bowl and pour in the warm tea. Leave the raisins to soak for about 1 hour, until nice and plump, then drain them thoroughly.

Put the couscous into a bowl and pour in the boiling water with a pinch of salt. Cover the bowl and leave for 10–15 minutes, until the couscous has absorbed all the water. Drizzle the oil over the couscous and, using your fingertips, rub it in to separate and aerate the grains. Add the cane sugar, orange flower water, and half the cinnamon to the couscous. Toss in the soaked raisins and pack the mixture into a smaller bowl, so that it all fits in snugly. Invert the bowl onto a serving plate, so that you have a couscous dome.

Quickly melt the butter in a skillet or frying pan and stir in the pistachios for 1–2 minutes, until they emit a nutty aroma. Scatter them over and around the couscous dome.

Using your fingertips, rub the rest of cinnamon in decorative lines from the top of the dome to the base, and sift the icing sugar over the top and around the base. Heat the honey and drizzle it over the top of the couscous and serve, with a jug of cream or buttermilk to pour over if you like.

Sweet couscous with rose-scented fruit compote

Aside from its savoury role, couscous is also eaten as a dessert or a nourishing breakfast. This sweet, filling and nutritious dish is lovely served with a dried fruit compote and it is particularly popular with children in the mountainous regions of Morocco where the winters can be long and cold. Make it as sweet and creamy as you like. Served warm, it makes a delicious snack when the weather is chilly.

Serves six

300ml/½ pint/1¼ cups water

225g/8oz/1½ cups medium couscous, rinsed and drained

50g/2oz/⅓ cup raisins

50g/2oz/½ stick butter

50g/2oz/¼ cup caster (superfine) sugar

120ml/4½fl oz/½ cup milk

120ml/4½fl oz/½ cup double (heavy) cream

For the fruit compote

225g/8oz/1½ cups dried apricots

225g/8oz/1½ cup pitted prunes

115/4oz/¾ cup sultanas (golden raisins)

115g/4oz/1 cup blanched almonds

175g/6oz/generous ¾ cup caster (superfine) sugar

30ml/2 tbsp rose flower water

1 cinnamon stick

Prepare the fruit compote a couple of days in advance. Put the dried fruit and almonds in a bowl and pour in just enough water to cover. Gently stir in the sugar and rose water, and add the cinnamon stick. Cover and leave the fruit and nuts to soak for 48 hours, during which time the water and sugar will form a lovely golden-coloured syrup.

To make the couscous, bring the water to the boil in a pan. Stir in the couscous and raisins, and cook gently for 1–2 minutes, until the water has been absorbed. Remove the pan from the heat, cover tightly and leave the couscous to steam for 10–15 minutes. Meanwhile, poach the compote over a gentle heat until warmed through.

Tip the couscous into a bowl and separate the grains with your fingertips. Melt the butter and pour it over the couscous. Sprinkle the sugar over the top then, using your fingertips, rub the butter and sugar into the couscous. Divide the mixture among six bowls.

Heat the milk and cream together in a small, heavy pan until just about to boil, then pour the mixture over the couscous. Serve immediately, with the dried fruit compote.

Variations

The couscous can be served on its own, drizzled with clear or melted honey instead of with the dried fruit compote. The compote is also delicious served chilled on its own or with yogurt.

Yogurt cake with pistachio nuts and passion fruit

Some yogurt cakes are dry and served with tea, others are bathed in lemon syrup and served at room temperature, and then there is this type, which is delicious warm or chilled with a dollop of crème fraîche or yogurt and a spoonful of fresh passion fruit. In Morocco this type of moist cake isn't necessarily reserved for dessert; it can be enjoyed at any time of day.

Serves four to six

3 eggs, separated

75g/3oz/scant ½ cup caster (superfine) sugar

seeds from 2 vanilla pods (beans)

300ml/½ pint/1¼ cups Greek (strained) yogurt

grated rind and juice of 1 lemon

scant 15ml/1 tbsp plain (all-purpose) flour

handful of shelled, unsalted pistachio nuts, roughly chopped

4–6 fresh passion fruits

crème fraîche, to serve

Preheat the oven to 180°C/350°F/gas 4. Line a 25cm/10in square heatproof dish with baking parchment and grease well.

Beat the egg yolks with two-thirds of the sugar until pale and fluffy. Beat in the vanilla seeds and stir in the yogurt, lemon rind and juice, and the flour.

In a separate bowl, whisk the egg whites until stiff, then gradually whisk in the rest of the sugar to form soft peaks. Fold the whisked whites into the yogurt mixture. Turn the mixture into the lined dish.

Place the dish in a roasting pan and pour in cold water to come about halfway up the outside of the dish. Bake for about 20 minutes until the mixture is risen and just set.

Sprinkle the pistachio nuts over the cake and cook for a further 20 minutes, until browned on top.

Serve the cake warm or chilled with the passion fruit drizzled over the top, along with crème fraîche.

Deep-fried orange and honey puffs in syrup

Throughout the Islamic world, there are variations of this medieval dish of deep-fried dough bathed in syrup. The Moroccan trademark of fruity flavours makes these honey puffs unique, as the juice and zest of the oranges lift and enrich the puffs in both taste and colour.

Serves four to six

For the dough

3 medium eggs

juice of 1 orange

zest of 2 oranges

45ml/3 tbsp sunflower oil, plus extra for frying

30ml/2 tbsp runny honey

300g/11oz/2¼ cups plain (all-purpose) flour, plus a little extra for dusting

5ml/1 tsp baking powder

For the syrup

225g/8oz/generous 1½ cups caster (superfine) sugar

250ml/9fl oz/generous 1 cup water

juice of 1 lemon

5–10ml/1–2 tsp orange flower water

In a bowl, whisk the eggs with the orange juice, orange zest and oil until light and frothy, then stir in the honey. Sift the flour with the baking powder and beat it into the mixture with a wooden spoon to form a sticky mixture. Cover with cling film or plastic wrap and put aside for 1 hour.

Meanwhile, prepare the syrup. Put the sugar and water into a heavy-based pan and bring to the boil, stirring all the time, until the sugar has dissolved. Stir in the lemon juice, reduce the heat and simmer for 10–15 minutes, until it thickens a little and becomes syrupy. Stir in the orange flower water and keep the syrup warm, or heat it up when you are frying the honey puffs.

Beat roughly 1–2 tablespoons flour into the sticky dough, until you can handle it with ease and knead it. Pop the dough onto a lightly floured surface and roll it out, until roughly 5mm/¼in thick. The dough will be very elastic, so keep pulling at it, until it stops springing back. Using a cutter, or an inverted glass or jar, cut out equal-sized circles, which can be anywhere between 2.5–5cm/1–2in in diameter.

In a deep-sided pan, heat enough sunflower oil for deep-frying. Fry the dough in batches – they will puff up in the hot oil – remove with a slotted spoon, drain on kitchen paper, then drop them into the syrup. Serve while still warm, or at room temperature.

Gazelle's horns

Said to resemble the horns of the antelope that roam the Atlas Mountains, these sickle-moon shaped pastries, *kaab el ghzal*, are a delightful treat. Traditionally, they are served at celebrations, such as weddings, but they are also available in the street pastry shops to munch on at any time of day.

Makes about twenty

For the almond filling

250g/9oz/2 cups ground almonds

250g/9oz/1½ cups caster (superfine) sugar

2 eggs, lightly beaten

45ml/3 tbsp orange flower water

5ml/1 tsp ground cinnamon

For the pastry

250g/9oz/2 cups plain (all-purpose) flour, plus extra for dusting

pinch of salt

30ml/2 tbsp sunflower oil

100ml/3½fl oz/½ cup orange flower water

100ml/3½fl oz/⅓ cup water

icing (confectioners') sugar, for dusting

Preheat the oven to 180°C/350°F/gas 4. First prepare the filling. Combine all the ingredients in a wide bowl and, using your hand, work them into a stiff paste. Put aside.

To prepare the dough, sift the flour into a bowl with a pinch of salt. Make a well in the centre and pour in the sunflower oil, orange flower water and the water. Using your fingers, draw in the flour to form a dough. Knead the dough with your hand for about 10 minutes, until soft and springy. Divide the dough into 4 balls, cover and set aside to rest for about 20 minutes.

Place one of the balls on a lightly floured surface and roll it out to form a thin rectangle, roughly 1mm thick. Cut across the rectangle to create 4–5 smaller rectangles. Take a spoonful of the almond paste, roll it into a thin log and place it along the long edge of one of the rectangles, leaving a little gap at the edge and at each end. Fold the dough loosely over the almond paste, press your thumb in the middle and use your fingers to curve the dough into the shape of a crescent moon, or a gazelle's horn. Seal the edges with the prongs of a fork.

Repeat with the rest of the dough and almond paste until you have roughly 20 gazelle's horns. Place them onto a lightly oiled baking sheet and prick each one with a fork. Place them in the oven for 15–20 minutes until lightly browned. Transfer them to a wire rack and dust with icing sugar, while still hot. Serve warm or at room temperature.

Ghoriba

These crumbly, buttery cookies can be made with toasted sesame seeds or ground almonds and flavoured with orange flower water, rose water or vanilla. Everyone has their own *ghoriba* recipe and some have special moulds for shaping them. You can bake them smooth and stick an almond in the middles (see page 324), or you can leave them plain and let cracks form on the surface.

Makes about sixteen

200g/7oz/1¾ sticks butter

130g/4½oz/generous 1 cup icing (confectioners') sugar, sifted

5–10ml/1–2 tsp orange flower water

225g/8oz/1¾ cups plain (all-purpose) flour, sifted

5ml/1 tsp baking powder

100g/3½oz/¾ cup sesame seeds, toasted

15ml/1 tbsp vegetable oil, if needed

Preheat the oven to 180°C/350°F/gas 4. In a heavy-based pan, melt the butter and leave to cool to blood temperature. Stir in the icing sugar and orange flower water, then gradually beat in the flour, baking powder and toasted sesame seeds to form a smooth, stiff dough. If it's too stiff or crumbly, add 1 tablespoon of oil. Work the dough lightly into a ball and chill it for 15 minutes.

Break off small walnut-sized pieces of dough and roll them into balls. Place them on an oiled baking sheet and flatten each one with the palm of your hand. Pop them on the high rack in the oven for about 20 minutes, until golden with cracks forming on the surface. Leave to cool before eating.

Sellou

Every Moroccan family has its own method of making *sellou* as the way it is presented and enjoyed is personal. Also called *sfouf*, it is like a Middle Eastern festive *helwah* and is strongly associated with Ramadan and celebratory feasts in the same way. Toasted and nutty, flavoured with cinnamon and anise and sweetened with honey and icing sugar, *sellou* can be moulded into a single high cone or mound, or shaped into compact balls or squares. You can dry-roast the flour, nuts and seeds in a pan or toast them in the oven – I prefer to dry-roast the flour so I can keep an eye on it, and toast the almonds and sesame seeds in the oven. Traditionally, *sellou* is garnished with golden fried almonds but if you are rolling it into balls you can finish them with more toasted sesame seeds or, as here, a dusting of icing sugar.

Makes about forty balls

225g/8oz/scant 2 cups blanched almonds

225g/8oz/scant 2 cups sesame seeds

30ml/2 tbsp ground cinnamon

10ml/2 tsp ground aniseed

115g/4oz/1 cup icing (confectioners') sugar, sifted, plus extra for dusting

225g/8oz/2 cups plain (all-purpose) flour

115g/4oz/1 stick clarified or salted butter

30ml/2 tbsp honey

Preheat the oven to 200°C/400°F/gas 6. Spread the almonds and sesame seeds onto two separate baking trays and pop them into the oven for about 10 minutes, shaking them half way through, to make sure they are golden brown all over – the sesame seeds won't take as long as the almonds. Tip them into a bowl to cool.

Using an electric blender, grind the roasted almonds and tip them into bowl. Using a mortar and pestle, grind the roasted sesame seeds – you can use an electric blender but you have to be careful not to overgrind and work the natural oils as you will end up with a paste. Add them to the ground almonds. Stir in the cinnamon, aniseed and icing sugar. Add more spice at this stage, if you like.

Put a heavy-based pan over a medium heat and dry-roast the flour in batches, stirring all the time, until golden in colour and emitting a nutty aroma. While still warm, stir the toasted flour into the ground almond and sesame seed mixture.

Quickly melt the butter in a pan. Stir in the honey until it dissolves, then pour the mixture into the bowl. Mix well to form a thick paste. Using your hands, roll small portions of the mixture into cherry or plum-sized balls. Finish them with a dusting of icing sugar.

Medjool dates with scented almond paste

As dates play an important role in the culinary culture of Morocco, they are enjoyed fresh and dried and find their way into many sweetmeats, tagines and couscous dishes. The soft, sweet Medjool are ideal for this sweet treat, *tmar b'looz*.

Serves six to eight

115g/4oz/1 cup ground almonds

115g/4oz/¾ cup golden caster sugar

15–30ml/1–2 tbsp rose flower water or orange flower water

24 soft Medjool dates, pitted and ready-to-eat

Tip the ground almonds and caster sugar into a bowl. Add the scented water of choice and, using your fingers, work the mixture into a smooth, soft paste, adding more scented water if you need to.

Make sure all the dates are slit open – where the stone would have been removed from – and fill the hollow with a portion of the almond paste. You can do this by rolling it into a mini log before placing it in the hollow. Press the stuffed date gently to compress the filling and arrange the dates on an ornate serving dish to offer with coffee or a glass of mint tea.

(If there is any almond paste leftover, just roll it into little balls to enjoy in the same way.)

Spicy majoun

You will find these sweet, spicy balls in every street, bus station and port. They vary hugely in the quantity of spices and some *majoun* sellers in the Mediterranean ports add hashish to the mix. They are often enjoyed on their own as a sweet treat or served with slow-roasted meats.

Makes twenty to thirty

500g/1¼lb/4 cups blanched almonds
250g/9oz/2 cups walnuts
500g/1¼lb/4 cups raisins
130g/4½oz/1 stick butter plus 1 tbsp
250g/9oz/generous 1 cup honey
7.5ml/1½ tsp ras el hanout
7.5ml/1½ tsp ground ginger
60g/2oz/4 tbsp toasted sesame seeds, for rolling

Pound together the nuts and raisins in a pestle and mortar. Melt the butter in a heavy-based pan, stir in the honey and spices, and add the pounded nuts and raisins. Stir over a gentle heat until the mixture reaches an almost jam-like consistency.

Leave the mixture to cool a little so that you can handle it, then take portions of it in your fingers and to create balls about the size of a small plum. Roll the balls in toasted sesame seeds and serve.

Candied baby aubergines with mastic

Candied fruits and vegetables are very popular in Morocco, particularly amongst the Jewish communities who have always been at the root of the ancient preserving techniques. Fragrant and aromatic, they are often served as a sweet treat to accompany a glass of mint tea.

Serves four

8–12 firm baby aubergines (eggplants), with the stalks intact

225ml/8fl oz/scant 1 cup water

450g/1lb/2½ cups caster (superfine) sugar (reserve 1 teaspoon)

juice of 1 lemon

25g/1oz fresh ginger root, finely sliced

2 cinnamon sticks

6 cloves

2 pieces of mace

piece of mastic, the size of a small coin

Prick the aubergines with a fork and place them in a steamer. Steam for 15 minutes, drain off any water and leave them to cool.

Meanwhile, make the syrup. Pour the water into a heavy-based pan and add the sugar and lemon juice. Bring the water to the boil, stirring all time, until the sugar has dissolved. Add the spices, reduce the heat and simmer gently for 10 minutes, until the syrup is thick and coats the back of the spoon. Crush the mastic with the reserved teaspoon of sugar and stir it into the syrup.

Gently squeeze the aubergines to remove any excess water and place them in the syrup. Cook the aubergines in the syrup, partially covered, on a very low heat for about 1 hour, making sure they are submerged in the syrup and that the sugar doesn't begin to burn the bottom of the pan.

Remove the pan from the heat and leave the aubergines to cool in the syrup. Arrange the aubergines on a serving dish with the stalks pointing upwards, strain the syrup and drizzle it over them. Alternatively, you can store the aubergines in the strained syrup in a sealed, sterilized jar for several months.

Candied grapefruit rind

Sweet and savoury preserved fruits include watermelon, oranges, clementines, lemons, quinces and pears, which can be served as a sweet treat or added to both savoury and sweet dishes. The candied grapefruit rind adds a fragrant touch to sweet couscous, *seffa* (page 332), pastries and tagines.

Makes 500g/1¼lb

1kg/2¼lb grapefruits, rinsed and patted dry

300ml/½ pint/1¼ cups water

1kg/2¼lb/5 cups caster (superfine) sugar

juice of 1 lemon

115ml/4fl oz/scant ½ cup orange flower water

Using a sharp knife, carefully remove the peel from the fruits. Halve the fruits and squeeze to extract the juice. Put the juice in a pot with the peel and add the water. Bring the liquid to the boil for 15 minutes.

Tip the sugar into a pot with the lemon juice and grapefruit liquid and bring to the boil. Reduce the heat and simmer for 10–15 minutes to form a light syrup. Drop the grapefruit peel into the syrup and simmer gently for about 30 minutes, or until the peel is tender. Add the orange flower water. Turn off the heat and leave to cool in the syrup. Store the peel in a sterilized jar with enough syrup to cover it.

Almond milk

This is another wonderful legacy of the invading Arabs. It is enjoyed all over the Middle East and North Africa, wherever the Arab soldiers settled, but the Moroccans have turned it into a bit of a speciality by combining the subtle almond taste with the perfumed flavour of orange flower water or, in more modern versions, fresh orange rind. Served chilled, it is a deliciously refreshing alternative to the ubiquitous mint tea –wonderful on a hot day.

Serves eight to ten

500g/1¼lb/4 cups blanched almonds

1.2 litres/2 pints/5 cups water

200g/7oz/1 cup caster (superfine) sugar

15ml/1 tbsp orange flower water

Using a mortar and pestle or a blender, reduce the almonds to a smooth paste. Adding a splash of water will help to make the paste smoother.

Put the water and sugar in a large pan and bring to the boil, stirring until the sugar has dissolved. Stir in the almond paste and simmer for 5 minutes.

Turn off the heat and stir in the orange flower water. Leave the mixture to cool in the pan so that the flavours mingle, then strain through muslin (cheesecloth) or a fine sieve or strainer. Chill thoroughly before serving. If there is room in your freezer, it can be served as it is almost setting into ice.

Mint tea

Known as *atay bi naana*, this is the national drink of Morocco, drunk in the morning, offered throughout the day while bargaining, conducting business, or wandering about, and served at the end of a meal to aid digestion. A blend of Chinese gunpowder green tea and fresh mint, traditionally sweetened with an overly generous amount of sugar lumps per cup or glass, it is incredibly refreshing on a hot day. You can, of course, reduce or omit the sugar.

Serves two

10ml/2 tsp Chinese gunpowder green tea

a large bunch of fresh mint

sugar, to taste

Put the tea in a small pot and fill with boiling water. Stuff in all the mint leaves and leave it to infuse (steep) for 2–3 minutes. Stir in sugar to taste and pour into tea glasses or cups.

Serving mint tea

At feasts and on special occasions, the making of mint tea can be an elaborate ceremony: the best green tea is chosen and only fresh spearmint (*Mentha spicata*), of which a well-known cultivar called Moroccan, is used. A fine silver-plated, bulbous-shaped teapot is selected for brewing and the heavily sweetened tea is poured rhythmically into fine glasses. For an additional flounce of ceremony, a fresh, fragrant orange blossom or jasmine flower may be floated in each glass. In winter, wormwood is sometimes added for extra warmth, and infusions flavoured with aniseed or verbena are quite common.

Iced mint and orange tea

The ubiquitous glasses of hot, sweet mint tea are both delicious and refreshing but in some hot, dusty regions a chilled version is very welcome. Sitting on the rooftop of a cinnamon-coloured riad in the stifling summer heat of Marrakesh with a glass of chilled tea, garnished with slice of sweet orange, is a moment of bliss.

Serves four

2 oranges

1 lime

large bunch of fresh peppermint and spearmint

30ml/2 tbsp golden granulated sugar

15ml/1 tbsp green tea leaves

600ml/1 pint/2½ cups water

15–30ml/1–2 tbsp honey

Peel one of the oranges, remove the pith and roughly chop the rind. Do the same with the lime, then squeeze the oranges and the lime to extract the juice.

Using a mortar and pestle, bruise the peppermint and spearmint leaves with the orange and lime rinds, using the sugar as an abrasive.

Tip the orange and mint mixture into a heavy-based pan and add the green tea leaves. Pour in the water and bring it to the boil. Reduce the heat and simmer for about 5 minutes. Stir in the freshly squeezed orange and lime juice, sweeten with honey to taste, and leave the tea to cool in the pot.

Strain the tea into a jug and keep chilled in the fridge, or fill 4 tall glasses with crushed ice, pour in the tea and garnish with a slice of orange, a slice of lime, or a sprig of fresh mint.

Nutritional notes

The nutritional analysis given for each recipe is calculated per portion (i.e. serving or item), unless otherwise stated. If the recipe gives a range, such as Serves 4-6, then the nutritional analysis will be for the smaller portion size, i.e. 6 servings. The analysis does not include optional ingredients, where no measurement is given, such as salt added to taste.

p74 | **Ouarka** Per sheet: Energy 145kcal/607kJ; Protein 2.9g; Carbohydrate 16.9g, of which sugars 0.1g; Fat 7.1g, of which saturates 1g; Cholesterol 0mg; Calcium 26mg; Fibre 0.8g; Sodium 1mg

p74 | **Ras el hanout** Per 5ml/1tsp: Energy 6kcal/24kJ; Protein 0.2g; Carbohydrate 0.6g, of which sugars 0.1g; Fat 0.2g, of which saturates 0g; Cholesterol 0mg; Calcium 9mg; Fibre 0.5g; Sodium 76mg

p74 | **Tabil** Per 5ml/1 tsp: Energy 7kcal/27kJ; Protein 0.3g; Carbohydrate 0.4g, of which sugars 0g; Fat 0.3g, of which saturates 0g; Cholesterol 0mg; Calcium 14mg; Fibre 0.7g; Sodium 13mg

p77 | **Harissa** Per 15ml/1 tbsp: Energy 75kcal/308kJ; Protein 0.6g; Carbohydrate 1.2g, of which sugars 0.6g; Fat 7.3g, of which saturates 1g; Cholesterol 0mg; Calcium 16mg; Fibre 0.8g; Sodium 387mg

p77 | **Chermoula** Energy 307kcal/1267kJ; Protein 4.1g; Carbohydrate 5.3g, of which sugars 3.5g; Fat 28.9g, of which saturates 4.2g; Cholesterol 0mg; Calcium 159mg; Fibre 4.7g; Sodium 282mg

p77 | **Homemade smen** Energy 3366kcal/13836kJ; Protein 3.2g; Carbohydrate 3.9g, of which sugars 2.9g; Fat 370.2g, of which saturates 234.5g; Cholesterol 959mg; Calcium 169mg; Fibre 2.3g; Sodium 6924m

p77 | **Khlii eggs** Energy 356kcal/1485kJ; Protein 29.4g; Carbohydrate 3.7g, of which sugars 3.6g; Fat 24.8g, of which saturates 9.2g; Cholesterol 432mg; Calcium 62mg; Fibre 0.7g; Sodium 1016mg

p78 | **Preserved lemons** Per jar: Energy 183kcal/762kJ; Protein 6.3g; Carbohydrate 21.5g, of which sugars 21.5g; Fat 1.7g, of which saturates 0.6g; Cholesterol 0mg; Calcium 523mg; Fibre 28g; Sodium 68879mg

p78 | **Amlou** Per jar: Energy 2838kcal/11741kJ; Protein 63.5g; Carbohydrate 78.7g, of which sugars 76.9g; Fat 246.1g, of which saturates 19.6g; Cholesterol 0mg; Calcium 674mg; Fibre 27.2g; Sodium 252mg

p78 | **Amlou** Per 15ml/1 tbsp: Energy 107kcal/44kJ; Protein 2.4g; Carbohydrate 3g, of which sugars 2.9g; Fat 9.3g, of which saturates 0.7g; Cholesterol 0mg; Calcium 25mg; Fibre 1g; Sodium 10mg

p78 | **Dates with rose water and milk** Energy 109kcal/139kJ; Protein 1.2g; Carbohydrate 25g, of which sugars 24.4g; Fat 0.6g, of which saturates 0.4g; Cholesterol 2mg; Calcium 41mg; Fibre 2.4g; Sodium 7mg

p78 | **Zitoun mchermel** Energy 107kcal/443kJ; Protein 0.6g; Carbohydrate 0.3g, of which sugars 0.2g; Fat 11.1g, of which saturates 1.6g; Cholesterol 0mg; Calcium 40mg; Fibre 2.1g; Sodium 823mg

Kemia and salads

p83 | **Matisha ma'asala** Energy 113kcal471kJ; Protein 0.6g; Carbohydrate 8.8g, of which sugars 8.3g; Fat 8.2g, of which saturates 1.2g; Cholesterol 0mg; Calcium 29mg; Fibre 0.8g; Sodium 2g

p84 | **Bissara dip with zaatar** Energy 388kcal/1615kJ; Protein 23.2g; Carbohydrate 27g, of which sugars 5g; Fat 15.8g, of which saturates 2.2g; Cholesterol 0mg; Calcium 97mg; Fibre 22g; Sodium 11mg

p87 | **Serrouda** Energy 347kcal/1450kJ; Protein 14.1g; Carbohydrate 31.9g, of which sugars 3.9g; Fat 15.5g, of which saturates 4.6g; Cholesterol 13mg; Calcium 117mg; Fibre 11.8g; Sodium 347mg

p88 | **Zaahlouk** Energy 268kcal/1105kJ; Protein 2.8g; Carbohydrate 7g, of which sugars 6.2g; Fat 24.1g, of which saturates 3.5g; Cholesterol 0mg; Calcium 65mg; Fibre 5.8g; Sodium 17mg

p91 | **Chunky roasted cauliflower and courgette dip** Energy 116 kcal/484 kJ; Protein 3.9g; Carbohydrate 6.5g, of which sugars 4.7g; Fat 7.7g, of which saturates 1.1g; Cholesterol 0mg; Calcium 62mg; Fibre 2.9g; Sodium 11mg

p92 | **Grilled aubergine in honey and spices** Energy 229kcal/948kJ; Protein 1.7g; Carbohydrate 5.8g, of which sugars 4.4g; Fat 21.4g, of which saturates 3.1g; Cholesterol 0mg; Calcium 21mg; Fibre 3.6g; Sodium 5mg

p95 | **Spicy plaintain snacks** Energy 349kcal/1455kJ; Protein 1.7g; Carbohydrate 36.6g, of which sugars 7.8g; Fat 21.1g, of which saturates 2.6g; Cholesterol 0mg; Calcium 14mg; Fibre 3.2g; Sodium 7mg

p96 | **Roasted red peppers with feta, capers and preserved lemon** Energy 204kcal/843kJ; Protein 8.2g; Carbohydrate 3.4g, of which sugars 3.3g; Fat 17.1g, of which saturates 7.8g; Cholesterol 35mg; Calcium 188mg; Fibre 1.7g; Sodium 765mg

p99 | **Artichoke hearts with ginger, honey and preserved lemon** Energy 150kcal/620kJ; Protein 3.2g; Carbohydrate 7.6g, of which sugars 5.8g; Fat 10.6g, of which saturates 1.6g; Cholesterol 0mg; Calcium 49mg; Fibre 5.8g; Sodium 305mg

p101 | **Broad bean salad** Energy 477kcal/1998kJ; Protein 29.7g; Carbohydrate 34.4g, of which sugars 7g; Fat 19.8g, of which saturates 2.6g; Cholesterol 0mg; Calcium 138mg; Fibre 22.2g; Sodium 145mg

p101 | **Carrot salad** Energy 137kcal/569kJ; Protein 1.6g; Carbohydrate 12.1g, of which sugars 11.1g; Fat 7.7g, of which saturates 1.1g; Cholesterol 0mg; Calcium 81mg; Fibre 6.4g; Sodium 40mg

p102 | **Feggous salad** Energy 23kcal/95kJ; Protein 1.1g; Carbohydrate 2.8g, of which sugars 2.8g; Fat 0.6g, of which saturates 0.2g; Cholesterol 0mg; Calcium 25mg; Fibre 0.8g; Sodium 4mg

p105 | **Beetroot salad with oranges** Energy 67kcal/283kJ; Protein 2.1g; Carbohydrate 12.4g, of which sugars 11.7g; Fat 0.2g, of which saturates 0g; Cholesterol 0mg; Calcium 34mg; Fibre 3.7g; Sodium 75mg

p106 | **Lentil salad with red onion and garlic** Energy 282kcal/1181kJ; Protein 12.4g; Carbohydrate 28.3g, of which sugars 6.6g; Fat 11.7g, of which saturates 1.6g; Cholesterol 0mg; Calcium 79mg; Fibre 3g; Sodium 28mg

p109 | **Sautéed herb salad with chilli and preserved lemon** Energy 174kcal/716kJ; Protein 3.7g; Carbohydrate 2.4g, of which sugars 2g; Fat 15.9g, of which saturates 3.1g; Cholesterol 2mg; Calcium 152mg; Fibre 2.7g; Sodium 322mg

p110 | **Fresh country salad** Energy 97kcal/402kJ; Protein 1.7g; Carbohydrate 6.3g, of which sugars 5.7g; Fat 6.6g, of which saturates 1g; Cholesterol 0mg; Calcium 55mg; Fibre 3g; Sodium 404mg

p113 | **Pan-fried baby squid with spices** Energy 87kcal/365kJ; Protein 8.3g; Carbohydrate 3.2g, of which sugars 1.8g; Fat 4.4g, of which saturates 0.7g; Cholesterol 112mg; Calcium 19mg; Fibre 0.7g; Sodium 62mg

p114 | **Hot spicy prawns with coriander** Energy 226kcal/938kJ; Protein 20.7g; Carbohydrate 1.6g, of which sugars 0.8g; Fat 14.9g, of which saturates 2.2g; Cholesterol 169mg; Calcium 68mg; Fibre 1g; Sodium 251mg

p117 | **Mini saffron fish cakes with chilled sweet cucumber and cinnamon salad** Energy 261kcal/1092kJ; Protein 26.3g; Carbohydrate 8g, of which sugars 7.8g; Fat 13.3g, of which saturates 3.1g; Cholesterol 131mg; Calcium 73mg; Fibre 1.9g; Sodium 404mg

p118 | **Sautéed chicken livers with orange flower water and roasted hazelnuts** Energy 213 kcal/885kJ; Protein 21.5g; Carbohydrate 1.5g, of which sugars 1g; Fat 13g, of which saturates 2g; Cholesterol 426mg; Calcium 41mg; Fibre 1.6g; Sodium 381mg

Broths and soups

p122 | **Cinnamon-scented chickpea and lentil soup** Energy 3 47kcal/1458kJ; Protein 24.1g; Carbohydrate 36.7g, of which sugars 9.4g; Fat 8.2g, of which saturates 1.2g; Cholesterol 0mg; Calcium 121mg; Fibre 13.3g; Sodium 519mg

p122 | **Fennel and honey buns** Energy 114kcal/482kJ; Protein 4.2g; Carbohydrate 20.2g, of which sugars 2.5g; Fat 1.6g, of which saturates 0.7g; Cholesterol 21mg; Calcium 65mg; Fibre 0.9g; Sodium 31mg

p125 | **Chilled almond and garlic soup** Energy 526kcal
/2184kJ; Protein 14.8g; Carbohydrate 23.5g, of which sugars 10.8g; Fat 39.7g, of which saturates 4g; Cholesterol 0mg; Calcium 157mg; Fibre 6.9g; Sodium 117mg

p126 | **Velvety pumpkin soup with rice and cinnamon** Energy 222kcal/932kJ; Protein 13.5g; Carbohydrate 23g, of which sugars 15.4g; Fat 8g, of which saturates 4.9g; Cholesterol 23mg; Calcium 322mg; Fibre 2.4g; Sodium504 mg

p129 | **Chunky tomato and squash soup with ras el hanout and noodles** Energy 408kcal/1708kJ; Protein 9.6g; Carbohydrate 54.1g, of which sugars 32.9 g; Fat 14g, of which saturates 2.9g; Cholesterol 3mg; Calcium 266mg; Fibre 7.9g; Sodium 902mg

p130 | **Fish broth with lemon and harissa** Energy 449kcal/1897kJ; Protein 64.5g; Carbohydrate 9.9g, of which sugars 7.7g; Fat 11.9g, of which saturates 2.2g; Cholesterol 218mg; Calcium 142mg; Fibre 2.7g; Sodium 1051mg

p133 | **Chicken rice and saffron broth** Energy 368kcal/1533kJ; Protein 27.2g; Carbohydrate 16.1g, of which sugars 2.7g; Fat 20.9g, of which saturates 5.4g; Cholesterol 132mg; Calcium 69mg; Fibre 2.7g; Sodium 96mg

p134 | **Rfissa** Energy 856kcal/3560kJ; Protein 48.5g; Carbohydrate 39.3g, of which sugars 5.4g; Fat 35.2g, of which saturates 12.2g; Cholesterol 203.6mg; Calcium 105mg; Fibre 3.1g; Sodium 1294mg

p137 | **Harira** Energy 493kcal/2062kJ; Protein 32g; Carbohydrate 33.7g, of which sugars 11.9g; Fat 22.5g, of which saturates 7.4g; Cholesterol 66mg; Calcium 190mg; Fibre 14g; Sodium 555mg

Breads and savoury pastries

p141 | **Beghrir** Per pancake: Energy 116kcal/485kJ; Protein 3.2g; Carbohydrate 12.9g, of which sugars 0.6g; Fat 5.6g, of which saturates 2g; Cholesterol 27mg; Calcium 23mg; Fibre 0.7g; Sodium 110mg

p142 | **Poppy seed harcha** Energy 494kcal/2062kJ; Protein 8.4g; Carbohydrate 50.3g, of which sugars 7.7g; Fat 28.3g, of which saturates 13.4g; Cholesterol 51mg; Calcium 94mg; Fibre 2.2g; Sodium 581mg

p145 | **Kesra** Per loaf: Energy 1105kcal/4665kJ; Protein 33g; Carbohydrate 188.8g, of which sugars 3.8g; Fat 21.9g, of which saturates 8.5g; Cholesterol 27mg; Calcium 345mg; Fibre 10.1g; Sodium 1157mg

p146 | **Batbout** Energy 143kcal/603kJ; Protein 4.3g; Carbohydrate 24.9g, of which sugars 0.8g; Fat 2.6g, of which saturates 0.4g; Cholesterol 0mg; Calcium 28mg; Fibre 1.5g; Sodium 230mg

p149 | **Mhemmer** Energy 326kcal/1369kJ; Protein 15.2g; Carbohydrate 35.9g, of which sugars 2.3g; Fat 12.5g, of which saturates 2.7g; Cholesterol 270mg; Calcium 100mg; Fibre 5.1g; Sodium 339mg

p150 | **Roast chicken with cucumber and tomato salad in pitta pockets** Energy 448kcal/1885kJ; Protein 31.3g; Carbohydrate 51g, of which sugars 5.8g; Fat 12.1g, of which saturates 2g; Cholesterol 55mg; Calcium 242mg; Fibre 4.9g; Sodium 421mg

p153 | **Bruschetta with anchovies, quail's eggs and roasted cumin** Energy 459kcal/1939kJ; Protein 16.8g; Carbohydrate 72.1g, of which sugars 4.7g; Fat 10.5g, of which saturates 2.5g; Cholesterol 224mg; Calcium224 mg; Fibre 4.5g; Sodium 694mg

p154 | **Chollo** Per loaf: Energy 1185kcal/4985kJ; Protein 39.3g; Carbohydrate 167.7g, of which sugars 6.2g; Fat 37.8g, of which saturates 6.5g; Cholesterol 206mg; Calcium 433mg; Fibre 8.3g; Sodium 1256mg

p157 | **M'semen** Each: Energy 364kcal/1518kJ; Protein 6.1g; Carbohydrate 35.6g, of which sugars 0.9g; Fat 21.5g, of which saturates 4g; Cholesterol 4mg; Calcium 54mg; Fibre 1.6g; Sodium 399mg

p158 | **Minced beef rghaif** Energy 816kcal/3404kJ; Protein 21.6g; Carbohydrate 74.4g, of which sugars g4; Fat 46.8g, of which saturates 5.8g; Cholesterol 25mg; Calcium 151mg; Fibre 4.9g; Sodium 812mg

p161 | **B'stilla b'djej** Energy 492kcal/2049kJ; Protein 29.2g; Carbohydrate 23.7g, of which sugars 7g; Fat 29.7g, of which saturates 10.7g; Cholesterol 135mg; Calcium 147mg; Fibre 6.2g; Sodium 285mg

p162 | **Picnic pie with egg, cashew nuts, ginger and coriander** Energy 578kcal/2399kJ; Protein 18.7g; Carbohydrate 22.9g, of which sugars 3.4g; Fat 45g, of which saturates 15.8g; Cholesterol 245mg; Calcium 114mg; Fibre 3.5g; Sodium 342mg

p165 | **Fish and chermoula mini pies** Energy 341kcal/1428kJ; Protein 20.3g; Carbohydrate 23.1g, of which sugars 1.6g; Fat 18.2g, of which saturates 2.6g; Cholesterol 103mg; Calcium 91mg; Fibre 2.1g; Sodium 300mg

p166 | **Briouat** Energy 171kcal/707kJ; Protein 5.7g; Carbohydrate 4.9g, of which sugars 1.2g; Fat 14g, of which saturates 4.4g; Cholesterol 43mg; Calcium 89mg; Fibre 1g; Sodium 210mg

p169 | **Spring rolls with chicken, spring onions and almonds** Energy 631kcal/2632kJ; Protein 42.7g; Carbohydrate 28.7g, of which sugars 6.3g; Fat 37.1g, of which saturates 7g; Cholesterol 317mg; Calcium 173mg; Fibre 5.9g; Sodium 360mg

p170 | **Brik** Energy 522kcal/2176kJ; Protein 26.6g; Carbohydrate 27.8g, of which sugars 3.8g; Fat 33.1g, of which saturates 7.9g; Cholesterol 245mg; Calcium 150mg; Fibre 3.3g; Sodium 945mg

Vegetables and pulses

p175 | **Tagine of artichoke hearts, potatoes, peas and saffron** Energy 207kcal/868kJ; Protein 7.4g; Carbohydrate 26.7g, of which sugars 4.8g; Fat 6.1g, of which saturates 1.1g; Cholesterol 0mg; Calcium 81mg; Fibre 7.8g; Sodium 317mg

p176 | **Tagine of yam, carrots and prunes** Energy 358kcal/1505kJ; Protein 4.5g; Carbohydrate 58.4g, of which sugars 19g; Fat 9.3g, of which saturates 2.1g; Cholesterol 4mg; Calcium 94mg; Fibre 11.1g; Sodium 283mg

p179 | **Tagine of butter beans, cherry tomatoes and olives** Energy 209kcal/874kJ; Protein 7.4g; Carbohydrate 21.3g, of which sugars 6.7g; Fat 8.6g, of which saturates 1.3g; Cholesterol 0mg; Calcium 82mg; Fibre 8.4g; Sodium 88mg

p180 | **Baked vegetable tagine with harissa yogurt** Energy 426kcal/1782kJ; Protein 15.1g; Carbohydrate 58.3g, of which sugars 24.4g; Fat 11.2g, of which saturates 3.9g; Cholesterol 14mg; Calcium 357mg; Fibre 15.3g; Sodium 382mg

p183 | **Mixed bean and aubergine tagine with mint yogurt** Energy 424kcal/1772kJ; Protein 18g; Carbohydrate 37.4g, of which sugars 11.4g; Fat 19.6g, of which saturates 3.2g; Cholesterol 0mg; Calcium 190mg; Fibre 12.9g; Sodium 440mg

p184 | **Okra and tomato tagine** Energy 150kcal/624kJ; Protein 4g; Carbohydrate 12.3g, of which sugars 10.4g; Fat 8.1g, of which saturates 1.3g; Cholesterol 0mg; Calcium 180mg; Fibre 6.1g; Sodium 16mg

p186 | **Chickpea tagine** Energy 244kcal/1020kJ; Protein 10.2g; Carbohydrate 24.8g, of which sugars 7.4g; Fat 9.6g, of which saturates 1.1g; Cholesterol 0mg; Calcium 97mg; Fibre 8.8g; Sodium 463mg

p189 | **Spicy carrot and chickpea tagine** Energy 209kcal/872kJ; Protein 3.6g; Carbohydrate 20.7g, of which sugars 18.4g; Fat 11.1g, of which saturates 1.6g; Cholesterol 0mg; Calcium 74mg; Fibre 6g; Sodium 36mg

p190 | **Loubia** Energy 473kcal/1562kJ; Protein 17.7g; Carbohydrate 44.8g, of which sugars 15.6g; Fat 9.2g, of which saturates 1.3g; Cholesterol 0mg; Calcium 208mg; Fibre 20g; Sodium 90mg

p193 | **Berber lentils with coriander** Energy 270kcal/1135kJ; Protein 16.2g; Carbohydrate 32.5g, of which sugars 4.2g; Fat 6.8g, of which saturates 3.4g; Cholesterol 13mg; Calcium 73mg; Fibre 1.4g; Sodium 80mg

p195 | **Summer vegetable kebabs with harissa and yogurt dip** Energy 410kcal/1700kJ; Protein 11.2g; Carbohydrate 23.3g, of which sugars 20.9g; Fat 28.2g, of which saturates 9.8g; Cholesterol 19mg; Calcium 242mg; Fibre 8.6g; Sodium 776mg

p196 | **Butternut squash with caramelized pink shallots** Energy 521kcal/2178kJ; Protein 14.5g; Carbohydrate 47.5g, of which sugars 38.1g; Fat 27.7g, of which saturates 3.9g; Cholesterol 5mg; Calcium 283mg; Fibre 5.7g; Sodium 54mg

p199 | **Stir-fried carrots with mango and ginger** Energy 97kcal/405kJ; Protein 1.6g; Carbohydrate 10.5g, of which sugars 9.2g; Fat 4.4g, of which saturates 0.6g; Cholesterol 0mg; Calcium 44mg; Fibre 4.3g; Sodium 51mg

p200 | **Spiced pumpkin wedges** Energy 101kcal/415kJ; Protein 3g; Carbohydrate 7.9g, of which sugars 5.7g; Fat 5.6g, of which saturates 1g; Cholesterol 0mg; Calcium 117mg; Fibre 2.6g; Sodium 15mg

p200 | **Spinach with apple, pine nuts and cream** Energy 158kcal/653kJ; Protein 3.3g; Carbohydrate 7.4g, of which sugars 6.6g; Fat 12g, of which saturates 3.8g; Cholesterol 15mg; Calcium 148mg; Fibre 3.4g; Sodium 124mg

p203 | **Casablancan baked stuffed tomatoes** Energy 251kcal/1057kJ; Protein 6.9g; Carbohydrate 39g, of which sugars 7.9g; Fat 6.5g, of which saturates 0.9g; Cholesterol 0mg; Calcium 52mg; Fibre 4.3g; Sodium 369mg

Seafood tagines and meshwi

p207 | **Tagine of monkfish, potatoes, cherry tomatoes and olives** Energy 424kcal/1789kJ; Protein 40.1g; Carbohydrate 27.1g, of which sugars 5.9g; Fat 16.2g, of which saturates 2.5g; Cholesterol 31mg; Calcium 62mg; Fibre 5.5g; Sodium 699mg

p208 | **Moroccan fish tagine** Energy 295kcal/1237kJ; Protein 32g; Carbohydrate 12.7g, of which sugars 10.9g; Fat 11.7g, of which saturates 1.6g; Cholesterol 84mg; Calcium 97mg; Fibre 5.2g; Sodium 559mg

p211 | **Mixed seafood tagine** Energy 358kcal/1492kJ; Protein 36.8g; Carbohydrate 7.7g, of which sugars 5.3g; Fat 19.3g, of which saturates 3.4g; Cholesterol 211mg; Calcium 126mg; Fibre 2.7g; Sodium 650mg

p212 | **Baked fish tagine with lime and tomato salad** Energy 249kcal/1034kJ; Protein 16.1g; Carbohydrate 3g, of which sugars 2.8g; Fat 18.9g, of which saturates 5.7g; Cholesterol 13mg; Calcium 72mg; Fibre 1g; Sodium 130mg

p215 | **Fish and potato tagine with saffron and preserved lemon** Energy 421kcal/1763kJ; Protein 28.5g; Carbohydrate 23g, of which sugars 5.7g; Fat 23g, of which saturates 4.3g; Cholesterol 89mg; Calcium 67mg; Fibre 4g; Sodium 161mg

p216 | **Prawn tagine with ginger and harissa couscous** Energy 532kcal/2238kJ; Protein 21.6g; Carbohydrate 76.6g, of which sugars 13.1g; Fat 13.8g, of which saturates 3.6g; Cholesterol 69mg; Calcium 123mg; Fibre 7.2g; Sodium 438mg

p219 | **Shellfish k'dra with lemon couscous** Energy 642kcal/2704kJ; Protein 39.1g; Carbohydrate 79.9g, of which sugars 6.4g; Fat 14.1g, of which saturates 5.1g; Cholesterol 114mg; Calcium 135mg; Fibre 5.9g; Sodium 505mg

p220 | **Red mullet with chermoula and preserved lemon** Energy 364kcal/1513kJ; Protein 18.1g; Carbohydrate 13.2g, of which sugars 8g; Fat 25.4g, of which saturates 4.1g; Cholesterol 0mg; Calcium 138mg; Fibre 5.2g; Sodium 839mg

p223 | **Grilled fish in vine leaves with sweet and sour chilli dipping sauce** Energy 500kcal/2100kJ; Protein 37.9g; Carbohydrate 45.6g, of which sugars 43.5g; Fat 15.7g, of which saturates 2.3g; Cholesterol 104mg; Calcium 217mg; Fibre 11.1g; Sodium 842mg

p224 | **Spiced sardines with grapefruit and fennel salad** Energy 302kcal/1252kJ; Protein 11.8g; Carbohydrate 10.1g, of which sugars 8.9g; Fat 23g, of which saturates 3.7g; Cholesterol 25mg; Calcium 103mg; Fibre 4.1g; Sodium 546mg

p227 | **Griddled swordfish with roasted tomatoes and cinnamon** Energy 588kcal/2447kJ; Protein 47.9g; Carbohydrate 17.8g, of which sugars 17.4g; Fat 35g, of which saturates 7.3g; Cholesterol 154mg; Calcium 73mg; Fibre 4.5g; Sodium 273mg

p228 | **Seared tuna with warm ginger, chilli and watercress salad** Energy 380kcal/1594kJ; Protein 51.5g; Carbohydrate 3.1g, of which sugars 2.5g; Fat 17.7g, of which saturates 3.7g; Cholesterol 75mg; Calcium 40mg; Fibre 1.1g; Sodium 177mg

p231 | **Roasted shad stuffed with dates** Energy 813kcal/3381kJ; Protein 44g; Carbohydrate 63.6g, of which sugars 40.2g; Fat 49.8g, of which saturates 8.7g; Cholesterol 150mg; Calcium 241mg; Fibre 9.9g; Sodium 116mg

p232 | **Pan-fried sardine fillets with harissa and olive sauce** Energy 334kcal/1391kJ; Protein 26.1g; Carbohydrate 9.4g, of which sugars 8.4g; Fat 20.7g, of which saturates 4.1g; Cholesterol 62mg; Calcium 117mg; Fibre 3g; Sodium 492mg

Meat and poultry tagines and k'dras

p237 | **Chicken tagine with green olives and preserved lemon** Energy 595kcal/kJ; Protein 41.7g; Carbohydrate 4.5g, of which sugars 3.2g; Fat 44.6g, of which saturates 10.4g; Cholesterol 214mg; Calcium 76mg; Fibre 3.9g; Sodium 1309mg

p238 | **Tagine of poussins with dates and orange flower water** Energy 944kcal/3945kJ; Protein 48.2g; Carbohydrate 68.2g, of which sugars 64.1g; Fat 51.4g, of which saturates 12.3g; Cholesterol 237mg; Calcium 72mg; Fibre 8.2g; Sodium 183mg

p241 | **Chicken tagine with apricots, rosemary, ginger and harissa** Energy 449kcal/1883kJ; Protein 40.2g; Carbohydrate 31.6g, of which sugars 30.4g; Fat 17g, of which saturates 5.9g; Cholesterol 204mg; Calcium 104mg; Fibre 4.1g; Sodium 68mg

p242 | **Chicken tagine with courgettes, lemon and mint** Energy 387kcal/1626kJ; Protein 54.5g; Carbohydrate 6.5g, of which sugars 5.6g; Fat 15.3g, of which saturates 3g; Cholesterol 147mg; Calcium 89mg; Fibre 2.9g; Sodium 113mg

p245 | **Chicken tagine with roasted garlic and orange chermoula** Energy 585kcal/2441kJ; Protein 48.3g; Carbohydrate 24.9g, of which sugars 11.8g; Fat 30g, of which saturates 6g; Cholesterol 195mg; Calcium 144mg; Fibre 10.5g; Sodium 90mg

p246 | **Chicken k'dra with turnip and ras el hanout** Energy 410kcal/1711kJ; Protein 41.8g; Carbohydrate 15g, of which sugars 12.7g; Fat 19.3g, of which saturates 6.9g; Cholesterol 208mg; Calcium 113mg; Fibre 4.2g; Sodium 482mg

p249 | **Chicken k'dra with chickpeas and almonds** Energy 496kcal/2075kJ; Protein 52.1g; Carbohydrate 16.3g, of which sugars 6.4g; Fat 23g, of which saturates 8g; Cholesterol 149mg; Calcium 118mg; Fibre 7.3g; Sodium 574mg

p250 | **Tagine of duck with chestnuts and pumpkin seeds** If skin removed before serving: Energy 381kcal/ 1598kJ; Protein 16.7g; Carbohydrate 42.9g, of which sugars 20g; Fat 14.3g, of which saturates 6.3g; Cholesterol 86mg; Calcium 113mg; Fibre 7.1g; Sodium 459mg

p253 | **Duck tagine with saffron, caramelized pears and orange salad** Energy 418kcal/1748kJ; Protein 26.3g; Carbohydrate 20.8g, of which sugars 19.9g; Fat 22g, of which saturates 7.6g; Cholesterol 154mg; Calcium 68mg; Fibre 2.9g; Sodium 569mg

p254 | **Mrouzia goat tagine** Energy 849kcal/ 3558kJ; Protein 65.3g; Carbohydrate 57.6g, of which sugars 56g; Fat 37.8g, of which saturates 7.3g; Cholesterol 156mg; Calcium 212mg; Fibre 8.2g; Sodium 323mg

p257 | **Tagine of spiced lamb kefta with lemon** Energy 389kcal/1617kJ; Protein 24.4g; Carbohydrate 16.1g, of which sugars 12.3g; Fat 23.8g, of which saturates 12.2g; Cholesterol 108mg; Calcium 131mg; Fibre 5.9g; Sodium 169mg

p258 | **Tagine of lamb with prunes** Energy 760kcal/3191kJ; Protein 47.1g; Carbohydrate 76g, of which sugars 22.6g; Fat 28.1g, of which saturates 10.8g; Cholesterol 18mg; Calcium 82mg; Fibre 7.1g; Sodium 186mg

p261 | **Tagine of lamb with country salad** Energy 510kcal/2130kJ; Protein 36.8g; Carbohydrate 35.2g, of which sugars 33.3g; Fat 23.1g, of which saturates 7.1g; Cholesterol 123mg; Calcium 118mg; Fibre 6.7g; Sodium 136mg

p262 | **Tagine of baked lamb with chermoula, figs and honey** Energy 523kcal/2167kJ; Protein 27.9g; Carbohydrate 11.3g, of which sugars 10.6g; Fat 40g, of which saturates 18.8g; Cholesterol 137mg; Calcium 59mg; Fibre 2.7g; Sodium 293mg

p265 | **Tagine of beef with peas and saffron** Energy 531kcal/2227kJ; Protein 58.1g; Carbohydrate 24.5g, of which sugars 7.2g; Fat 19.6g, of which saturates 6.7g; Cholesterol 126mg; Calcium 69mg; Fibre 12g; Sodium 188mg

p266 | **Beef tagine with sweet potatoes** Energy 593kcal/2484kJ; Protein 60.1g; Carbohydrate 25.4g, of which sugars 8.7g; Fat 26.9g, of which saturates 9.8g; Cholesterol 177mg; Calcium 64mg; Fibre 4.6g; Sodium 182mg

p269 | **Merguez and black-eyed bean tagine** Energy 243kcal/1014kJ; Protein 11.4g; Carbohydrate 19.6g, of which sugars 5.6g; Fat 9.8g, of which saturates 4.8g; Cholesterol 29mg; Calcium 71mg; Fibre 6.1g; Sodium 89mg

Meat and poultry meshwi

p272 | **Fiery chicken wings with blood oranges** Energy 727kcal/3030kJ; Protein 56.9g; Carbohydrate 24.4g, of which sugars 23g; Fat 43.7g, of which saturates 10.3g; Cholesterol 240mg; Calcium 147mg; Fibre 4g; Sodium 1012mg

p275 | **Pan-fried quail with ginger and grapes** Energy 520kcal/2165kJ; Protein 30.4g; Carbohydrate 19g, of which sugars 18.3g; Fat 35.5g, of which saturates 12.5g; Cholesterol 140mg; Calcium 34mg; Fibre 1.6g; Sodium 173mg

p276 | **Roast duck legs with quince, ginger, honey and cinnamon** Energy 370kcal/1552kJ; Protein 23.1g; Carbohydrate 30g, of which sugars 9.2g; Fat 16.5g, of which saturates 4.8g; Cholesterol 125mg; Calcium 68mg; Fibre 5g; Sodium 152mg

p279 | **Kouah** Energy 181kcal/746kJ; Protein 26g; Carbohydrate 0.7g, of which sugars 0.3g; Fat 8.2g, of which saturates 2.2g; Cholesterol 539mg; Calcium 42mg; Fibre 0.5g; Sodium 97mg

p280 | **Dafina** Energy 486kcal/2044kJ; Protein 34.4g; Carbohydrate 49.3g, of which sugars 20.7g; Fat 14.7g, of which saturates 3.9g; Cholesterol 250mg; Calcium 99mg; Fibre 9.6g; Sodium 155mg

p283 | **Tangia** Energy 439kcal/1833kJ; Protein 56.1g; Carbohydrate 1.2g, of which sugars 0.3g; Fat 23.1g, of which saturates 10.2g; Cholesterol 187mg; Calcium 30mg; Fibre 0.7g; Sodium 284mg

p284 | **Roast leg of lamb with dates and almonds** Energy 719kcal/2668kJ; Protein 59.6g; Carbohydrate 11.5g, of which sugars 10.7g; Fat 47.9g, of which saturates 23.9g; Cholesterol 263mg; Calcium 76mg; Fibre 3.1g; Sodium 573mg

p287 | **Mechoui** Energy 525kcal/2195kJ; Protein 52.8g; Carbohydrate 9.3g, of which sugars 8.4g; Fat 30.3g, of which saturates 14g; Cholesterol 204mg; Calcium 63mg; Fibre 2.2g; Sodium 161mg

p289 | **Bus-station kefta with egg and tomato** Energy 394kcal/1642kJ; Protein 25.2g; Carbohydrate 15.1g, of which sugars 9g; Fat 25.2g, of which saturates 8g; Cholesterol 353mg; Calcium 137mg; Fibre 3.3g; Sodium 277mg

p290 | **Merguez** Energy 291kcal/1208kJ; Protein 17.5g; Carbohydrate 1g, of which sugars 0.1g; Fat 23.9g, of which saturates 10.6g; Cholesterol 55mg; Calcium 43mg; Fibre 1.2g; Sodium 68mg

p293 | **Spicy minced beef kebabs with hot chickpea purée** Energy 515kcal/2140kJ; Protein 26.9g; Carbohydrate 22.7g, of which sugars 6.6g; Fat 33.5g, of which saturates 11.7g; Cholesterol 66mg; Calcium 124mg; Fibre 6.9g; Sodium 524mg

Couscous

p296 | **Plain buttery couscous** Energy 403kcal/1688kJ; Protein 11.9g; Carbohydrate 42.8g, of which sugars 2g; Fat 19.5g, of which saturates 4.8g; Cholesterol 14mg; Calcium 66mg; Fibre 4.4g; Sodium 372mg

p299 | **Green couscous with a spring broth** Energy 597kcal/2515kJ; Protein 31.6g; Carbohydrate 86.9g, of which sugars 8.8g; Fat 8.5g, of which saturates 2.5g; Cholesterol 5mg; Calcium 167mg; Fibre 23.3g; Sodium 876mg

p300 | **Couscous with dried fruit and nuts** Energy 746kcal/3126kJ; Protein 20g; Carbohydrate 93.5g, of which sugars 33g; Fat 30.2g, of which saturates 4.1g; Cholesterol 4mg; Calcium 124mg; Fibre 9.7g; Sodium 404mg

p303 | **Casablancan couscous with roasted summer vegetables** Energy 743kcal/3107kJ; Protein 15.2g; Carbohydrate 84.1g, of which sugars 17.8g; Fat 36g, of which saturates 6.7g; Cholesterol 9mg; Calcium 107mg; Fibre 10.8g; Sodium 439mg

p304 | **Spicy couscous with aromatic shellfish broth** Energy 670Jcak/2807kJ; Protein 30.8g; Carbohydrate 64.1g, of which sugars 2.8g; Fat 31.4g of which saturates 14.1g; Cholesterol 158mg; Calcium 108mg; Fibre 8.1g; sodium 1158mg

p307 | **Couscous with lamb cutlets, harissa and fennel** Energy 1076kcal/4483kJ; Protein 35.9g; Carbohydrate 80.4g, of which sugars 14.8g; Fat 64.9g, of which saturates 27.2g; Cholesterol 126mg; Calcium 176mg; Fibre 13.6g; Sodium 608mg

p308 | **Cinnamon couscous with beef tfaia** Energy 735kcal/3086kJ; Protein 40.8g; Carbohydrate 87.5g, of which sugars 22.2g; Fat 22.6g, of which saturates 8.1g; Cholesterol 95mg; Calcium 111mg; Fibre 8.1g; Sodium 434mg

Sweet treats, preserves and tea

p312 | **Watermelon and spiced orange granitas with grilled fruits** Energy 471kcal/2000kJ; Protein 2.3g; Carbohydrate 113.1g, of which sugars 111.1g; Fat 0.5g, of which saturates 0.1g; Cholesterol 0mg; Calcium 52mg; Fibre 2.9g; Sodium 8mg

p315 | **Minted pomegranate yogurt with grapefruit salad** Energy 271kcal/1146kJ; Protein 8.5g; Carbohydrate 36.9g, of which sugars 36.6g; Fat 9.4g, of which saturates 5.3g; Cholesterol 13mg; Calcium 189mg; Fibre 3.6g; Sodium 57mg

p316 | **Poached pears in scented honey syrup** Energy 125kcal/526kJ; Protein 0.7g; Carbohydrate 28g, of which sugars 27.9g; Fat 0.2g, of which saturates 0g; Cholesterol 0mg; Calcium 12mg; Fibre 3.9g; Sodium 4mg

p319 | **Almond and pistachio ice creams** Energy 837kcal/3477kJ; Protein 15.9g; Carbohydrate 52.3g, of which sugars 50.5g; Fat 61.7g, of which saturates 27.2g; Cholesterol 349mg; Calcium 234mg; Fibre 4.3g; Sodium 63mg

p320 | **Jabane** Energy 566kcal/2383kJ; Protein 9.7g; Carbohydrate 96g, of which sugars 93g; Fat 15g, of which saturates 2g; Cholesterol 0mg; Calcium 47mg; Fibre 3.9g; Sodium 35mg

p323 | **Burnt mulhalbia with rose-petal jam** Energy 237kcal/1002kJ; Protein 5.6g; Carbohydrate 40.9g, of which sugars 34.4g; Fat 5.7g, of which saturates 3.6g; Cholesterol 18mg; Calcium 188mg; Fibre 0.3g; Sodium 69mg

p324 | **Saffron and cardamom crème caramel** Energy 729kcal/3048kJ; Protein 14.9g; Carbohydrate 77.2g, of which sugars 46.1g; Fat 39.4g, of which saturates 21.2g; Cholesterol 219mg; Calcium 214mg; Fibre 3g; Sodium 351mg

p327 | **M'hanncha** Energy 479kcal/1989kJ; Protein 12g; Carbohydrate 27.4g, of which sugars 19.5g; Fat 34.4g, of which saturates 9g; Cholesterol 51mg; Calcium 129mg; Fibre 5.7g; Sodium 152mg

p328 | **Silky milk b'stilla with cinnamon** Energy 582kcal/2431kJ; Protein 14.6g; Carbohydrate 56.7g, of which sugars 31.6g; Fat 31.7g, of which saturates 11.4g; Cholesterol 45mg; Calcium 261mg; Fibre 5.5g; Sodium 312mg

p331 | **Apricot parcels with honey glaze** Energy 388kcal/1007kJ; Protein 9.7g; Carbohydrate 45.1g, of which sugars 32.2g; Fat 18.2g, of which saturates 1.4g; Cholesterol 0mg; Calcium 117mg; Fibre 6g; Sodium 88mg

p332 | **Seffa** Energy 467kcal/1972kJ; Protein 12.4g; Carbohydrate 83.6g, of which sugars 28.8g; Fat 8g, of which saturates 2.8g; Cholesterol 9mg; Calcium 53mg; Fibre 5.6g; Sodium 84mg

p335 | **Sweet couscous with rose-scented fruit compote** Energy 775kcal/3255kJ; Protein 13.3g; Carbohydrate 113.5g, of which sugars 87.2g; Fat 27.9g, of which saturates 11.6g; Cholesterol 51mg; Calcium 170mg; Fibre 8.5g; Sodium 87mg

p336 | **Yogurt cake with pistachio nuts and passion fruit** Energy 255kcal/ 1056kJ; Protein 9.1g; Carbohydrate 18.3g, of which sugars 16.3g; Fat 15.5g, of which saturates 7.3g; Cholesterol 121mg; Calcium 95mg; Fibre 2g; Sodium 83mg

p339 | **Deep-fried orange and honey puffs in syrup** Energy 580kcal/2431kJ; Protein 8.8g; Carbohydrate 81.2g, of which sugars 44.2g; Fat 24g, of which saturates 3.4g; Cholesterol 102mg; Calcium 78mg; Fibre 2.2g; Sodium 127mg

p340 | **Gazelle's horns** Energy 197kcal/825kJ; Protein 5.2g; Carbohydrate 22.7g, of which sugars 13.2g; Fat 9.1g, of which saturates 0.9g; Cholesterol 20mg; Calcium 47mg; Fibre 2g; Sodium 23mg

p343 | **Ghoriba** Energy 222kcal/924kJ; Protein 2.8g; Carbohydrate 18.7g, of which sugars 8.2g; Fat 14.9g, of which saturates 7.3g; Cholesterol 27mg; Calcium 61mg; Fibre 0.7g; Sodium 123mg

p344 | **Sellou** Energy 125kcal/519kJ; Protein 3.3g; Carbohydrate 8.2g, of which sugars 3.9g; Fat 8.5g, of which saturates 2.3g; Cholesterol 6mg; Calcium 64mg; Fibre 1.2g; Sodium 22mg

p347 | **Medjool dates with scented almond paste** Energy 318kcal/801kJ; Protein 4.8g; Carbohydrate 56.4g, of which sugars 55g; Fat 8.1g, of which saturates 0.6g; Cholesterol 0mg; Calcium 75mg; Fibre 5.7g; Sodium 3mg

p348 | **Spicy majoun** Energy 424kcal/1763kJ; Protein 10g; Carbohydrate 29.3g, of which sugars 11g; Fat 28.4g, of which saturates 5.6g; Cholesterol 14mg; Calcium 109mg; Fibre 5.8g; Sodium 61mg

p351 | **Candied baby aubergines with mastic** Energy 494kcal/2096kJ; Protein 1.6g; Carbohydrate 116.9g, of which sugars 115.8g; Fat 1g, of which saturates 0.3g; Cholesterol 0mg; Calcium 46mg; Fibre 5.4g; Sodium 14m

p352 | **Candied grapefruit rind** *Per jar:* Energy 4265kcal/18132kJ; Protein 6.2g; Carbohydrate 1049g, of which sugars 1049g; Fat 4g, of which saturates 0.5g; Cholesterol 0mg; Calcium 264mg; Fibre 6.2g; Sodium 0mg

p352 | **Candied grapefruit rind** *Per 100g:* Energy 207kcal/880kJ; Protein 0.3g; Carbohydrate 50.9g, of which sugars 50.9g; Fat 0.2g, of which saturates 0g; Cholesterol 0mg; Calcium 13mg; Fibre 0.3g; Sodium 3mg

p355 | **Almond milk** Energy 378kcal/1573kJ; Protein 12.8g; Carbohydrate 22.5g, of which sugars 22.2g; Fat 25g, of which saturates 1.9g; Cholesterol 0mg; Calcium 136mg; Fibre 6.2g; Sodium 1mg

p356 | **Mint tea** Energy 3kcal/10kJ; Protein 0.4g; Carbohydrate 0.1g, of which sugars 0.1g; Fat 0g, of which saturates 0g; Cholesterol 0mg; Calcium 5mg; Fibre 0.2g; Sodium 2mg

p359 | **Iced mint and orange tea** Energy 37kcal/157kJ; Protein 0.8g; Carbohydrate 7.7g, of which sugars 7.7g; Fat 0.2g, of which saturates 0g; Cholesterol 0mg; Calcium 17mg; Fibre 0.9g; Sodium 2mg

Index

About the author

Ghillie Başan is a writer, broadcaster and food anthropologist with a degree in Social Anthropology and a Cordon Bleu Diploma. She grew up in East Africa, worked as journalist in Istanbul and as a freelance food and travel writer in India, Southeast Asia and North Africa. Her interest in culinary cultures has culminated in over 50 books – eight have featured Morocco – and she has been described as 'one of the finest writers on Middle Eastern food'. Her books have been shortlisted for numerous awards – *The Lebanese Cookbook* (also from Lorenz Books) won Best in the World in the Gourmand International Cookbook Awards 2021. She has many BBC credits as a presenter and contributor and produces her own podcast, Spirit & Spice, featuring food and drink stories in Scotland. Spirit & Spice is also the name of her Whisky and Food Experience business in a remote part of the Scottish Highlands where she hosts visitors from all over the world.

Additional captions **Front endpaper: A camel caravan wends its way between the Lake of the Bride (Lac Tizlit) and the Bridegroom (Lac Izli); according to legend, when the lovers separated, they cried enough tears to fill two lakes. Back endpaper: Juniper tree berries are famously used to make gin, but not in Morocco – here they are eaten by the goats and also used for herbal remedies. Page 1, clockwise from top left: The sage seller of Marrakesh (a bundle costs 2 dirhams – less than 2 pence); Apples from the orchards of the High Atlas mountains; The two little girls, Sofia and Khadija, are dressed up in their best to enjoy the Aid celebrations and the requisite mint tea; A kitten having a nap in a handmade pottery plate from Safi. Page 5: Painted blue door in the city of Chefchaouen.**

Author's acknowledgements

Over the last 30 years, I have written a number of books on Morocco's culinary culture and its 'perfumed soul'. This is my last. So, I would like to thank my Moroccan friends and many strangers who have accompanied me on my journeys for their warm welcomes and generous hospitality. I have eaten my way around Morocco and the food has always been a surprise and a delight, but it is the hospitality that I will never forget. That is why I keep coming back!

I would like to thank the Adventurer, Alice Morrison, who lives in Imlil and has travelled in the deserts with camels. Her expeditions have been documented in films and books and her stunning photographs have given this book some real cultural body and soul.

It has also been an honour to work with the publisher, Joanna Lorenz, over these years and I must thank her for having faith in me to deliver several books on Morocco, Turkey, Lebanon, Syria, Jordan and most of the regions of Southeast Asia. In our long journey together, she has always been easy to work with and ever so patient. I would also like to thank the acclaimed photographer, Martin Brigdale, who has photographed many of the books that Joanna and I have worked on together and I would like to thank the team on this book – Ian Garlick, Simon Daley, Valentina Harris, Felicity Barnum-Bobb, Fergal Connolly, Sunil Vijayakar, Clare Emery and Catherine Atkinson.

Cook's notes

Bracketed terms are intended for American readers.

For all recipes, quantities are given in both metric and imperial measures and, where appropriate, in standard cups and spoons. Follow one set of measures, but not a mixture, because they are not interchangeable.

Standard spoon and cup measures are level.
1 tsp = 5ml, 1 tbsp = 15ml, 1 cup = 250ml/8fl oz.

Australian standard tablespoons are 20ml. Australian readers should use 3 tsp in place of 1 tbsp for measuring small quantities.

American pints are 16fl oz/2 cups. American readers should use 20fl oz/2½ cups in place of 1 pint when measuring liquids.

Since ovens vary, you should check with your manufacturer's instruction book for guidance.

This edition is published by Lorenz Books
an imprint of Anness Publishing Ltd
www.annesspublishing.com; info@anness.com

A CIP catalogue record for this book is available from the British Library.

Publisher: Joanna Lorenz
Design: Simon Daley
Recipe photography: Ian Garlick and Martin Brigdale
Food styling: Valentina Harris, Felicity Barnum-Bobb, Fergal Connolly and Sunil Vijayakar
Nutritional consultant: Clare Emery
Index: Cathy Heath
Production: Ben Worley

Location photography by Alice Morrison: 2, 6, 7, 26b, 27b, 30tl, 31, 43t, 46b, 62, 64t, 67t, 67b, and endpapers. With additional thanks to Alamy 11, 15b, 25b, 26t, 27t, 33b, 34b, 43, 55t, 56t, 56b, 59t, 60b, 68t, 68b and Shutterstock 5, 8, 12t, 12b, 15t, 16, 19t, 19b, 20t, 20b, 23t, 23b, 24, 25, 29, 30tr, 30bl, 30br, 33tl, 34t, 37t, 37b, 38t, 38b, 40, 41t, 41b, 44, 45t, 45b, 46t, 48, 51, 55b, 59b, 60t, 63t, 63b, 64b, 71tl, 71tr, 71bl, 71br, 72t, 72b.

Some material in this book has been previously published in *The Food and Cooking of Morocco*, updated and revised in this extended new edition.